THE ENGLISH EMBLEM AND
THE CONTINENTAL TRADITION

AMS Studies in the Emblem: No. 1
ISSN 0892-4201
Other titles in this series:
No. 2   John Manning, ed. *The Emblems of Thomas Palmer: Sloane MS 3794.* 1988
No. 3   Alan R. Young, *The English Tournament Imprese.* 1988

THE ENGLISH EMBLEM
AND
THE CONTINENTAL TRADITION

Edited by Peter M. Daly

AMS PRESS
NEW YORK

i 00313275X

Library of Congress Cataloging-in-Publication Data

The english emblem and the continental tradition

    (AMS studies in the emblem; no. 1)
    Bibliography: p.
    Includes index.
    1. Emblem books, English—History. 2. Emblems—
England. 3. Emblem books—History. 4. Emblems.
I. Daly, Peter M. (Peter Maurice) II. Series.
Z1021.3.E54 1988   686   87-/45812
ISBN 0-404-63701-9

AMS PRESS, INC.
56 East 13th Street
New York, N.Y. 10003

MANUFACTURED IN THE UNITED STATES OF AMERICA

This volume, the first in the series "Studies in the Emblem," is dedicated to Karl Josef Höltgen (Erlangen, Federal Republic of Germany), on the occasion of his sixtieth birthday in appreciation of his many and varied contributions to emblem studies.

CONTENTS

LIST OF ILLUSTRATIONS

Figure 9
The Christians Zodiake, Emblem 8. Etching by Hollar. Department of Prints and Drawings, British Museum, P 191.

Figure 10
The Christians Zodiake, Emblem 9. Etching by Hollar. Department of Prints and Drawings, British Museum, P 192.

Figure 11
The Christians Zodiake, Emblem 10. Etching by Hollar. Department of Prints and Drawings, British Museum, P 193.

Figure 12
The Christians Zodiake, Emblem 11. Etching by Hollar. Department of Prints and Drawings, British Museum, P 194.

Figure 13
The Christians Zodiake, Emblem 12. Etching by Hollar. Department of Prints and Drawings, British Museum, P 195.

Figure 14
The engraved title-page for *The Christian Zodiack* (Rouen, 1633), Hollar's model for *The Christians Zodiake* (see Figure 13). British Library, C 111. d. 23.

Figure 15
Title-page for Wenceslaus Hollar's *Emblemata Nova* (London, ?1641-44). Hollar Collection, Thomas Fisher Rare Book Library, University of Toronto, P 446 i.

Figure 16
Revised title-page with Peter Stent's imprint for Hollar's *Emblemata Nova* (London, c. 1646). Department of Prints and Drawings, British Museum, P 446 ii.

Figure 17
Revised title-page with John Overton's imprint for Hollar's *Emblemata Nova* (London, 1665). Department of Prints and Drawings, British Museum, P 446 iii.

PREFACE

Several of these essays were presented as conference papers at a symposium held at McGill University in April, 1982. I am grateful to their authors for permission to include them in this volume.

With the exception of the first essay, which attempts to provide an review of the cultural context surrounding the production of emblem books in England, the essays are arranged chronologically in order to reflect something of the development of the emblem in England during the sixteenth and seventeenth centuries. It was not our purpose to write a new history and evaluation of the English emblem, although that should also be done. Rather we set out to show in closer detail the relation of emblems in England to the older and richer Continental tradition. In effect, the authors provide case studies of various aspects of this large topic.

Alan R. Young shows that Continental imprese had been an important influence long before any books of imprese had been translated into English. Drawing on a scarcely known, yet significant German manuscript source he establishes that over 800 tournament imprese are known to have been created in England for royal entertainments up to 1611.

John Manning finds further, unexplored evidence of Geffrey Whitney's use of Continental emblems in the manuscript version of his *Choice of Emblemes.* He also shows that the published version and manuscript serve different political purposes--the manuscript is a private act of homage to his patron the Earl of Leicester, the published *Choice* is addressed to a more general readership--and this will account both for the authorial decision on what to include and the treatment of that material.

Mason Tung discusses various ways in which Henry Peacham modelled many of his emblems on the personifications of Caesare Ripa's *Iconologia,* revealing new evidence of Peacham's wit and inventiveness.

In a second essay, Alan R. Young reports on two hitherto unidentified emblem books by the Bohemian artist Wenceslaus Hollar, who created the engravings for London printings of Drexel's *Christians Zodiake* and van Veen's *Moralia Horatiana.*

G. Richard Dimler, S. J. provides a close examination of Edmund Arwaker's translation of Hermann Hugo's *Pia desideria,* which indicates that the Protestant Archdeacon of Armagh was guided by neo-classical and pietistic principles of translation. The resulting work is meditative in a Protestant sense, and more subjective than the Catholic original. However, theologically Arwaker found little to criticize in the Jesuit source.

In the final essay, Michael Bath discovers the influence of the emblem in some unlikely documents: the Household Accounts of Queen Elizabeth. The collared stags and bridled lions evidently owe much to Continental traditions. In mapping the complex interrelationships between emblems and mythography, Bath shows something of the process of historical accretion and development. This should serve as a warning to those unwary literary historians who with more speed than circumspection grasp at emblems for analogues to elucidate verbal images in literary works.

I wish to acknowledge the assistance of McGill University, which co-sponsored the initial symposium that provided the focus for these studies. McGill also provided a grant towards the costs of publication of this volume. My thanks go to the Social Sciences and Humanities Research Council of Canada, which over the years has co-funded a number of symposia on research in the field of emblem studies and generously supported my on-going work on the Index Emblematicus. I also wish to express my gratitude to the Guggenheim Foundation for a fellowship which provided me with the most precious of all commodities, time.

ENGLAND AND THE EMBLEM: THE CULTURAL CONTEXT OF ENGLISH EMBLEM BOOKS

PETER M. DALY
McGill University

During the reigns of Elizabeth and James, Englishmen were far more aware of emblems than some earlier historians of English literature would have us believe, especially those historians whose knowledge of the emblem was confined to the printed book, and often to those in English. The fact that the number of surviving English emblem books is small in no way reflects the pervasiveness of the phenomenon. It is a curious circumstance that it should have taken over half a century after the appearance of Alciato's *Emblematum liber* (Augsburg, 1531) for an Englishman[1] to publish a book of emblems. It is equally odd that only six[2] emblematic works were printed in English during the sixteenth century. However, we should neither overlook, nor underestimate the influence of Continental emblem books in England. There is still much work to be done on this subject.

Emblem Books

English literary historians tend to see the emblem largely through the eyes of Mario Praz and Rosemary Freeman.[3] To these writers we owe what has become a traditional conception of the emblem, as well as certain aesthetic and value judgements about the phenomenon and a general sense of the pervasiveness of emblematic modes in the various art forms of the sixteenth and seventeenth centuries. It is unnecessary to rehearse the achievements of Praz and Freeman here, nor do I wish to elaborate on those areas where modern theories of the emblem differ, a subject on which I have written elsewhere.[4] Suffice it to say that scholarship never stands still, and earlier theories and accounts will always stand in need of revision and correction as knowledge increases and as perspectives change. For my purposes here it is enough to note that Freeman's conception of the emblem is narrower than that of Praz and therefore her bibliography of English emblem books is smaller, thereby creating the impression that especially in England the emblem is a "secondary cultural phenomenon," Joseph Mazzeo's term,[5] or even a "fad" in the view of Lisolette Dieckmann.[6] Freeman's narrow, literary theory of the emblem restricts the term to the three-part combination of text and picture introduced by Alciato, and that is an oversimplification that can falsify our view of the workings of the emblematic mode. In order to gain an overview of these related forms and to avoid pedantic distinctions, I also include imprese and iconographic allegorizations under the general heading of emblem.

The emblem, both as an art form and as a mode of thought, played a greater role in book making and printing in England than Freeman's study suggests. Her bibliography, based on a restrictive conception of the emblem, lists only twenty-four books in a total of forty-six printings. According to my bibliography, which covers the same time period but is based on a broader conception of the emblem, some fifty books were published in English in at least 130 editions and printings up to the year 1700. Of these titles, eight also appeared in at least 111 editions and printings after 1700, and this does not include modern reprints and microforms. The eight titles include one love, two moral, and five religious emblem books. These emblematic publications may be divided into four groups:

1. emblem books in the strict sense, i.e. the tight three-part form introduced by Alciato;
2. expanded forms: e. g. van der Noot, who adds a book-length prose commentary to his collection of emblems, or Hawkins who employs a complex nine-part structure;
3. emblematically illustrated works such as meditations where the plate becomes an integral part, e. g. Drexel;
4. theoretical discussions of emblem and impresa which provide many examples of actual imprese, e. g. Giovio and Estienne.

Although this larger number of English emblem books is still small in comparison with the approximately one thousand emblem books published on the Continent during the same period, the English contribution is more significant than hitherto realized. Furthermore, I have omitted manuscript collections and those many illustrated, book-length descriptions of coronations, royal entries, progresses and pageants, which were so often emblematic in character.[7]

English emblem books were, then, more numerous and more important than has been thought. However, we still have lamentably little information on the details of book production and distribution. How large were the editions produced at the time?

Who bought them, and who read them, and how influential were they for writers and artists? The only statistics that I have come across derive from the archives of the Plantin Press, which have miraculously survived to the present day. In a fascinating study based on the accounts of the Plantin Press in Antwerp, Leon Voet has unearthed details of costing and numbers of copies printed.[8] Plantin printed an Alciato edition in 1565 in 1,250 copies, and a further edition in 1567 of 1,000 copies. There was an edition of Faerno fables in 1566 of 1,600 copies, and a year later another printing of 1,250 copies. Plantin also published Junius' emblems into French in 1565 in 1,250 copies, in 1566 a further 850 copies, and a translation in 1567 in 1,000 copies. It is rare to have such accurate information, but from it we can see that dur-ing a three-year period one publisher printed no fewer than 8,200 copies of three emblem books, an eloquent witness to the popularity of this kind of book.

Poetics and Cultural Handbooks

It is evident that educated Englishmen were aware of Conti-nental emblems and imprese long before any emblem book had been published in England, or in English. Thomas Palmer compiled an emblematic manuscript entitled *Two hundred poosees*, which he dedicated to Robert Dudley as Earl of Leicester and Chancellor of the University of Oxford, which allows us to date the manu-scrip to the year 1565. Palmer's unpublished manuscript may thus lay claim to being the earliest known English emblem book. It also documents the reception of Continental emblem books in England. John Manning[9] has recently shown that Palmer drew upon Aneau's *Picta poesis* (1552) for thirteen emblems, Wechel's bilingual Latin-German edition of Alciato (Paris, 1542) for thirty-two emblems, de Tournes's edition of Alciato (Lyons, 1547, fre-quently reprinted) for a further five emblems, Coustau's *Pegma* (Lyons, 1555) for nine emblems and Paradin's *Heroica symbola* (Antwerp, 1562) for seven more emblems. Furthermore, Palmer used Valeriano's *Hieroglyphica*, two editions of Aesop and two printers' devices.

George Puttenham wrote on the subject of emblematics in *The Arte of English Poesie*, which, although published in 1589, was apparently written between 1565 and 1585. Scholars disagree as to the dating of Puttenham's section "Of the device or emb-leme." Puttenham's editors, Willcock and Walker, suggest that the passage was added in 1589, whereas John F. Leisher[10] argues convincingly that it was part of the 1585 manuscript, which was published in 1589. Puttenham's five page discussion of the emblem is a little masterpiece of condensed information and argumentation. He aptly concludes his discussion with the following summary of the "vse and intent" (p. 107) of "liueries, cognizances, emblemes, enseigns and impreses" as follows:

> . . . the vse and intent . . . is to insinuat some secret, wittie, morall and braue purpose presented to the beholder, either to recreate his eye, or please his phantasie, or examine his judgement, or occupie his braine or to manage his will either by hope or by dread, euery of which respectes be of no litle moment to the interest and ornament of the ciuill life: and therefore giue them no litle commendation. (p. 107)

Leisher dispells the myth that George Puttenham held emblems in contempt, a notion that derives from Friedrich Brie's misunderstanding of Elizabethan English. Leisher concludes that interest in emblem and impresa "has passed beyond the stage of the courtly novelty and had by 1585 become a serious, well-known genre commanding the attention of the sober literary critic." (p. 3)

A year before Puttenham's poetics appeared, Abraham Fraunce published an important work in Latin on things emblematic, entitled *Insignium, Armorum, Emblematum, Hieroglyphicorum, et Symbolorum, quae ab Italis Imprese nominantur* (London, 1588). In the third book Fraunce reviews at some length impresa theory and the five rules for the creation of the perfect impresa, naming amongst others Giovio, Ruscelli, Fara, Contile, Bargagli and Paradin. Reviewing the most important emblem writers, Fraunce enumerates Alciato, Sambucus, de Bèze, Aneau, Reusner, Faerno and Junius. There is no reason to regard this as mere name-dropping. More concerned with practice than theory, Fraunce provides lists of imprese, giving the name of the bearer, describing the *figura* or picture, naming the *vox* or motto, and indicating the source where known. Fraunce himself wrote an emblem book, *Emblemata varia*, which exists in an undated manuscript version in the Bodleian. The forty oval emblems have mottoes, Latin epigrams, and are accompanied by notes on facing pages.

In 1598 Frances Meres published his *Palladis Tamia* where amongst other things he praises the English emblem writers

Whitney, Willet and Combe, whom he associates with the Continental writers Alciato, Reusner and Sambucus. Thomas Combe's translation of La Perrière's *Theatre des bons engins* doubtless dates from 1593.[11] Although the unique complete copy belongs to the 1614 edition, the work was entered in the Stationer's Register on May 9, 1593. Meres writes of the English emblematists as though they were household names. The interest in emblems and imprese continued under the Stuarts. The English nobility was much given to the fashion for imprese, as we know from portraits, accounts of tournaments, and personal possessions which have survived. William Camden's book, first published in 1605, *The Remaines concerning Britaine* contains lengthy descriptions of the imprese of the English aristocracy (pp. 158-176). Judging by its ten printings, this must have been a popular work.

In 1612 Henry Peacham incorporated sections of Ripa's *Iconologia* in his popular *Gentleman's Exercise*, as Alan Young has established.[12] Peacham's cultural and educational handbook thus provides further evidence of the general and serious acceptance of the emblem.

The Cultural Context of English Emblem Books

I wish to leave the printed emblem book in order to review the role of the emblem in art as the broader cultural context of emblem books. The importance of the emblem as an expression of the cultural life of the Renaissance and Baroque is no longer in question. The combination of motto, picture and epigram is best regarded both as an art form and as a mode of thought.[13] It finds expression in illustrated books, but perhaps even more importantly it helped to shape all the visual arts. Combinations of mottoes and pictures, as well as emblematic motifs with their implied meanings, are to be found in paintings and portraits, wall and ceiling decorations of all kinds, carving, stained glass and jewelry. Ephemeral and fragile, but equally significant, were the emblematic designs etched on to glass, embroidered on to cushions and bed valances, and woven into table carpets and tapestry wall hangings. The public was further made aware of emblems by the preacher in his sermon.[14] They saw and heard emblems on the stage, in pageants, entries, and street processions. Perhaps it is not an exaggeration to suggest that emblems were as immediately and graphically present in this period as illustrated advertising is today.

In the following I shall review briefly the role of emblem and impresa in art, i.e. portraiture, wall and ceiling decoration, wood carving, tapestry and painted cloths, embroidery and jewelry. Space does not allow for a consideration of the use of emblem and impresa in drama, pageants and tilts, although much work has been done on the subject.[15] The second general area I wish to review might be called the emblem and book production, which will include title-pages, frontispieces, printers' devices and illustrations, and lastly illustrated broadsides.

Painting and Portraiture

Elizabethan painting and portraiture aimed at the stylized, heroic and allegorical representation of its subjects. The flattery inherent in portraits often took the form of hierarchical, political and symbolic allusion. Portraits of Elizabeth I were thus endowed with the qualities associated with icons, and Roy Strong's choice of the terms "icon" and "cult" in the titles of his studies[16] is particularly appropriate. He shows how two decades of destruction of religious art and artifacts led to the impoverishment of all English art, not only by virtue of the destruction of existing art, but because it also discouraged the production of new art. Just as the Byzantine icon emerged after a period of iconoclasm, so too the flowering of Elizabethan art followed the Protestant-inspired destruction of religious art in England.

Elizabethan painting harks back to the symbolic modes of the Middle Ages, but it is enriched with Renaissance hieroglyphs, imprese and emblems to produce a style that is essentially anti-naturalistic, strangely unlike the realism and psychological individualization that characterizes much Dutch art of the same period. The sitter was just as concerned to project his conception of himself and his role in society, as he was with the re-creation of his physical likeness. To fulfil this purpose artists resorted to the use of costume, accoutrements and symbols, even verbal statements, to translate into visual and external terms notions of self and the social and political status of the sitter. The way of thinking that produced imprese and emblems thus shaped the art of portraiture during the period.[17]

Whereas art historians increasingly recognize the emblematic quality of Elizabethan painting, literary scholars appear, perhaps understandably, less aware of the fact, and yet painting forms part of the cultural context of printed emblems. This emblematic quality resides in the use of mottoes, even explanatory poems or statements, inserted emblem or impresa pictures, and isolated emblematic motifs. Perhaps the best known motto on a portrait of Elizabeth is the famous NON SINE SOLE IRIS [No rainbow (Iris) without the sun], which accompanies the celebrated Rainbow Portrait[18] of the queen as the royal Astraea, variously attributed to Marcus Gheeraerts, the Younger and Isaac Oliver (Figure 1). Holding the rainbow in her left hand, Elizabeth is associated with the sun, without which there can be no rainbow. This is as much a political statement, underscoring the divine right of the sovereign, as it is a promise of peace for the realm. There is more than an echo of the Old Testament, where the rainbow is a sign of the covenant between God and his people, thereby reinforcing the notion of the divinely sanctioned monarch. Elizabeth had always insisted that England would enjoy peace and prosperity as long as a united people obediently followed the dictates of its sovereign, who was ultimately responsible to God alone. As a motto NON SINE SOLE IRIS is a many faceted political statement, which captures in words the significance of the portrait.

Elizabeth's servants, suitors, and courtiers frequently chose to incorporate mottoes, indeed impresa-like statements, in their portraits, which were often intended as a compliment, or tribute, or a plea, to their sovereign. Thus Sir Walter Raleigh stresses both his love and his personal excellence in the motto "Amor et virtute" [Love and by virtue] in a portrait, attributed to the monogrammatist H, which abounds with visual, symbolic references to the queen.[19] Similarly, Robert Cecil, 1st Earl of Salisbury, included in his portrait the motto SERO, SED SERIO [Late, but serious] as an impresa-like statement of his own high seriousness. Evidently Cecil, delayed for an important meeting of the Council, excused himself wittily with these words.[20] Sir Henry Lee, long time Queen's champion at the Accession Day Tilts, liked to have his portrait rendered the more significant by the inclusion of his impresa-like motto "Fide et constantia" [By faith and constancy].[21] These few examples are typical of the Elizabethan use of mottoes in portraits, the significance of which is not always obvious at first sight.

In structural terms a portrait becomes most obviously emblematic when the pictured subject, as an icon, is accompanied

not only by a motto but also by an explanatory poem, usually
placed in a cartouche towards the bottom of a painting. The
poem, like the *subscriptio* of an emblem, explicates the picture
by both describing and interpreting individual motifs.

A picture by Marcus Gheeraerts, the Younger, which is
known as either "The Lady in Fancy Dress" or "The Persian
Lady"[22] shows a woman in rich floral dress, standing next to a
stag. Above her head a swallow sits on the branch of a tree,
which is inscribed with three mottoes. Although it is difficult
to decipher them from the black and white photograph provided
·by Roy Strong in his *Icon*, I suggest the following alternative
readings: "Iniusti iusta querela" [The just complaint of the unjust];
"Mea sic mihi" [What is mine is mine], and finally "Dolor est
medecina amori[s]" [Grief is the remedy for love].[23] A sonnet
explaining the lady's love-lorn situation is inscribed in the cartouche, bottom right. The first quatrain equates the "restless
swallow," shown in the picture, with the speaker's "restless
minde," reviving "renewing wronges" and expressing her "Just
complaintes of cruelly vnkinde." The second quatrain directs attention to the stag: "With pensive thoughtes my weeping Stagg I
crowne." In fact, she crowns the stag with a garland of pansies,
while a long bracelet of pearls, themselves emblematic of sadness,
hangs from her wrist over the stag's head.

The proverbial association of the stag and melancholy finds
expression in the second line of the second quatrain: "Whose
Melancholy teares my cares Expresse." The stag's famous tears,
together with the speaker's sighs, are said to be the only "phys-
icke that my harmes redresse." The concluding sestet speaks of
the "goodly tree" that the speaker "did plant in love," but to no
avail, for "the shales be mine, the kernels others are." The "love
tree" is not identified in the sonnet, as were stag and swallow,
but it appears to be a peach tree, a fruit often associated with
love in the emblematic tradition.[24] At least since the Egyptian
hieroglyphics, the peach fruit had been associated with the heart,
and during the Renaissance by extension and perhaps by conflation
with the apple also with notions of love. It became enshrined in
the hieroglyphics of Valeriano. Both Plutarch and Valeriano note
that the heart-shaped fruit of the peach is sacred to Isis, the
goddess of fertility associated by the Greeks with Demeter.[25]
In this highly emblematic and literary picture the three mottoes
and the three motifs of swallow, peach tree and stag serve to
explain the pensiveness of the standing woman. Although the

sonnet offers a fuller elucidation, somewhat in the manner of an emblematic *subscriptio*, much of the meaning is implied by the visual motifs rather than stated in the verse.

Finally, we might return to Sir Henry Lee, whom Marcus Gheeraerts the Younger once painted (ca. 1590-1600) together with his dog, Bevis, with the motto "More faithfull then favoured."[26] The dog was, of course, proverbial for trust and faithfulness, and this aspect is emphasized by Lee's gesture of placing his left hand on the dog's head. The poem, comprising ten iambic pentameters, expounds on the nature of "love and faith," contrasting Lee's own undivided loyalty and the "very scante" faithful friends; Lee's dog is compared with Ulysses' dog, which proved "true and kinde." It is interesting to note that this poem is said to commemorate an incident in which Lee was rescued by his dog. However, as in the emblem proper, which generalizes the particular in order to make valid statements, there is no reference in the picture or poem to the biographical incident.

Some portraits contain complete emblem pictures set into the top corner. In his study *The English Icon* Roy Strong reproduces four examples: ". . . a queen issues from a castle to view weapons enmeshed. . . , a Cupid aims his dart at a chaste unicorn. . . , a man stands in the midst of a circular maze. . . , [and] a lady sits unharmed amidst reptiles. . . ."[27] In many instances a Latin motto appears in or beneath this inset emblem picture. Although the references are now frequently lost to us, it is evident that these emblematic pictures were meant to convey something of importance about the sitter.

The relationship of inset picture to sitter is usually clear in the case of an impresa. A miniature portrait by Nicholas Hilliard shows the Duke of Cumberland wearing his armour; in the background we see his impresa of a fork of lightning and the motto "Fulmen acquasque fero" [I bear lightning and the waters].[28] Another full length portrait of Cumberland as the queen's Champion and Knight of Pendragon Castle, also by Hilliard, shows his impresa shield on a tree behind him. The device features a centred earth, above it the sun and beneath it the moon; it is accompanied by the motto "Hasta quan[do]" [When the spear], indicating as Roy Strong suggests that "Cumberland would wield the lance (hasta) as Champion until the sun, moon and earth went into eclipse."[29]

Equally emblematic is the use in portraits of isolated motifs, which are intended to make allegorical statements about the sit-

ter.   The Ermine Portrait of the Queen (1585), variously attributed to Sir William Segar and Nicholas Hilliard, shows Elizabeth
with a small ermine, a gold coronet around its neck, looking up
at the queen and placed above her left wrist (Figure 2).   The
ermine was a common emblem of purity, but in this case the
golden coronet directly associates the purity of the ermine with
the queen.   Elizabeth holds in her right hand an olive branch,
while the handle of the massive sword of state can be seen close
to her left hand.   The sword and olive branch are emblems of
justice and peace, which she embodies just as the ermine alludes
to her personal moral virtue.[30]   Examples could be multiplied.
There is the famous Sieve portrait (ca. 1580), attributed to
Cornelius Ketel, which celebrates the queen as the Roman vestal
virgin Tuccia, by virtue of the sieve she carries in her hand.
There are layers of significance here.   Educated Elizabethans
might well have recognized in the sieve an emblem or impresa of
discerning knowledge and virtue, for such was its meaning in
Paradin's collection of *Heroicall Devices* (p. 184), published in
English translation by P. S. in 1591.
     Pearls, emblematic of purity, were so much the favoured
jewel of the queen that many of her courtiers had themselves
portrayed wearing not only the queen's colours of black and white
but also pearls as a compliment to the monarch.   In Nicholas
Hilliard's portraits of a "Young Man amongst Roses"[31] and of Sir
Walter Raleigh (1588)[32] both men wear pearl-embroidered garments.   Raleigh also wears a pair of pearl earrings in one ear.
To make the reference even clearer, there is in the top left
corner of the portrait the crescent moon of Cynthia, an allusion
to Elizabeth as the moon-goddess.   This crescent moon stands
directly above the motto "Amor et virtute" [Love and by virtue],
indicating emblematically the object of his love.   In the portrait
of the "Young Man amongst Roses" it is the eglantine, Elizabeth's
favourite flower symbol, which emblematically identifies the royal
object of love.
     Colours could also be emblematic, conveying precise meanings.
Elizabeth's preferred colours were white for purity and black for
constancy, and this was well known to courtiers and commoners
alike.   Reference has been made to the portraits of rival courtiers
in which the subjects wear black and white, but the colours were
also worn by Elizabeth's champions at the tilt, and by her dancers
at court.   Leaving the court for the cities, the town of Sandwich
was decked out in black and white to greet Her Majesty in 1573

and 200 men, dressed in white doublets, black hose and white garters came out to greet her.[33] Generally speaking, emblematic language, i.e. specific motifs and colours and their meanings, was well understood in the sixteenth and seventeenth centuries. It is only the more riddling use of certain impresa that was exclusive and recondite. Copies of emblematic portraits of Elizabeth I, or icons as Roy Strong prefers to call them, circulated widely. Both the queen and Council tried on several occasions to control the production of portraits for propaganda purposes to ensure a certain kind of uniformity.

Wall and Ceiling Painting

As emblematic structures and motifs played such an important part in Tudor and Jacobean painting, it comes as no surprise to find something similar in the decoration of secular and ecclesiastical buildings. Just how important emblems and imprese were is difficult to ascertain, since so many buildings have disappeared, and in the cases of those that remain changes in taste led to the replacement of one set of decorations by another. I am not aware of any inventory that draws together the information that is available in a scattered form. Our knowledge tends to be rather accidental.

Even in its day, Blickling Hall in Norfolk, was an exceptionally fine, although still characteristic example of contemporary decoration. The ceiling of the Long Gallery, some 123 feet long, is an elaborate example of Jacobean plaster work. The eleven central panels are dedicated to five heraldic patterns and allegories of the Five Senses and of Learning. The sense of hearing carries the motto "Auditus" and shows a man playing a lute sitting next to an amply bodied female singer holding a large book.[34] The side rows on the ceiling contain virtues and assorted emblems, largely deriving from Peacham's *Minerva Britanna* (London, 1612). Two examples must suffice: "Pulchritudo foeminea" [Feminine beauty] shows a naked virgin sitting on dragon, taken from Peacham, p. 58; the motto "Non invicta recedo" [Not unconquered-I retire] accompanies a rhinoceros that derives from Peacham, p. 106.

The great Gallery at Lanhydroc House near Bodmin, Cornwall, 116 feet long, is all that remains of the original house built 1630-40. The impressive plasterwork on the barrel-vaulted ceiling is presumed to have been finished before the outbreak of Civil

War in 1642. It is made up of some twenty-four panels illustrating Old Testament scenes from the Creation to the Burial of
Isaac (Figure 3).[35] These panels are arranged twelve on each side
and are interspersed with other smaller circular panels depicting
various birds and beasts, many of them as in nature but others
of heraldic, mythological and emblematic provenance. In the
centre of each half ceiling and making up a sequence of large
circles are panels depicting birds which appear to have thematic
significance. For instance, a crane clutching a stone separates
the scene showing the sacrifice of Cain and Abel from the next
panel which illustrates Cain killing Abel. The crane was, of
course, a common emblem of prudence and watchfulness, virtues
that Abel apparently lacked. Among the other birds one can
recognize a dragon-tailed bird holding a mirror, which may represent prudence (Figure 4). There is also an ostrich with a
horseshoe in its mouth, emblematic of fortitude[36] and fortitude
in adversity,[37] an eagle with crown and sceptre, and the pelican
in her piety (Figure 5). The left-hand side of the half barrel
ceiling repeats what is to be found on the right-hand side, thus
all the beasts and birds of the one side are reflected in the
patterns of the other. Although there are no mottoes or inscriptions on the ceiling, the birds clearly embody an abstract meaning
that makes them emblematic rather than merely decorative.

The Palace of Whitehall, which had played such a central
role in the cultural and political life of Elizabethan England,
was ravaged by fire in the year 1619. The impresa shields used
in the Accession Day Tilts were on permanent display in the
Waterside Gallery for all to see. Writing in 1598, the German
visitor Paul Hentzner alludes briefly to them.[38] However, the
published information available is scanty, although uniquely
interesting manuscripts exist. Reference is occasionally made to
the lengthy descriptions recorded by another German traveller,
probably Johannes Georg Dehn Rotfelser, a member in the entou-
rage of Otto of Hesse who visited London in 1611. His account
has never been translated into English, and only briefly excerpted
in German.[39]

After the great fire, the Banqueting House at Whitehall was
rebuilt by Inigo Jones and finished in 1622. Peter Paul Rubens
was commissioned to decorate the ceiling, and as this room was
the principal room of state, decorations were a matter of political
importance. The paintings celebrate the absolute monarch from
whom peace and plenty flow. This is the burden of Rubens's

iconographic decorations, which are mythological in the main, but frequently employ emblematic pictorial language. Art historians have pointed to the influence of Ripa (Liberty), Alciato (Cupid driving a lion-drawn chariot), and van Veen (Hermathena), reflecting the emblematic and iconographical tradition.[40]

Windsor Castle must also have had its share of emblematic embellishment. Paul Hentzner mentions a "gallery everywhere ornamented with emblems and figures" (p. 134) that caught his eye when visiting the third court at Windsor.

The taste for emblem and impresa was not confined to the monarchy and aristocracy. Landed gentry and the rising middle class liked to decorate their homes with emblems. Hawstead Hall in Suffolk, the home of Sir Robert Drury, had a painted wainscoted closet, often referred to as the oratory of Lady Drury.[41] The emblematic panels are now preserved in the Branch Museum, Christchurch Mansion, Ipswich. The four walls are decorated with a total of sixty-one painted panels and seven thematic statements set in cartouches. No fewer than forty-three are emblematic combinations of motto and symbolic picture, for which Norman K. Farmer, Jr. has established sources or analogues in the works of Continental writers such as Camerarius, Paradin, Reusner, Valeriano and Ripa, as well as the Englishman Whitney. The oratory is a kind of emblem theatre--the phrase was often used in the titles of emblem books--a theatre for spiritual contemplation. The subjects of meditation are introduced by general statements, e.g. "Frustra nisi Dominus" [In vain without the Lord], which appear just below the ceiling. These thoughts are then focussed by the single emblems beneath. As Farmer observes, the emblems "take the thinker directly into the heart of the meditation on such subjects as the relation of the individual to the world, the desirability of living within one's own center, the psychology of assertiveness, fear, anxiety, and the mysteries of the world itself" (pp. 104f.).

Carving

From Gabriel Harvey's *Marginalia* we know that his father's house in Saffron Walden boasted a fine chimney mantle, carved in clunch, which may be seen in the Museum at Saffron Walden (Figure 6).[42] The three panels and certain individual motifs derive from Alciato emblems: the bee hive and the laden ass flank the much larger central panel depicting Ocnus in contemporary dress making rope (Figures 7, 8 and 9). Since John Harvey was a farmer who apparently made much of his wealth from rope-making, it was natural that he should choose the motif of Ocnus. But it is even more understandable that he should replace Alciato's original motto warning against wasting money on harlots[43] with a new riddling motto NEC ALIIS NEC NOBIS [Neither for others nor ourselves], which only makes sense when one recognises that the ass is eating the rope laboriously produced by Ocnus. The rope is destined neither for Ocnus nor his clients. Each of the Alciato emblem pictures is given a new moralising motto, so that together they form a series of related statements on the value of labour. ALIIS ET NOBIS [For others and ourselves] is illustrated by bees returning to their beehive; NEC ALIIS NEC NOBIS [Neither for others nor ourselves] shows the work of the rope maker Ocnus destroyed by the ass; and ALIIS NON NOBIS [For others not ourselves], is exemplified by the ass, which though laden with food stuffs, eats thistles. While there is no doubt that Alciato is the source for the emblematic motifs on the Harvey chimney mantle, they convey quite different meanings in the Italian's emblem book. Alciato's beehive stands for the clemency of the prince, and the laden ass eating thistles connotes greed. There is nothing capricious about this re-interpretation. Whoever designed the mantle piece re-interpreted the Alciato emblems within the spectrum of possible meanings established by tradition for each of the dominant motifs. The educated Elizabethan visitor to Harvey's house would have had little difficulty in "reading" the meaning of the emblematic panels as he warmed himself before the fire.

During the second half of the sixteenth century wood panelling, often embellished with carving, was increasingly used for interior decoration. Such panelling frequently replaced or covered up earlier wall painting. Emblems, indeed, programmes involving emblematic designs were probably not uncommon, if the examples preserved in University College, Oxford are any indication. The Summer Room is decorated with twenty-eight carved oak panels that were moved to the College from a house built in 1572 (Figure 10). Peter C. Bayley[44] has shown that twenty of these carved pictures derive from the emblems of Alciato. They include Ganymede and the eagle, Tantalus, Prometheus and the eagle, the ass bearing Isis on its back, the three girls playing at dice, the lame man carrying the blind man (Figure 11), and the figure of constrained genius whose hand is weighted down by a stone (Figure 12).

Wood, no less than silver and gold, was used to embody emblematic compliments to the queen and impresa-like statements of a subject's loyalty. On occasions the carver was instructed to cut a verbal motto into the wood, the words of which replace actual emblem pictures. Without knowing the heraldic and emblematic meanings of certain flowers and animals, the visitor to Hardwick Hall would be hard pressed to understand the following inscription carved deep into a table:

> The redolent smell of Eglantine
> We stags exalt to the Divine.[45]

The stag was, however, the heraldic animal of the Cavendish family and the eglantine was one of the most important floral emblems of Elizabeth. Bess of Hardwick was giving expression to the loyalty of the Cavendish family to the crown.

Tapestries

From the early sixteenth century onwards wealthy Englishmen began adorning their manors and mansions with tapestries from the Continent. By the time of his death, Henry VIII had collected over 2,000 pieces of tapestry, which are listed in the inventory made at the time. By the end of the century, however, tapestry had ceased to be a collector's item for the very wealthy. Visiting London in 1598 Hentzner noted that Englishmens' "beds are covered with tapestry, even those of farmers."[46] In 1611 Johannes Georg Dehn Rotfelser filled two sides of his diary with a description of the "emblems worked into the old tapestry," which he observed in the great hall at Richmond.[47] In 1638 the historiographer of France, Sieur de la Serre, recorded the visit of Mary de Medicis, the Queen Mother of France to England. Like earlier Continental visitors he, too, was struck by the richness of the tapestries hanging at the Palace of Whitehall. Of the tapestries in the bed chamber he writes that it was a "new tapestry, all of silk, just new from the hands of the workman, representing the Twelve Worthies; and certainly this work was so rare and precious, that Europe cannot boast anything similar. . . ."[48] The Frenchman admits that "to express to you the great number of chambers, all covered with tapestry. . . would be impossible."[49]

While the major themes of these tapestries derive largely from Biblical, classical and mythological sources, as well as from contemporary Elizabethan life, the borders are frequently embellished with heraldic, allegorical and emblematic devices.   There are also armorial tapestries,[50] and yet others in which emblematic and allegorical representations play a significant role. This fact was not always recognized by scholars and antiquarians who described these tapestries in the early decades of this century.   Art historians and literary scholars today still have insufficient information to allow them to know just how pervasive the emblem tradition was in this particular art form.   Such tapestries are rare and frequently belong to private collections, inaccessible to most of us.

One of the greatest examples of Jacobean tapestry to have survived is the set of "Four Seasons" tapestries, originally made in 1611 for Sir John Tracy of Toddington, and now hanging in Hatfield House.[51]   The designer, Francis Hyckes, had enjoyed a classical education at Oxford and retained a life-long interest in Latin and especially Greek.   He was also very knowledgeable about Continental emblems and imprese.

Francis Hyckes based his designs for the "Four Seasons" upon engravings by Martin de Vos, but he added wide borders containing no fewer than 170 emblems, each comprising a Latin motto and a circular picture, nine inches in diameter (Figure 13).

The first attempts undertaken in this century to identify and interpret the emblem borders of the "Four Seasons" tapestries were made by writers who pursued the subject with much devotion but little knowledge of emblematic traditions or iconographical conventions.   Consequently, these writers frequently failed to identify correctly the iconographical motifs, and this in turn must lead to a misinterpretation of the tapestry.   Thus W. G. Thomson in his study *Tapestry Weaving in England. From the Earliest Times to the End of the XVIIIth Century* (London [1915]) describes Spring emblem 37 (Figure 14) "Consilium" [Counsel] as a "figure holding a horn-book" (p. 61).   One may well wonder what a "horn-book" is, and what kind of "counsel" might derive from it. On close examination the "horn-book" turns out to be the tables of the law, surmounted by a cornucopia.   The picture and text together suggest that the "counsel" is the law of God, which, if observed, will result in the abundance and prosperity denotated by the cornucopia.

A comparison of the tapestry emblems with the emblem books reveals that there are three apparent sources for the forty-two emblems that frame the "Spring" panel. These are: Geffrey Whitney's *A Choice of Emblemes* (Leyden, 1586), as A. F. Kendrick[52] had suggested earlier, but even more importantly, Joannes Sambucus' *Emblemata*, in the Antwerp edition of 1566,[53] and Andrea Alciato's *Emblemata*, in all likelihood a Plantin edition.[54] There is some doubt whether Whitney was a source at all since all of the fifteen Whitney emblems that Kendrick regarded as sources derive either from Alciato or Sambucus. Furthermore, I have discovered that twenty of the emblems derive from Alciato and twenty-one from Sambucus, the remaining emblem being a traditional representation of justice. Since all the "Spring" emblems derive directly or indirectly from Alciato and Sambucus, and none is an original creation of Whitney, it seems reasonable to conclude that Hyckes drew on these two Continental sources. Interestingly enough, Plantin was the publisher of Sambucus and the some of the most influential Alciato editions, probably the one used by Hyckes. Plantin also issued the Whitney compilation, which drew heavily on plates already used for Alciato, Sambucus and others.

Although my research into the sources of the emblems in the borders of the other three tapestries is not yet concluded, it is evident that Francis Hyckes utilised at the very least the following Continental emblem writers: Andrea Alciato, Joannes Sambucus, Guillaume de la Perrière, Georgette de Montenay, Gabriello Faerno and others in addition to the collection made by Geffrey Whitney. All this indicates how influential the Continental tradition was in Jacobean England.

The "Four Seasons" tapestries are not unusual in including emblematic and iconographic materials in larger designs. Another Sheldon tapestry, measuring 16' 3" by 6' 2" and depicting the Expulsion from Paradise, hangs in the library at Sudeley Castle in Gloucestershire. Mr Dudley B. Sidgwick, the Curator at Sudeley Castle, informs me[55] that John Humphreys visited the castle in 1923 to make the description of the tapestry that appeared in his book on *Elizabethan Sheldon Tapestries*.[56] Humphreys provides a full account of the rich background of Elizabethan flowers and assorted animals together with the border depicting the hunt. But the description of the eight medallions is iconographically inaccurate and incomplete. By virtue of their mottoes, one Latin and six English, and iconographically significant details, these medallions must be considered emblematic. I offer here my description of the medallions, the panels and two other allegorical figures (Figure 15).

Starting from the left, we observe a trinity of Christian virtues. There is first the figure of Hope, a woman standing before an anchor and wearing a blue dress inscribed with the word "Hope." Beneath stands the figure of Faith holding a cross, whose dress bears the inscription "Faithe." To the right and centred between Hope and Faith is Charity holding a baby in her arms and surrounded by three other children. This medallion is inscribed "Charatie" at the top (Figure 16). To the right of Charity stands Judith, holding a sword in her right hand and the head of Holofernes in her left hand (Figure 17). This figure is not placed within a medallion, but rather stands in the background of English flowers and animals. To the right of Judith are the two central panels dedicated to the Expulsion and Justice.[57] The top panel depicts Adam and Eve being expelled from Paradise by the angel brandishing a flaming sword; the apple tree is featured in the background. Directly beneath this is a medallion inscribed IVDICES [Judges]. To the left under the inscription is a pair of scales beneath which there is an open book bearing the words SECVND LEGEM, which means either "according to the law," i.e. "Secund[um] legem" or "second law," i.e. "Secund[am] legem." Under the inscription we see a robed judge standing on a pedestal or cube, denoting constancy. At the top right is situated a two-headed bust, a Janus figure, representing prudence,[58] and below to the right of the judge there is a seated lion which is frequently associated with power,[59] vengeance[60] and revenge.[61] I shall return to this panel and its Latin motto later.

To the right and centred stands another female figure holding a bag. She may be the maid who frequently accompanies Judith in paintings and tapestries, including a piece by Sheldon now in the Metropolitan Museum of Art in New York (No. 42.27). There follows a trinity of moral virtues, Temperance, Justice and Prudence,[62] that balance the Christian virtues on the left of the panel (Figure 18). In the centre is a medallion inscribed "Temperance," depicting a woman who pours water from a jug into a wine goblet. She also wears a blue dress. To the right again, and placed on a level with the Expulsion from Paradise is a medallion inscribed IVSTICE. This features a woman holding an upright sword in her right hand, from which a pair of scales hangs down. Her left hand holds the tables of the law, lightly balanced against her left knee. Her right foot is placed squarely on a cube. This figure of Justice is similar to that in the "Spring" panel (emblem 27) of the "Four Seasons" tapestries. Beneath Justice is a medallion inscribed PROVIDENC, which depicts a woman holding a mirror in her right hand and a snake encircling her left arm.

The central panels deserve closer attention. The Expulsion from Paradise, IVDICES, and Judith embody the themes of justice and retribution. Whereas God punishes the disobedient Adam and Eve, and Judith is Jehovah's agent of retribution, the IVDICES panel is a hieroglyphic combination of motifs illustrating justice. The motto IVDICES suggests not only judges, but also the Old Testament book of Judges. The motif of the open book with its inscription SECVND LEGEM may hold a clue to the central meaning of the whole tapestry, a meaning that seems to have eluded earlier commentators. One must first decide whether SECVND is an abbreviation of "secundum" [according to] or "secundam" [second]. If "secundum," then the open book is the book of the law. But the phrase may also be construed as referring to the second law or commandment: "Thou shalt not make unto thee any graven image" (Exodus 20,4). The two panels can be regarded as embodying in pictorial form the first two commandments brought down by Moses. The transgression of Adam and Eve was in two ways a sin against what would later be established as the first commandment: "Thou shalt have no other gods before me" (Exodus 20,3). Firstly, they had followed the advice of the serpent thereby rejecting the will of God, an act that set the serpent "before" the Lord. Secondly, in disobeying Jehovah's ordinance not to eat of the tree of the knowledge of good and evil, they were assuming a God-like prerogative, for the Lord had reserved the knowledge of good and evil to himself. Although not depicted in the Expulsion from Paradise, the serpent is none the less an implied link to the IVDICES picture beneath. The association becomes the more significant when we recall that the children of Israel worshipped a graven image in the form of the brasen serpent, which the Lord charged Moses to create in order to cure the repentant people from the plague of fiery serpents. We read in II Kings that during the reign of Hezekiah the king "did that which was right in the sight of the Lord" by breaking into pieces the "brasen serpent that Moses had made: for unto those days the children of Israel did burn incense to it. . . . " (II Kings 18,4). Furthermore, the book of Judges (IVDICES)

is a history of the Israelites' "whoring after other gods" (Judges
2,11f.), and of God's punishment and subsequent deliverance of his
his people.   If, then, the reference to SECVND LEGEM, is an
allusion to the second commandment, then the whole tapestry is,
quite literally, centered on the first two of the ten commandments, which enshrine the worship of God as laid out in the Old
Testament.

Painted Cloths

Whereas the wealthy purchased, or commissioned, expensive
tapestries, the less well-to-do bought the ubiquitous substitute
of painted cloths.   Done in oil on canvas or cloth, they depicted
classical, mythological and Biblical themes, as well as scenes from
Elizabethan life.   The pictorial subjects were often supported by
proverbs and mottoes, and presumably emblems.   Painted cloths
were sufficiently important to be listed in inventories and wills.
In 1558 a French visitor wrote: "The English make great use of
Tapestries, and of painted linens . . . for you can enter but few
houses where you do not find these tapestries."[63]   Harrison
informs us: "In the days of Elizabeth, the walls of our houses on
the inner side are either hanged with tapestry, arras work, painted
cloths, wherein either divers histories, or herbs, beasts, knots,
and such like are stained."[64]   Such painted cloths were used in
homes, inns and taverns, and temporary buildings of all kinds;
they functioned as a backdrop on stage and for other entertainments.   Unfortunately, only a very few examples have withstood
the ravages of time, the earliest dating from the end of the
seventeenth century.   From the brief descriptions available it is
impossible to determine to what extent painted cloths were emblematic.   But it is inconceivable that the emblem, popular for its
decorative beauty as well as its moral seriousness, should not have
been influential.[65]

Embroidery

Emblems, imprese and allegories also contribute to the
designs in embroidery,[66] whether used as cushion covers, table
carpets, decorative panels for wall hangings, or simply to embellish
garments.   One set of Hardwick embroideries depicts Penelope
and other worthies of antiquity flanked by the iconographically
represented virtues of Sapientia and Prudentia.[67]   Roy Strong

suggests that Bess of Hardwick was celebrating herself through Penelope as the exemplary wife and widow both in this embroidery and in the painting "Ulysses and Penelope."[68] In such cases the emblem or iconograph takes on the function associated with impresa.

Mary Queen of Scots[69] has gone down in history as, amongst other things, a great needlewoman. Destined to become Queen of France, she was brought up from the age of six in France by her grandmother, the Duchess Antoinette de Guise, and her powerful uncles. In her carefully supervised education, languages played a significant role: French, Italian, Latin, Spanish and some Greek. She also learned the social graces and activities prized at a Renaissance court: horse riding, dancing, singing, playing the lute, sewing and embroidery. The Continental tradition of imprese, augmented by the growing emblem literature--Wechel in Paris took the lead in publishing the first translations of Alciato into French and German--was imprinting its stamp on the cultural life of the French court. Henry II chose as his personal impresa three crescent moons, which symbolize the goddess Diana and her namesake his mistress Diane de Poitiers, with the motto "Donec totum impleat orbem" [Till he fills the whole world]. Mary's mother, Marie de Guise, took the phoenix rising from the flames, with the motto "En ma fin git ma commencement" [In my end lies my beginning], an appropriate impresa for a woman who had suffered widowhood twice. Marguerite, the sister of Francis, had chosen for herself an impresa which can either be construed as spiritually lofty or aristocratically superior: the marigold which always follows the sun, accompanied by the motto "Non inferiora secutus" [Not following lower things]. The flower actually depicted in the picture is not the marigold but the marguerite, a pun on the bearer's name. Mary later was to take this same emblem and attach to it a French motto "Sa virtu m'atire" [Its strength draws me]. If the letters of the motto are transposed it will be noted that they produce the name Marie Stvart. The emblem and impresa would later play a significant role in the embroidery of the Queen of Scots.

Within an eighteen month period death took off Henry II of France, Mary's mother, the Queen of Scotland and finally Mary's husband, Francis, who had succeeded to the French throne. Rather than become a second dowager Queen of France she returned to Scotland in August 1561 to claim the throne. Mary brought with her not only hangings and tapestries, beds and cushions, but two professional embroiderers and three upholsterers to improve her Scottish residences.

It is probably to this period that the embroidered royal bed belonged, which William Drummond saw in Edinburgh in 1619. Its embroideries were attributed to Mary. Since the bed no longer exists, Drummond's description in a letter to Ben Jonson, dated July 1, 1619, is the only surviving evidence. That he should have described and interpreted the imprese in such detail reveals not only his own knowledge and interest, but also the importance of emblems and imprese in the cultural life of the times. The thirty-two imprese include those of the French court mentioned earlier, as well as the imprese of Francis II, her uncle, the Cardinal of Lorrain, Henry VIII, and the Duke of Savoy. Drummond gives Mary's own impresa pride of place in his description, perhaps because it was indeed the central element in the political and moral programme of emblematic embellishments, but also, one assumes, because the Queen of Scots was no longer the enemy of Elizabeth's England, but in Drummond's words "the late Queen mother to our sacred Soveraign."[70] Mary's impresa was a load-stone turned towards the pole, its motto her name and its ana-gram: "Maria Stuart, sa vertue m'attire" [Its strength draws me]. Drummond comments on the political implications of two imprese which appear to allude to Elizabeth. "Two Women upon the Wheels of Fortune, the one holding a Lance, the other a Cornu-copia; which *Impressa* seemeth to glaunce at Queen *Elizabeth* and her self, the word [i.e. motto] *Fortunae Comites* [Companions of Fortune]." The other impresa features an eclipse of the sun and moon.

Mary's marriage to Lord Darnley, son of the Earl of Lennox, a Catholic claimant to the throne of England, infuriated Queen Elizabeth. The birth of Mary's son, James, who would later unite the kingdoms of Scotland and England, dashed Darnley's ambitions to become the ruler of Scotland. The murders of Mary's Italian secretary, David Rizzio, and later of Darnley himself, and Mary's subsequent marriage to Bothwell, who was widely suspected of having initiated Darnley's murder, all added to the notoriety of the Scottish Queen. Her subjects rose against her. Bothwell fled the field of battle, leaving Mary to be taken back to Edinburgh as a prisoner. She remained a captive in the castle on Lochleven for the next ten and a half months, during which time it is presumed she produced a number of large pieces of embroidery subsequently attributed to her. In her captivity she asked, amongst other things, for an embroiderer who would "drawe forth such worke as she would be occupied about."[71]

Mary escaped, but defeated in her attempt to regain the Scottish throne, she was forced to seek sanctuary in Elizabeth's England. Her uninvited presence in England was both an embarrassment and a source of danger to Elizabeth, who had little choice but to keep the Catholic Queen and heir to England's throne in near regal captivity. Nearly eighteen years later, execution ended her imprisonment.

From the beginning of 1569 Mary was in the custody of George Talbot, sixth Earl of Shrewsbury, and his second wife Elizabeth, Bess of Hardwick. Mary and Bess would spend a great deal of time together devising and executing various embroideries: Bess for her Cavendish home that she was re-building, and Mary to pass the time. The two women signed their creations with ciphers and monograms. Continental imprese and emblems frequently served as models for their work.

Mary was an intelligent and scheming woman: she used her needle as well as her pen to communicate with would-be allies. The Queen of Scots had a distinct purpose in mind when in 1570 she sent to the Duke of Norfolk a cushion embroidered by her own hand, depicting a hand holding a pruning knife, cutting away the unfruitful branch of green vine in the foreground (Figure 19). The emblem bears the motto "Virescit vulnere virtus" [Virtue flourishes by wounding].

Mary signed the design by placing directly beneath the first word of the motto her cipher, made up of the letters MA within the Greek letter O for her first husband, Francis. While the motif of the pruning of the vine could be understood as a religious emblem, admonishing patience and pious resignation, or a personal impresa, witnessing the stoic fortitude of the bearer, Mary's intention was different. Norfolk understood the message, which encouraged him to cut down the unfruitful branch, Elizabeth, to make way for the flourishing of the fruitful branch, Mary. The Queen of Scots had already indicated her willingness to share her matrimonial bed and the crown of England with the ambitious earl who in 1572 paid for his treachery with his head.

Even when Mary's use of emblem and impresa was not subversive, it was frequently allusive, conveying a hidden meaning to the alert and sympathetic observer. The story is told that she received an English envoy sitting under her cloth of estate which was decorated with Marie de Guise's impresa of the phoenix (see above).   The envoy, Nicholas White, did not understand the "riddle,"[72] but it was presumably intended as a statement of personal commitment, to make a new beginning herself when she had arisen from the ashes of her captivity.

Mary continued to take a genuine interest in the children of the Duke of Norfolk after his death.   His eldest son Philip Howard had been married during childhood to Ann Dacre, to whom the condemned Duke entrusted all his young children before his death.   When it appeared that the marriage of Ann and Philip was endangered by Philip's ambitions at Elizabeth's court, Mary "devised a cryptic embroidery for Ann Dacre."[73]   It showed two turtle doves in a tree, the right side leafy, the left leafless. The motto "Amoris sorte pares" [Equals by the fortune of love] referred as much to Mary's own mourning for the executed Duke as it expressed sympathy with Ann.   Later in 1585 Philip, who had become a Catholic, was apprehended attempting to leave the country.   He died in the tower six years later.

A piece of emblematic embroidery exists which it is thought was made for the ill-fated Philip Howard (Figure 20).   It depicts an armillary sphere above a stormy sea with sea monsters and ships.   The Spanish motto reads "Las pennas passan y queda la speranza" [Sorrows pass but hopes arise].   A series of imprese fills the border urging fortitude and apparently expressing the hope for succour or reward.   The borders also contain the arms of France, Spain, England and Scotland.   Some of the emblems derive from Paradin's collection of imprese, although Marguerite Swain does not note this.[74]   One picture shows a hand to which is attached a snake above a fire with the motto "Quis contra nos" [Who is against us (if God be for us)?], which was taken from Paradin, p. 187.   Similarly, the sword cutting through the Gordian knots with the motto "Nodos virtute resoluo" [I resolve the knots through virtue] also derives from Paradin (p. 214).   The remaining imprese are too faint to identify from photographs, but they may also derive from Continental sources.[75]

A particularly interesting and complicated example of emblematic embroidery is the coverlet depicting "The Shepheard Buss"[76] (Figure 21).   The love-sick shepherd, whose name is embroidered above his head, strikes a languishing pose in a stylized arbor. A Latin motto surrounds the picture, accompanied by four impresa pictures which make visual statements on the dangers of love. A rectangular outside border explains the meaning of the whole design in a statement made up of words and rebus devices:

False *Cupid* with misfortunes *wheel* hath wounded *hand* and *heart*.
Who *siren* like did *lure* me with *lute* and charmed *harp*.
The *cup* of care and sorrow's *cross* do clips my *star* and *sun*
My *rose* is blasted and my *bones*, lo, *death* inters in *urn*.[77]

The four impresa pictures derive from Paradin's *Devises*: a snake
in a strawberry plant, the sunflower drawn to the sun, a dog
jumping from a sinking ship and a hand holding a fan of peacock's
feathers with bees.   These imprese lack mottoes, which suggests
knowledgable observers were able to decipher them without the
aid of textual elucidation.   Whether they derive from the translation of Paradin published in 1591, as Roy Strong asserts, or
from the earlier original is not clear.[78]
    Ladies used their embroidery needles not only to decorate
cushions and covers, but also to embellish articles of clothing.
In his essay on the Hatfield tapestries, A. F. Kendrick refers to
an embroidered tunic, which is said to have belonged to Queen
Elizabeth herself.   It is a linen tunic embroidered in black silk
and adorned with flowers, birds, animals and mythical beasts, as
well as "a few emblematical subjects, and three of these are
found in Whitney's book."[79]   Unfortunately, neither Kendrick nor
Nevinson[80] identifies the emblems and their precise sources.
    Although very few garments have survived from the Eliza-
bethan period, contemporary paintings and portraits give us a
lively impression of what embroidered garments looked like.   In
the Rainbow Portrait the left sleeve of Elizabeth's dress is embroidered with a curled snake from the mouth of which hangs
what appears to be a jewelled heart, red in colour, indicating that
wisdom governs the heart or emotions of the monarch.   Elizabeth
is also wearing a cloak embroidered with eyes and ears, signifying either the constant watchfulness or the omniscience of the
sovereign.

Emblematic Jewelry and Silverware

    Jewelry, like every other art form, was influenced by the
Renaissance delight in emblem and impresa.   Unfortunately, the
the Civil War destroyed much of the art of the English Renaissance, just as the Reformation had earlier destroyed many of the
treasures of the Middle Ages.   Many of the surviving pieces of
Tudor and Jacobean jewelry were reset in the course of time as

taste changed. As Lesley Parker has observed, settings "were modified to comply with the demands of fashion, fortune and felony."[81] Although relatively little remains, contemporary portraits and inventories are an additional source of valuable information.

Two famous examples from Elizabeth's collection will illustrate emblematic jewelry: the Phoenix Jewel and the Pelican Jewel. The Phoenix Jewel (Figure 22) shows the profile image of the queen cut from a gold medal struck in 1574 while the obverse depicts the mythical bird in a flaming fire, signifying legendary uniqueness and solitariness. The queen's heraldic flowers, Tudor roses and eglantine, surround the royal portrait in translucent red and green enamel.[82] The Pelican Jewel (Figure 23), prominent in the Pelican Portrait and attributed to Nicholas Hilliard, features the pelican in her piety, thereby associating the monarch with Christ, and underscoring not only the divine right of the king, but perhaps more importantly, the notion that the good king lives out a kind of *imitatio Christi*.[83]

Household silverware was often embellished with emblematic designs. One of the rare pieces to have survived is the Vyvyan Salt, once owned by the Vyvyan family of Trelowarren in Cornwall and now in the Victoria and Albert Museum. The verre-eglomisé panels are decorated with designs, which, as Joan Evans notes,[84] were probably copied from Whitney. There are: a vine encircling a tree, "Prudente[s] vino abstinent" [Prudent men abstain from wine]; a snake hiding in strawberry plants, "Latet anguis in herba" [The snake lurks in the grass]: crowned Tantalus, trapped in a lake, unable to pluck fruit from a near-by tree, "Avaritiae stipendium" [The reward of avarice], and roses, from which spiders and flies draw nourismhemt, "Vitae aut morti" [For life and for death]. If Whitney was the source, the Vyvyan Salt is no slavish copy. Whereas Whitney entitles the Tantalus emblem simply "Avaritia," the artist, or the person who commissioned the Salt, improved on the original motto by adding the interpretational key word "stipendium."

Printing and Book Making

Title-Pages and Frontispieces

No history of emblematic forms would be complete that ignored the influence of emblem in the creation of title-pages and frontispieces for books in general. With the exception of some comments on individual works by McKerrow and Ferguson in their collection of title-page borders,[85] some references by Johnson in his catalogue of English title-pages[86], the methodologically important study of twenty frontispieces by Corbett and Lightbown[87] and relevant essays by Farmer and Höltgen little has been done on the subject to my knowledge.[88] And yet it is also here that one could expect to trace the influence of emblematic and hieroglyphic forms in the art of the woodcut and engraving during the period.

Emblematic frontispieces and title-pages were carefully devised by authors in order to make visual statements about the books they introduced. Virtually every motif carries significance; little if anything is purely decorative. Thus the relationship between frontispiece and book is closer than many a modern reader would imagine. Corbett and Lightbown discuss the frontispiece to Sidney's *Arcadia* (Figure 24), which is typical in most ways. At the top, a cartouche frames Sidney's crest of a porcupine passant. A shepherd and an amazon, dressed in costumes that correspond closely with descriptions in the romance, stand to the left and right of the frontispiece. At the bottom there is an emblem, which depicts a boar backing away from a marjoram bush. The motto NON TIBI SPIRO [I breathe (sweet scents) but not for you] captures the meaning of the scene. In Sanford's fore-word "To The Reader" the marjoram bush is explained as the ethical treasures of the *Arcadia*, which are presumably enjoyed only by the virtuous-minded. This emblem can be traced to Camerarius, and even further to Horapollo. A single title-page was frequently re-used by the printer for several different works. Thus one emblematic design was often more significant in terms of its distribution than it might at first appear. A case in point is the edition of *The Psalmes of David*, which H. Bynneman published in 1571. The emblem which interests us is found at the base of an arch. The motto "Non vi sed virtute" [Not by strength but by virtue] is printed at the top of an oval, which shows a dragon sprawled on its back on the ground with a

panther(?) at its throat.[89]   The printer used this title-page with
its emblem for at least twenty-six different works that appeared
in thirty-one editions between 1570 and 1629.

   Some of the emblematic combinations of motto and picture
found on title-pages are in fact printer's devices.   One of the
emblematic panels of the title-page introducing *A shorte introduction of grammar* (London, 1574) depicts three sweet williams
growing out of a cask or tun, which is inscribed with the letters
NOR.   At the root of the sweet william plant a "W" may be detec-
ted.   This was the punning emblem or rebus for the printer
William Norton.[90]

   These illustrated title-pages and frontispieces are deeply
indebted to allegorical, emblematic and hieroglyphical traditions,
which are to be understood both as an art form and a symbolic
mode of thought.   While the emblematic mode is clearly important,
frontispieces should not be simply regarded as emblems.   Corbett
and Lightbown point out that no matter how similar, the frontispiece does not exist in its own right, as does an emblem, nor
does it make a self-contained philosophical or moral statement.
Rather it introduces, even epitomizes, the book that follows. The
term "frontispiece" can mean both the entrance to a book and
to a building; as Höltgen points out, there are also close links
between emblematic title-pages and architectural allegories such
as triumphal arches for state entries.   Höltgen also describes
and illustrates for the first time the sub-genre of emblematic
brasses: they are monumental mural brasses, engraved in a shallow
technique, and for the most part executed during the first half
of the seventeenth century.[91]

Printers' Devices

   In the early sixteenth century, printers' devices tended to
be uncomplicated signs associating the printer with his place of
work.   For instance, James Gaver's collophon informs us that he
was "dwellynge at the sygne of the Sonne,"[92] hence his choice of
the sun as a device.   During the later sixteenth century, however, emblematic forms greatly influenced the creation of printers'
devices, which frequently asssumed the function of an impresa
rather than a geographic sign.   Thus William Leake who lived at
the Crane, the White Greyhound and the Holy Ghost used none
of these as his sign, but took the emblematic combination of a
globe of the world surmounted by a winged death's head, which

in turn was topped by a small hourglass before a larger open book inscribed with the motto "I live to dy. I dy to live" (Figure 25).[93] This printer's device derives from the emblem "In morte vita" [Life in death] (Figure 26) in Sambucus' collection (p. 99 of the 1566 ed.).

Several of Alciato's emblems re-appear with minor modifications as printers' devices. During the years 1571-4 William Williamson used a device showing Triton on a dolphin encircled by the snake of eternity, accompanied by the motto "Immortality is gotten by the study of letters." This derives ultimately from Alciato's emblem 133, but since it was used earlier by Jean Waesbergh of Antwerp and Rotterdam (1557-88) Williamson may have simply adopted the device of the Continental printer. Maurice Sabbe has written a brief study of the relation of Alciato emblems to some Continental printers' devices.[94]

John Wolfe adapted a Whitney emblem, which derives ultimately from Hadrianus Junius, for his Italian books with their fictitious imprints. The device portrays a palm tree with serpents and toads scrambling around its base, with the motto "Il vostro malignare non jiova nulla" [Your maligning is of no avail].[95]

On the basis of his study of hundreds of printers' and publishers' devices used in England and Scotland between 1485 and 1640 Ronald B. McKerrow concluded that "perhaps the majority [of such devices] are based ultimately on emblems. But it does not follow that they were in all cases taken directly from emblem books. Many came to England through the medium of the device of a foreign printer" (p. xxv). Thus the Plantin device of a pair of compasses with the motto "Labore et Constantia" [Through labour and constancy] was used by John Harrison and Nicholas Oakes; Wechel's Pegasus surmounting a caduceus over crossed cornucopias was copied by John Nicholas III from about 1660 to 1684.

In our enthusiasm for the emblem and impresa we should guard against the temptation to exaggerate the importance of some of our discoveries. The fact that printers and publishers employed emblems so readily does not necessarily imply that they were avid readers or collectors of emblem books. However, since each title published was sold in the hundreds of copies, it does mean that the emblematic device on title-pages, frontispieces and colophons appeared many thousands of times. In terms of distribution and frequency, then, the emblematic printer's device played a small and yet significant role. Precisely how significant we do not yet know, since much of the earlier research was done without the knowledge of emblem books available to us today. McKerrow does not notice that R. Wolfe's device showing three boys throwing sticks at a tree in order to obtain the fruit derives from Alciato's emblem 193, and the early date of 1549 precludes any reliance on Whitney. A fuller knowledge of the emblem tradition will in fact contribute to the correct interpretation of printer's devices. McKerrow (p. xxiv) admits being unable to decipher the meaning of the complex hieroglyphic device which Islip used in 1598 and 1613 (Figure 27) and which derives from Sambucus (1566, p. 97) "Quibus respublica conservetur" [By means of these the state may be kept safe] (Figure 28). When Thomas Scarlet and Richard Bradick use Camerarius' emblem 9 from his collection *Symbolorum et emblematum ex volatilibus et insectis* (1596) showing an eagle holding up its young to the sun with the motto "Sic crede" [You must believe in this] the printer is not merely referring to his "first class work" as McKerrow remarks (p. xxiv), but rather the printer is claiming the truth, in some instances perhaps the divine inspiration for the books he publishes.

It would appear that the Continental emblem writers from whom English printers most frequently borrowed emblems were Alciato, Sambucus, Camerarius and Junius. Frequently, Whitney was an intermediary.

Illustrated Initials

The illustrated initial, which dates back to early medieval illustrated manuscripts, has never completely disappeared; from time to time it makes a minor come-back. The smallest form of book illustration, it is perhaps hardly surprising to find the omnipresent emblem incorporated into illustrated initials. The title-pages for the domestic accounts of Elizabeth's household were illustrated with line drawings of emblematic and heraldic motifs and imprese. Michael Bath reproduces and discusses the cerf volant,[96] which with its crown and motto "Hoc Caesar me donavit" [Caesar gave me this] embellishes the accounts for the year 1580. The cerf volant was one of the badges of the kings of France, borrowed by Elizabeth I in keeping with her title of Queen of England, France and Ireland, as the title-page of the account states. Elizabeth's household accounts and other royal papers will doubtless yield further evidence of the pervasive emblematic mode, and a study of sources is likely to underscore yet again the importance of Continental traditions in England.[97]

Broadsides

Broadsides, being ephemeral and fugitive material, are notoriously difficult to study. They are dispersed throughout the libraries of the world and usually inadequately catalogued. This makes it doubly difficult to make any reliable pronouncements. There are a few printed collections and catalogues.[98] The British Library probably has the largest, if scattered collection, accompanied by information on some holdings at other libraries. The University of Texas possesses an important collection of seventy-four illustrated broadsides; however, only five are in English.[99]

From an examination of the 516 broadsides collected by the Society of Antiquaries of London, and described in their catalogue[100] it would appear that emblematically illustrated broadsides were something of a rarity in England. There seem to be broadly two kinds of emblematic illustration, the portrait and the hieroglyphic combination of motifs.

No. 101 is described as "The Rare Print of the Portrait of Queen Elizabeth in the Clouds." The whole broadside has a perfectly emblematic structure. At the top we read the motto PER TAL VARIAR SON QUI [The world may change but I am here]. Beneath is the portrait of Elizabeth who holds a fan of ostrich feathers in her right hand; above her head is a circle of stars. Beneath the print we read the following epigram:

> Lo here her Type who was of late The Prop of Belgia, Stay
> of France,
> Spaines Foyle, Faiths Shield, and Queen of State, of Armes
> and Learning, Fate and Chance,
> in briefe, of women, nere was seene, so greate a Prince, so
> good a Queen.

We are not surprised to find that Nicholas Hilliard designed the portrait. There are other similar broadside portraits of the Earl of Cumberland, Robert Cecil, and Prince Henry.

Perhaps the most impressive of these emblematic and hieroglyphic portraits is the broadside, dated March 4th, 1619, which marks the death of Queen Anne.

The closest relative of the printed emblem is the illustrated broadside, which introduces its emblematic design with the self-conscious use of the term "emblem." The year 1647 saw the appearance of an illustrated broadside entitled "An Embleme of the Times,"[101] setting out God's gracious dealings with England. The large picture graphically sets out instances of "legall punishments" in the shape of a soldier identified as "war," a two-headed woman identified as "hypocrisy" and an angel, sword in hand, identified as "pestilence." Biblical texts frame the picture on both sides, while beneath the illustration rhyming pentameters develop the themes of peace and religion, which are the subject of the broadside.

The English Emblem and the Continental Tradition

Whereas we know of the translation and borrowing done by English writers, we still have but the vaguest notion of the role Continental emblem books played in the original. Some information is available on the use to which Ben Jonson and Inigo Jones put Ripa's *Iconologia* in the creation and production of court masques. The emblematic interpretation of literature and drama, especially studies of source and influence, has remained largely speculative. Such literary criticism is likely to remain speculative until more accurate information on the emblems themselves is available.

Leaving aside translations and borrowings, we need to establish which Continental emblem books were available in their original languages in England, and how widely they were distributed, read and used. What is required is the compilation of an inventory of Continental emblem books in England and references to Continental emblem writers in English during the sixteenth and seventeenth centuries. One could start with public and private libraries where careful research would be required to collect the information that will begin to provide a more accurate picture. However, the mere fact that a sixteenth-century emblem book exists in an old library does not necessarily prove that it was there in the sixteenth century. Happily, some libraries, such as the Bodleian, possess catalogues dating back to the period.[102] Some of the colleges at Oxford[103] and Cambridge, the Inns of Court, and various of the great houses in England possess catalogues from the period. A catalogue of Robert Cecil's library, dating from 1615, is preserved at Hatfield House. It will be interesting to see which emblem books, if any, Elizabeth's first minister possessed.[104]   We know that Thomas Palmer dedicated a manuscript emblem book to him in 1598 as a new year's gift.[105] The library of Sir Thomas Knyvett of Ashwellthorpe (ca. 1539-1618) is known to have included two Alciato editions (Lyons, 1551 and Lyons, 1573), the Altdorf emblems, Bargagli, Camden, Camerarius, Canisius, Contile, Giovio, Junius, Ruscelli, Sambucus, Strada, Typotius, Van Veen (*Moralia Horatiana*) and Valeriano.[106] There are some printed records of private libraries of the period in existence, such as that of Sir Thomas Browne, Ben Jonson, Henry Pyne,[107] and the list of the books owned by William Drummond and others read by him during the years 1604-14.[108]

Proof of ownership, whether indicated by name, initials or an ex libris, occasionally allows us to date the presence of an emblem book in a given place. Princeton University Library possesses a copy of Sambucus' *Emblemata*, printed with blank pages as an album amicorum, and which had been owned by the influential German baroque writer Georg Philip Harsdröffer. The British Library has a copy of Hawkin's *The Devout Hart* with the entry "Anne Fortescue her Book 1683, given mee by my Cosin . . ."[109]

In addition to the evidence provided by libraries and by translators of Continental emblems, English writers and artists occasionally refer to emblem writers in letters, diaries and published works. In a letter to Edmund Spenser, Gabriel Harvey writes of "Jouios and Rassellis Emblemes in Italian, Paradines in Frenche. . . ."[110] John Harington had evidently seen an Alciato in England in the late 1580's. In an "Advertisement to the Reader," which prefaces his *Orlando Furioso* (London, 1591) he comments somewhat disparagingly on the use of woodcuts in Alciato and Whitney whereas his illustrations, which he himself designed, "are all cut in brasse" (sig. A).[111] William Drummond, who in 1619 described in detail the imprese adorning the state bed of Mary Queen of Scots for Ben Jonson, also wrote "A short Discourse upon Impresa's" in the form of a letter to the Earl of Perth.[112] He provided the Earl with a succint review of imprese theory expressed in thirteen points, demonstrating his mastery of the subject. The undated letter was evidently written between 1611 and 1633.

Continental Emblems as Sources

While it was not uncommon for German Baroque dramatists to annotate printed editions of their plays with references to emblem writers, this was much less the case with men of the Elizabethan and Jacobean theatre. As far as I am aware, painters did not follow any such practice, either in England or on the Continent, although it is possible that some artists' notebooks may contain references to emblem writers. It is, then, to modern scholarship that we must look for information on emblem books, and especially Continental emblem books as the sources for both writers and artists. Source hunting is, of course, a precarious activity, because emblems are highly derivative in two senses of the word. Firstly, later emblem writers re-use, one might almost say re-cycle, the emblems of earlier authors. Secondly, the emblem itself is a repository for the knowledge and lore, the traditions and attitudes of its time. A. F. Kendrick suggests that the embroidery known as "The Shepheard Buss" has "emblems worked upon it which are to be found in Whitney's volume" (p. 97), but he gives neither descriptions nor evidence for the statement; Roy Strong states the same emblems "are from the 1591 translation of Paradin's Devises."[113] But Strong does not tell us why the Paradin imprese derive from the English translation rather than one of the earlier original versions. Paradin's imprese were known to English devisers of tournament imprese as early as 1560, as Alan R. Young has demonstrated.[114]

While it is often impossible to identify sources, we can at least point to a Continental tradition. Peter Bayley has established Alciato as the source for the wood carvings that now decorate the Summer Room in University College, Oxford. Kendrick and others have demonstrated that Richard Hyckes drew extensively on the emblem books of such Continental writers as Alciato, Sambucus, La Perrière and de Montenay for the borders of his "Four Seasons" tapestries. Michael Bath has been able to establish Paradin as a source for the illustrated initials in Elizabeth's account book for 1580, and since no English translation of Paradin was made before 1591, the illustrator must have used an earlier Continental version such as that published in 1567. However, in order to ascertain precise sources or even an emblematic tradition deriving from the Continent, we need much more accurate information on the reception of European emblems in England.

Figure 1
Rainbow Portrait of Elizabeth I, Hatfield House.
Reproduced by courtesy of The Marquess of Salisbury.
Photograph provided by the Courtauld Institute of Art, London.

Figure 2
The Ermine Portrait of Elizabeth I, Hatfield House.
Reproduced by courtesy of The Marquess of Salisbury.
Photograph provided by the Courtauld Institute of Art, London.

Figure 3
The barrel-vaulted ceiling of the Gallery of Lanhydroc House, Cornwall. Reproduced by courtesy of The National Trust.

Figure 4
Dragon-tailed bird holding a mirror, ceiling at Lanhydroc House, Cornwall. Reproduced by courtesy of The National Trust.

Figure 5
The pelican in her piety, ceiling at Lanhydroc House, Cornwall. Reproduced by courtesy of The National Trust.

Figure 6
The carved chimney mantle from John Harvey's house at Saffron
Walden. Reproduced by courtesy of the Museum at Saffron Walden.

Figure 7
Laden donkey eating thistles, John Harvey's chimney mantle.
Reproduced by courtesy of the Museum at Saffron Walden.

Figure 8
Ocnus spinning rope eaten by a donkey, John Harvey's chimney mantle.   Reproduced by courtesy of the Museum at Saffron Walden.

Figure 9
Beehive, John Harvey's chimney mantle.   Reproduced by courtesy of the Museum at Saffron Walden.

Figure 10
Carved oak panels from the Summer Room, University College,
Oxford. Reproduced by courtesy of University College, Oxford.

Figure 11
The lame man carrying the blind man, Summer Room, University
College, Oxford. Reproduced by courtesy of University College,
Oxford.

Figure 12
Figure of constrained genius, the Summer Room, University College,
Oxford. Reproduced by courtesy of Univesity College, Oxford.

Figure 13
Spring panel of the Four Seasons tapestries, Hatfield House. Reproduced by courtesy The Marquess of Salisbury.

Figure 14
"Consilium" emblem on the Spring tapestry, Hatfield House.
Reproduced by courtesy of The Marquess of Salisbury.

Figure 16
Faith, Hope and Charity,
The Expulsion from Paradise.
On view at Sudeley Castle,
Winchcombe, Gloucestershire.

Figure 15
Sheldon's tapestry The Expulsion from Paradise. On view at
Sudeley Castle, Winchcombe, Gloucestershire.

Figure 17
Judith, The Expulsion from Paradise. On view at Sudeley Castle,
Winchcombe, Gloucestershire.

Figure 17 (continued)
Judges,
The Expulsion from Paradise.
On view at Sudeley Castle,
Winchcombe, Gloucestershire.

Figure 18
Justice, Temperance and Prudence, The Expulsion from Paradise.
On view at Sudeley Castle, Winchcombe, Gloucestershire.

Figure 19
Mary Queen of Scots's embroidered emblem "Virescit vulnere virtus," Oxburgh Hall, Norfolk. Reproduced by courtesy of The National Trust.

Figure 20
Mary Queen of Scots's embroidered emblem "Las pennas passan y
queda la speranza," Oxburgh Hall, Norfolk. Reproduced by
courtesy of The National Trust.

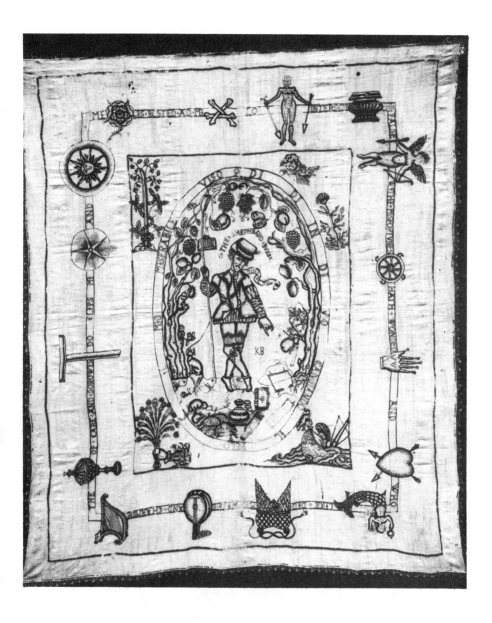

Figure 21
"The Shepheard Buss" embroidery, Victoria and Albert Museum,
London. Reproduced by courtesy of the Victoria and Albert
Museum, London.

Figure 22
The Phoenix Jewel. Reproduced by courtesy of The British
Museum.

Figure 23
The Pelican Jewel, from the Pelican Portrait of Elizabeth I.
Reproduced by courtesy of The Trustees of the National
Museums and Galleries on Merseyside (Walker Art Gallery).

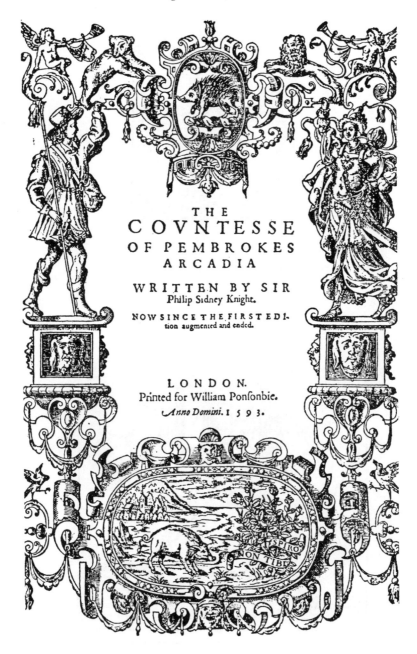

Figure 24
Emblematic title-page to Sir Philip Sidney's *Arcadia*.

Figure 25
William Leake's printer's device.

Figure 26
Joannes Sambucus, *Emblemata* (1566), p. 9.

Figure 27
John Islip's printer's device.

Figure 28
Joannes Sambucus, *Emblemata* (1566), p. 97.

NOTES

1. Whitney's is the first English emblem book in the strict sense that it is modelled on Alciato's volume. It is predated by Daniel's translation of Giovio in 1585 and the English version of van der Noot's *Theatre for worldlings* that appeared in 1569.

2. The six titles are: Jan van der Noot, *Theatre for worldlings* (London, 1569); Samuel Daniel's translation of *The Worthy Tract of Paulus Jovius* (London, 1585); Geffrey Whitney, *A Choice of Emblemes and other Devises* (Leyden, 1586); P. S.'s translation of *The Heroicall Devises of M. Claudius Paradin* (London, 1591); Andrew Willet, *Sacrorum emblematum centuria una* [London, 1592?]; and Thomas Combe, *Theater of Fine Devices* [London, 1593?]. However, since Daniel's volume contains an unacknowledged selection from the imprese of Ludovico Domenichi, and P. S's translation includes imprese by Gabriel Simeoni, a total of eight separate works are represented by these six English titles.

3. One of the few exceptions is the article by Jerome Dees on "Studies in the English Emblem," *English Literary Renaissance, 16 (1986), 391-420.*

4. Peter M. Daly, *Emblem Theory. Recent German Contributions to the Characterization of the Emblem Genre* (Nendeln: Kraus-Thompson Organization, 1979).

5. Joseph Mazzeo, "A Critique of Some Modern Theories of Metaphysical Poetry," *Modern Philology*, 50 (1952), 93.

6. Liselotte Dieckmann, *Hieroglyphics. The History of a Literary Symbol* (St. Louis, Mo.: Washington University Press, 1970), p. 45.

7. For example, John Ogilvy, *The Entertainment of. . . Charles II* (London, 1662); *A Description of General Solemnities* (London, 1675); Francis Sanford, *The History of the Coronation of James II* (London, 1687); and *An exact Relation of the Entertainment of. . . William III* (London, 1691).

8. Leon Voet, *The Plantin Press (1555-1589). A Bibliography of Works Printed and Published by Christopher Plantin at Antwerp and Leyden*, 6 vols. (Antwerp: Van Hoeve, 1980-83).

9. John Manning, "Continental Emblem Books in Sixteenth-Century England: The Evidence of Sloane MS 3794," *Emblematica* 1 (1986), 1-11.

10. John F. Leisher, "George Puttenham and Emblemata," *Boston University Studies in English*, I (1955-6), 1-8.

11. Peter M. Daly, "The Case for the 1593 Edition of Combe's *Theater of Fine Devices*," *Journal of the Warburg and Courtauld Institutes*, 49 (1986), 255-257.

12. Alan Young, "Henry Peacham, Ripa's *Iconologia*, and Vasari's *Lives*," *Renaissance and Reformation*, 9 (1985), 177-188.

13. Albrecht Schöne, *Emblematik und Drama im Zeitalter des Barock*, (Munich: Beck, 1964; 2nd ed. 1968); Dietrich Walter Jöns, *Das 'Sinnen-Bild'. Studien zur allegorischen Bildlichkeit bei Andreas Gryphius* (Stuttgart: Metzler, 1966); Daly, *Emblem Theory*. Peter M. Daly, *Literature in the Light of the Emblem. Structural Parallels between the Emblem and Literature in the Sixteenth and Seventeenth Centuries* (Toronto: University of Toronto Press, 1979).

14. Jenner informs us that he based his emblem book *The Soules Solace* on sermons that he heard in London. It is known that certain preachers employed emblems in their sermons and in fact preached emblematically. See Dietrich Walter Jöns, "Die emblematische Predigtweise Johann Sauberts" in *Rezeption und Produktion zwischen 1570 und 1730*. Festschrift für Günther Weydt zum 65. Geburtstag, ed. Wolf Dietrich Rasch, Hans Geulen und Klaus Haberkamm (Bern and Munich: Francke, 1972), pp. 137-158.

15. For a review of the emblematic aspects of various forms of drama, see Daly, *Literature in the Light of the Emblem*, ch. 4, pp. 134-167.

16. Roy Strong, *The English Icon: Elizabethan and Jacobean Portraiture* (London: Paul Mellon Foundation in association with Routledge & Kegan Paul; New York: Pantheon Books, 1969); Roy Strong, *The Cult of Elizabeth. Elizabethan Portraiture and Pageantry* (London: Thames and Hudson, 1977).

17. Leslie Duer, "The Painter and the Poet: Visual Design in *The Duchess of Malfi*," *Emblematica* I (1986), 293-316.

18. Reproduced in colour in Strong, *Cult*, plate 1 [p. 9].

19. Reproduced in Strong, *Cult*, p. 74.

20. Strong, *Icon* p. 260 and Roy Strong, *Tudor and Jacobean Portraits*, (1969), p. 275.

21. Marcus Gheeraerts, The Younger's portrait is reproduced and discussed by Strong in *Icon*, p. 281; see also pp. 282 and 290.

22. Reproduced in Strong, *Icon*, p. 288.

23. Strong reads the first motto as "Iniusti Iusta querela"; the second word seems to me to be "iusta," which also appears

to make more sense; and in the third motto "Dolor est medecina ed lori (?)" the last two words are probably "amori[s]," which suits the grammar of the motto, expresses the theme of the painting, and harmonizes with the sonnet in the cartouche.

24. A characteristic example may be found in Otto van Veen's *Amorum emblemata* (Antwerp, 1608), p. 70, where a Cupid holds a branch with peach leaves and fruit, gesturing silence. The emblem is reproduced and discussed in Daly, *Emblem Theory*, pp. 103-107.

25. Piero Valeriano, *Hieroglyphica*, Bk 54 "De persico": Cor; see also "De Malo" Bk. 54. The edition used is Lyons, 1602, pp. 573-578.

26. Reproduced in Strong, *Icon*, p. 290.

27. Strong, *Icon*, p. 31.

28. Reproduced in Strong, *Cult*, p. 142.

29. Reproduced in Strong, *Cult*, pp. 156f. The motto, previously thought to be Spanish, eluded explanation until it was discovered that the miniature had been trimmed, resulting in the loss of the letters "do." See *Artists of the Tudor Court. The Portrait Miniature Rediscovered 1520 - 1620*, by Roy Strong with contributions from V. J. Murrell (London: Victoria and Albert Museum, 1983), p. 134.

30. Reproduced in colour in Strong, *Cult*, pp. 148f.

31. Reproduced in Strong, *Cult*, plate 2 [p. 10]. See also pp. 56-83.

32. Reproduced in Strong, *Cult*, p. 74.

33. Strong, *Cult*, p. 71.

34. The panel "Auditus" is reproduced in the National Trust guide.

35. The panel depicting Adam and Eve is reproduced in Arthur Foss, *Country House Treasures* (London: The National Trust / Weidenfeld and Nicolson, 1980), p. 208.

36. Joachim Camerarius, *Symbolorum et emblematum ex volatilibus et insectis* (1596), No. 19.

37. Juan de Boria, *Empresas morales* (1581), No. 89.

38. Paul Hentzner, *Travels in England during the Reign of Queen Elizabeth* in James Beeverell, *The Pleasures of London* (London: Witherby & Co, 1940), p. 117. This volume is translated and annotated by W. H. Quarrell who added Walpole's translation (1797) of Hentzner from the French. Hentzner (1558-1628) was a Silesian whose travels were published as *Itinearium Germaniae, Galliae; Angliae; Italiae* (Nuremberg, 1612); another edition Nurem-

berg, 1629; under a somewhat different title another edition Breslau 1617.

39. The manuscripts, 4 Ms. Hass. 68, belong to the Kassel Landesbibliothek and Murhardschee Bibliothek.

40. *The Renaissance Imagination.* Essays and Lectures by D. G. Gordon, collected and edited by Stephen Orgel, (Berkeley: University of California Press, 1975) pp. 24-50; Pamela Wachna, "Rubens at Whitehall," M.A. Thesis, McGill University, 1979.

41. Norman K. Farmer, Jr., *Poets and the Visual Arts in Renaissance England* (Austin: University of Texas Press, 1984).

42. G. C. Moore Smith (ed), *Gabriel Harvey's Marginalia* (Stratford upon Avon: Shakesepeare Head Press, 1913), pp. 7-8.

43. The motto to Alciato's Ocnus emblem (Padua 1621, no. 92) reads "Ocni effigies, de iis qui meretricibus donant, quod in bonos usus verti debeat" [A picture of Ocnus; on those who give to harlots what should be turned to better use]. I am indebted to Mr. Bari Hooper of Saffron Walden for sending me his description of the mantlepiece, which has suffered some damage, making it difficult to identify all the details from the photograph. Mr. Hooper had also recognised Alciato as the source for the main panels.

44. Peter C. Bayley's articles "The Summer Room Carvings" appeared in *The University College Record*, 3 (1958), pp. 192-201; 4 (1950), pp. 252-256; 5 (1960), pp. 341-346.

45. Strong, *Cult,* p. 70.

46. Paul Hentzner, "Travels in England" in James Beeverell, *The Pleasures of London,* p. 139.

47. 40 MS. Hass. 68, fol. 79^v.

48. Sieur de la Serre, "History of the Entry of Mary de Medicis, the Queen Mother of France, into England, anno 1638" in James Beeverell, *The Pleasures of London,* p. 89.

49. Cit. from Beeverell, p. 90

50. John Humphreys, *Elizabethan Sheldon Tapestries* (Oxford: Oxford University Press, 1929), pp. 19, and 24f.

51. Peter M. Daly, "'The Four Seasons' Tapestries (1611) made for Sir John Tracy of Toddington," forthcoming in the *Proceedings of the Manorial Society of Great Britain.*

52. A. F. Kendrick, "The Hatfield Tapestries of the Seasons," *Walpole Society,* 2 (1913), pp. 89-97.

53. A comparison of the motto of Spring no. 35 "Animi sub vulpe laetentes" with Sambucus texts shows that the source is not the first edition of 1564, where the same emblem (p. 124) bears

the motto "Fictus amicus" but the edition of 1566, or perhaps one of even later date, with the identical motto "Animi sub vulpe laetentes" (p. 171). Whitney could not have been the source since he modified the 1564 motto to read "Amicitia fucata vitanda" (p. 124).

54. "Spring" emblem 10 may be taken as evidence of Hyckes's use of the Plantin edition of Alciato. Whereas the earlier Wechel Paris editions (emblem 5), and the Roville/Bonhomme Lyons printings (emblem 30) had depicted a stork in flight carrying another on its back, the Plantin editions and the tapestry depict a stork flying with food in its beak to its nest where three young birds are waiting.

55. Letter from Dudley B. Sidgwick dated August 25, 1982.

56. Humphreys, pp. 20-2.

57. These panels and Judith are reproduced in colour in *Sudeley Castle. An Illustrated Guide.*

58. Alciato, *Emblemata* (Padua: Tozzi, 1621), emblem 18.

59. Ripa, Hertel ed., p. 31.

60. Ripa, Hertel ed., p. 47.

61. Ripa, Hertel ed., pp. 60, 169.

62. These three are reproduced in Humphreys, plate VII.

63. Quoted from Humphreys, p. 9.

64. Quoted from Humphreys, p. 9.

65. For further information on painted cloths and Shakespeare, see Arthur H. R. Fairchild, "Shakespeare and the Arts of Design," *The University of Missouri Studies*, 12 (1937), pp. 1-191.

66. George Wingfield Digby, *Elizabethan Embroidery* (London: Faber & Faber, 1963); A. F. Kendrick, *English Needlework*, 2nd ed. revised by Patricia Wardle (London: Black, 1967); John L. Nevinson, *Catalogue of English Domestic Embroidery of the Sixteenth and Seventeenth Centuries*, 2nd ed. (London: H. M. Sationary Office, 1950); Patricia Wardle, *Guide to English Embroidery* (London:H. M. Sationary Office, 1970).

67. Reproduced in Strong, *Icon*, p. 41.

68. Strong, *Icon*, p. 41.

69. The fullest account of the embroidery done by Mary Queen of Scots during her captivity in Scotland and in England is found in Marguerite Swain's book, *The Needlework of Mary Queen of Scots* (London and New York: Nostrand-Reinhold, 1973). This study describes and reproduces all the work bearing her monogram or cipher, as well as pieces attributed to her.

70. Quoted from Wingfield Digby, p. 49, where the letter is cited in its entirety.

71. Quoted from Swain, p. 42.

72. Quoted from Swain, p. 63.

73. Quoted from Swain, p. 78.

74. Quoted from Swain, p. 87.

75. This armilliary embroidery is also reproduced in Wardle, *Guide*, plate 28C. For a full account of the Oxburgh hangings, see Swain, pp. 95-120.

76. The coverlet belongs to the Victoria and Albert Museum and is reproduced by Strong, *Cult*, p. 76, and Wardle, *Guide*, plate 29.

77. I have underlined the rebus.

78. Strong, *Cult*, p. 76.

79. Kendrick, "The Hatfield Tapestries of the Seasons," p. 97. Kendrick, *English Needlework*, p. 75.

80. Nevinson, p. 78.

81. Lesley Parker, *Renaissance Jewels and Jeweled Objects* (Baltimore: The Baltimore Museum of Art, 1968), p. 15.

82. Reproduced by Strong, *Cult*, p. 73, and Joan Evans, *English Jewelry*, plate 19.

83. Reproduced by Strong, *Icon*, p. 161.

84. Joan Evans, *Pattern. A Study of Ornament in Western Europe from 1180 to 1900.* (New York: Hacker Art Books, 1975), first published Oxford, at the Clarendon Press, 1931.

85. R. B. McKerrow and F. S. Ferguson, *Title-Page Borders used in England & Scotland 1485-1640* (London: Bibliographical Society at the Oxford University Press, 1932). This represents a collection of over 300 titlepages described and reproduced in facsimile.

86. Alfred Forbes Johnson, *A Catalogue of Engraved and Etched English Title-pages down to the Death of William Fairthorne, 1691* (London: Bibliographical Society at the Oxford University Press, 1934).

87. Margery Corbett and R. W. Lightbown, *The Comely Frontispiece. The Emblematic Title-Page in England 1550-1660* (London: Routledge & Kegan Paul, 1979).

88. Most recently, Norman K. Farmer, Jr., "Renaissance English Title-Pages and Frontispieces: Visual Introductions to Verbal Texts," in *Proceedings of the IXth Congress of the International Comparative Literature Association*, vol. 3 (Innsbruck, 1981), pp. 61-5. See Karl Josef Höltgen. "Emblematic Title-Pages

and Brasses," in his *Aspects of the Emblem. Studies in the English Emblem Tradition and the European Context.* With a foreword by Sir Roy Strong. (Kassel: Reichenberger, 1986).

89. McKerrow, No. 133.

90. McKerrow, Nos. 143, 144, also R. B. McKerrow, *Printers' Devices* (1913), No. 174.

91. Höltgen, "Emblematic Title-Pages and Brasses," *Aspects of the Emblem*, pp. 122-131, 135-140.

92. McKerrow, No. 90.

93. McKerrow, No. 341.

94. Maurice Sabbe, "Le symbolisme des margues typographiques," *De Gulden Passer. Le Compas d'Or* N.S. 10 (1932), 93-119.

95. McKerrow, No. 278 (Whitney, p. 118 and Junius [1569], No. 9).

96. Michael Bath, "The legend of Ceasar's deer," *Medievalia et Humanistica*, N.S. 9 (1979), 53-66, and "The white hart, the *cerf volant*, and the Wilton Diptych," *Third International Beast Epic, Fable and Fabliau Colloquium.* Münster 1979. Proceedings (Cologne and Vienna: Bohlau, 1981), pp. 25-42.

97. See below, Michael Bath, "Collared Stags and Bridled Lions: Queen Elizabeth's Household Accounts."

98. Many German illustrated broadsides were collected and published in two volumes by William A. Coupe, *The German Illustrated Broadsheet in the Seventeenth Century* (Baden-Baden: Heitz, 1966). Wolfgang Harms is currently editing the collection in the Herzog August Bibliothek, Wolfenbüttel. See Wolfgang Harms (ed), *Deutsche Illustrierte Flugblätter des 16. und 17. Jahrhunderts*, Band I: *Die Sammlung der Herzog August Bibliothek in Wolfenbüttel*, Kommentierte Ausgabe, Teil 1: Ethica, Physica. Herausgegeben von Wolfgang Harms und Michael Schilling zusammen mit Barbara Bauer und Cornelia Kemp (Tübingen: Niemeyer, 1985). Band II: *Die Sammlung der Herzog August Bibliothek*, Teil 2: Historica. Herausgegeben von Wolfgang Harms zusammen mit Michael Schilling und Andreas Wang (Munich: Kraus International Publications, 1980), now available from Niemeyer (Tübingen). Three further volumes are in preparation.

99. The collection is described in *Emblem Books at the Humanities Research Center. A Checklist with Selected Emblematic Broadsides*, introduced by Norman K. Farmer, Jr., (Texas, Austin, [1979]). The broadsides are described in a little more detail in Norman K. Farmer, J., "Popular Imagery," *The Library Chronicle*, N.S. 4 (1972), 48-57.

100. *Catalogue of a Collection of Printed Broadsides*, compiled by Robert Lemon (London, 1866).

101. Wing E-703.

102. The Thomas James Catalogue of 1605, and 1620; a list of books donated by Robert Burton, 1639; the catalogue of Thomas Hyde, 1674; the donation of books made by the second earl of Essex in 1600. See also Lucy Gent, *Picture and Poetry 1560-1620*. Relations between literature and the visual arts in the English Renaissance (Leamington Spa: James Hall, 1981), which also contains an inventory of library catalogues.

103. For instance, N. R. Ker, *Records of All Souls College Library 1437-1600* (London: for the Oxford Bibliographic Society, by the Oxford University Press, 1971).

104. Karl Josef Höltgen has now examined the manuscript catalogues of 1615 and 1637 at Hatfield House. He informs me that he has found only one entry for a book of emblems or imprese, *Cent. imprese d'huomini d'arme 4* (Cecil Papers, FP 5/22, fol. 37ᵛ).

105. The MS. is I. Bod. Ashmole MS 767. See Rosemary Freeman, p. 235. Palmer produced two other MS collections: BL Sloane 3797 (see Note 8) and BL Additional MS 18040.

106. The British Library has several seventeenth-century catalogues of the libraries of "eminent persons" whose books were put up for auction: "A Catalogue of the Libraries of 2 Eminent Persons (1684)" (BL 821.i.4[4]) and many others. There is also the list of English books printed not later than 1600; "Part II History [Library of Henry Pyne]" (London 1847; BL 011904.h.45). The BL catalogues of special purchases from great houses might also yield information (See Reader's Guide 9).

107. D. J. McKitterick (ed.), *The Library of Sir Thomas Knyvett of Ashwellthorpe, c. 1539-1618* (Cambridge: Cambridge University Library, 1978).

108. The list is printed by French Rowe Fogle in his *A Critical Study of William Drummond of Hawthornden* (New York: King's Crown Press, Columbia University Press, 1952), pp. 179-186.

109. Robert Burton's name, or initials, often accompanied by his own mark of three dog's heads (derived from his coat-of-arms), adorn the books that he donated to the Bodleian and Christ Church. From the list of Burton's books (see *Oxford Bibliographical Society, Proceedings and Papers*, vol. 1, 1922-26, pp. 222-246) Karl Josef Höltgen reports the following items: Abraham Fraunce, *Insignium Explicatio* (London, 1588), Horapollo, *De Hiero-*

glyphicis Notis (Basel, 1518), Hadrianus Junius, *Emblemata* (Antwerp, 1566) and Joannes Sambucus, *Emblemata* (Antwerp, 1566).

110. Edward J. L. Scott (ed.), *Letter-book of Gabriel Harvey, A.D. 1573-1580*, Camden Society Publications, new series, vol. 33 (Westminster: Camden Society, 1884), pp. 78-79.

111. John Harington, *Orlando Furioso in English Heroical Verse* (London: Richard Field, 1591).

112. The "Discourse" was printed in John Sage and Thomas Ruddiman (ed.) *The Works of William Drummond, of Hawthornden* (Edinburgh: James Watson, 1711); rpt Hildesheim and New York: Olms, 1970

113. Strong, *Cult*, p. 76.

114. See below Alan R. Young, "The English Tournament Imprese."

THE ENGLISH TOURNAMENT IMPRESE

ALAN R. YOUNG
Acadia University

It is generally acknowledged that the English fashion for imprese dates from the 1570's, the period when Gabriel Harvey complained of the lamentable manner in which English scholars were, in his opinion, wasting their time reading the works of men like Giovio, Ruscelli and Paradin.[1] In what follows I shall make three points that somewhat qualify the view that the fashion was very much a mid sixteenth-century phenomenon in England. I would like to argue first that the impresa was a familiar art form to the English from at least as early as the end of the fifteenth century. Secondly, I will suggest that there is evidence that the first Continental collections of imprese quickly made their way to England and were immediately used as sources for imprese as early as 1560. Thirdly, I will show that while published English impresa books may have been few in number, relative to their European counterparts, we have to balance this by the obvious wealth of surviving English imprese, and particularly by the large number of surviving tournament imprese. As I will make clear, descriptions and mottoes of over five hundred English tournament imprese are extant. Although they have never been studied in any detail, they represent a major addition to the corpus of existing English material that needs to be considered in any examination of the history of English emblematic art.

As the Elizabethan herald and historian, William Camden, explains in his *Remaines of a Greater Worke* (1605), "An Imprese (as the Italians call it) is a devise in picture with his Motte, or Word, borne by noble and learned personages, to notifie some particular conceit of their owne."[2] Whereas the emblem had a tri-partite structure of motto, picture and poem, and expressed some general truth, the impresa omitted the poem and expressed, as Camden explained, a particularity. As is well known, the impresa was subjected in the sixteenth and early seventeenth centuries to the conflicting attempts of theorists to establish laws for such matters as the proper relationship between its verbal and visual components, the languages to be used, the length of the motto, the appropriate subjects for pictures, and the degree to which an impresa should provide a witty and tantalizing interpretive challenge to the viewer. Such rules seem to have been made to be broken, and they were. Furthermore, as students of English emblem books are aware, the distinctions between "emblem" and "impresa" were frequently and deliberately ignored, as is evident in the conglomeration to be found in Henry Peacham's *Minerva Britanna* (1612), aptly sub-titled *A Garden of Heroical Devises, furnished, and adorned with Emblemes and Impresas of sundry natures*.   As Harvey's strictures in the 1570's regarding scholars wasting time reading Giovio, Ruscelli, and Paradin make clear,[3]   before any English treatises or emblem and impresa collections appeared, their European precursors were already well-known from Continental imports and from the works of European theorists, and certainly by 1585 the impresa (like the emblem) had become a serious genre commanding the attention of the sober literary critic,[4] something apparent from Puttenham's succinct and masterly discussion in *The Arte of English Poesie*. This was printed in 1589, but its section dealing with the impresa was probably in manuscript form in 1585, the very year in which Giordano Bruno's *De Gl'Heroici Furori* with its series of imprese was dedicated to Philip Sidney and published in London, and the same year in which Samuel Daniel published his translation of Giovio's *Dialogo dell'Imprese militari et amorose*.   Three years later, in 1588, Abraham Fraunce dedicated to Robert Sidney his Latin treatise on *Insignium, Armorum, Emblematum, Hieroglyphicorum et Symbolorum*, the third part of which drew upon various Italian theorists--chiefly Giovio, Ruscelli, Farra, Contile, and Bargagli.

However, the English person's contact with imprese was by no means confined to such treatises, for the impresa from the 1570's on can be found in literature.   George Whetstone introduced one in his prose romance *The Rock of Regard* (1576), and Sidney, before he died in 1586, introduced over twenty into his unfinished manuscript of the *Arcadia*, which was subsequently published in 1590.   In the early 1590's Spenser included imprese in his descriptions of two tournaments in *The Faerie Queene* (IV iv 39; V iii 14), and Daniel drew upon them in the *Delia* sonnets, which he published in 1593.[5]   In fact, as art historians in particular have noted, the impresa was pervasive and appeared in many different manifestations during the 1580's and 1590's in portraits, embroidery work, wall and ceiling paintings, wood carvings, tapestries and painted clothes, jewelry, plaster ceiling-work, and armour.   Thus, the hundreds of Elizabethan and Jacobean tournament imprese that are known to us are no isolated phenomenon; however, this should not mislead us into thinking that imprese were in any way an Elizabethan discovery. The history of the English impresa goes back much further.

In his *Remaines*, William Camden traced the origin of the impresa to the time "some hundred yeeres since, when the French and Italian in the expedition of Naples, under *Charles* the eight beganne to leave Armes [i.e. "coats-of-arms"], happly for that many of them had none, and to beare the curtaines of their mistresses beddes, their mistresses colours, or these Impreses in their banners, shields, and caparisons: in which the English have immitated them." Camden then gives some early English examples of imprese that he calls "imperfect" because they lack mottoes and goes on to suggest that the fully-fledged impresa began to appear in England on Henry VIII's accession when "the English wits beganne to imitate the French and Italian in these devises, adding the Mots."[6] But the use of imprese in English tournaments in fact began somewhat earlier than Camden suggested. Impresa-like devices were used at the English tournament to celebrate the marriage of Prince Richard in 1477, an innovation apparently inspired by the Burgundian tournament practices,[7] and at Henry VII's tournament in 1494 in honour of the creation of Prince Henry as Duke of York, the challengers entered the Westminster tiltyard on the second day of the tournament beneath portable pavilions, each of which was topped by an impresa-like device. At the 1494 tournament, for example, the Earl of Suffolk entered the lists beneath a pavilion of red sarcenet. On it was embroidered his motto: "For to accumplisshe." On top was his crest, a golden lion, the tail fourchy [i.e. divided into two], with white and green plumes (the Tudor colours), and dotted with spangils.[8] Closest to the type of impresa familiar from the later Tudor period was Henry Wynslow's deliberately comical picture painted upon his horse's bard. It showed two men playing at dice and was accompanied by "certain othes writtyn" but, according to the discreet chronicler, "nott wrothey her to be rehearsed."[9]

The 1494 tournament is the only tournament to provide clear evidence of the use of imprese at such events during Henry VII's reign, but from Henry VIII's accession onwards one can find a continual stream of allusions to apparel with "curious deuises, of cuttes and of embrouderies, as well in their coates, as in trappers for their horses" (Coronation tournament of 1509), to bases and bards "broudered with greate letters" (1517 tournament), and to bases and trappers "embroidered with true loves" (a wedding tournament in 1519).[10] Far more explicit, however, is the information concerning the Henrican tournaments of 1511 (January), 1515 (February), 1518 (October), 1520 (Field of the Cloth of Gold), 1522 (March), 1522 (June), 1526 (February), and 1527 (May). At all of these, impresa-like devices of one kind or another were placed on the horse bards of their bearers and were subsequently described in varying degrees of detail.[11]   One example will suffice by way of illustration.

In March 1522, elaborate revels were held at Greenwich to entertain the ambassadors of Charles V.   The revels included a tournament at which Henry led one group of jousters, his base and horse bard in cloth of silver, embroidered with three letter "L's" in gold, and "vnder the letters a harte of a manne wounded, and greate rolles of golde with blacke letters, in which was written, *mon nauera*." As the chronicler Edward Hall explains, the letter "L," the picture, and the motto signified "ell mon ceur a nauera, she hath wounded my harte," an allusion no doubt to Henry's queen who sat in the place of honour. The impresa of Sir Nicholas Carew, also on his base and horse bard, consisted of an embroidered picture of a prison with a man looking out at a grate, above which was written, "in prison I am at libertie, and at libertie I am in prison."[12]   As in the tournament at the Field of Cloth of Gold two years previously, it is these imprese, witty and ingenious in their composition and lavishly presented in complex embroidery work, that seem to have caught the attention of observers.[13]   Indeed, it would appear that such imprese often provided the chief vehicle of pageantry and display, coming into their own as an important part of tournament ritual at the very time when the use of other forms of scenic display, for various reasons, began to decline.[14]

Surviving descriptions of the tournaments held during the reigns of Edward VI and Queen Mary do not mention the use of imprese, but this by no means should be taken as indicating that imprese were not employed.   The Revels Office accounts for both reigns show in fact that bards and bases from past tournaments were carefully stored and then on occasion had their mottoes and embroidered pictures reworked for subsequent tournaments. The challengers for the tournament held in January 1552 during the fifth year of Edward VI's reign, for example, were so furnished from the Revels Office store.   The accounts for this event also note various payments for work done to prepare additional bases, bards, and caparisons for other participants, and there are references to the work involved in "the payntinge of the poesies written in the skertes of the barbes Caparrysons baces and skutchens" of the challengers.[15]

The evidence is equally scanty, but for one significant exception, for the tournaments of the first twenty years of Queen Elizabeth's reign. This one exception, however, is very considerable and is of special importance because it clearly demonstrates that the impresa collections of Giovio and Paradin were not only known at a very early date in England but were used as sources for tournament imprese. In the College of Arms there is a document containing a series of pictures of pairs of knights jousting. Above each knight is depicted his impresa. The first drawing (Figure 1) shows a knight with the Dudley family ragged staff on his horse bard jousting against another knight who has a star on his horse bard. Dudley's impresa is an ostrich with a key in its beak and the motto "Spiritus durissima coquit" [A noble mind digests even the most painful injuries]. The other knight has a picture of waves breaking against a rock and the motto "Conantia frangere frangunt" [They break those who are trying to break them]. There are then two further knights, one with a rampant lion on his bard, the other with the Dudley ragged staff (this latter also bearing a crescent, a second son's heraldic mark of "difference"). The first of these two knights has an impresa consisting of a pot with steam rising from it and the motto "Sic tua nos virtus" [Thus are we by your virtue], and the other has a pyramid encircled with ivy and the motto "Te stante virebo" [With you standing I will flourish]. The second drawing shows two further knights (Figure 2), one with a swan on his bard, the other with a bird (perhaps a blackbird). Both knights also have imprese. The first shows three feathers and the motto "Semper" [Always] and the second shows the sun breaking from behind clouds and the motto "Obstantia nubila soluent" [They dissolve obstructing clouds]. Finally there are two knights, one with a unicorn on his horse bard, the other with a bull. The first knight's impresa shows a unicorn dipping his horn in water and the motto "Venena Pello" [I banish poisons] and the second knight's shows a rock of diamonds with the motto "Naturae non artis opus" [A work of nature not of art]. Below this second knight is a note identifying him as Lord Darcy.[16]

The presence of the two Dudley brothers and Darcy helps one to associate these pictures with a particular tournament. Lord Darcy appeared in tournaments in 1558;[17] on 16 January, 1559; on 5 November, 1559; and in the tournament held on 21

and 28 April the following year.   Thereafter no Lord Darcy
appears other than in the barriers on 1 January, 1582.   The
Dudley brothers, Ambrose and Robert, took part in a number of
tournaments in Queen Mary's reign and in the early years of
Elizabeth's reign, but the only tournaments in which it is known
that both brothers participated alongside Lord Darcy are that of
5 November, 1559, and that of 21 and 28 April, 1560.[18]   The
heralds' score cheques for these events include the names of Lord
Windsor, whose crest was a unicorn; William Howard, whose crest
was a lion; Lord Hundson, whose crest was a swan; and Lord
Scroop, whose crest was a cornish chough or blackbird.   The Earl
of Sussex, whose family device sometimes included a star, participated in the 1560 tilt on 28 April, but the identification of the
star in the College of Arms drawing with the Sussex family device
is at best only tenuous, and it would probably be wiser to conclude that the drawings could refer to either of the tournaments.[19]

The surviving heralds' score cheques in the College of Arms,
with their lists of the names of participants, when matched
against the names of the various bearers of the imprese just
mentioned, thus show that imprese were in use in a tournament
within a year or so of the beginning of Elizabeth's reign.   Far
more important, however, is the fact that all of the imprese
described, except for two, appear in Giovio's *Dialogo*,[20] first
published in Rome in 1555, its first illustrated edition appearing
in Lyons in 1559.   In 1556 in Venice an edition was published
with Lodovico Domenichi's *Ragionamento* appended to it and this
was again included in the 1559 edition.   It seems clear that it
was one of these two editions with the Domenichi appendix that
was used as the source for the English tournament imprese since
one of the imprese not in Giovio ("Sic tua nos virtus"--"Thus
are we by your virtue") is nonetheless to be found in the Domenichi section.   The other impresa not in Giovio ("Te stante virebo"
--"With you standing I will flourish"), one adopted by Robert
Dudley, the future Earl of Leicester, and perhaps suggesting
something about his relationship to the Queen, appears in Claude
Paradin's *Devises heroiques* (1557 ed., p. 72).   The English must
have been quite quick to obtain copies of both Giovio and Paradin
and obviously they lost no time in making use of such ready-made
sources.   This, however, remains a somewhat isolated example of
such borrowing, although a number of examples can be found in
Camden and in the Kassel list of imprese (an important source

that will be discussed below) of possible borrowings from Alciato,[21] Giovio,[22] and Paradin.[23] In fact most later English tournament imprese do not appear to derive from such external sources, something which suggests that the personal nature of the impresa and the importance of displaying one's own powers of ingenious invention in its creation tended to prevent close imitations of the kind displayed by the Dudley brothers and their companions.

There is no further record of such devices appearing in the tiltyard following this early Elizabethan use of imprese by Robert and Ambrose Dudley and their fellow knights until a tournament held on 17 November (probably in 1577) at which Sir Philip Sidney, the nephew of Robert Dudley, appears to have presented himself in the guise of his pseudonym "Philisides, the Shepherd Knight." He was accompanied by a group of ploughmen, his impresa being a harrow with the motto "Nec habent occulta sepulchra" [Graves have no secrets].[24] Sidney appears to have had a special talent for the composition of imprese,[25] and it was possibly the enthusiasm for them that he and others generated that led to the custom at English tournaments of each knight presenting his impresa to the monarch as part of the ceremonial accompanying his entry into the tiltyard. A possible source for the custom is to be found in Italy where each knight's "divisa" (a motto or verse alluding to his cause) was presented upon his entry into the tiltyard and recited by a herald at the sound of a trumpet. This ritual was apparently well-established by the fourteenth century. At a tournament in Rome in 1332, for example, Galeotto Malatesta da Rimini, dressed in green, presented a device on a pennon which said "Alone like Horace," while that of Lodovico da Polenta, who was dressed in red, said "If I die in blood, what a sweet/soft ['douce'] death."[26] Another possible origin of the Elizabethan custom may have been the older requirement that each knight present his coat-of-arms before the start of a tournament. In 1494, for example, every participant was ordered to "bring with him a scuction of his Armes and deliver it to the Officers of Armes"; in November 1501 at Westminster there was erected a tree of chivalry surrounded by a fence, upon the bars of which "were hanged the scochions and shieldes with the armes" of the challengers and defendants; in June 1509 the conduit at Westminster was transformed into a scenic castle and "the targettes of the armes, of the defendauntes, appointed for the saied Iustes, there vpon sumptuously set"; the articles for the tournament in May 1540 stipulated that a tree of chivalry would be erected, on which would be hung "the escutcheons with the arms of the six challengers," and that a place would be provided for the presentation of the "escutcheons of arms" of the defendants; in Sir Thomas Pope's Hatfield entertainment for Princess Elizabeth in 1556 the arms of the challengers were placed upon a scenic castle; and in 1565 at the Whitehall marriage tournament for Ambrose Dudley, the retinue of each knight included an amazon with a sword by her side, a mask on her face, long hair hanging down to her boots, and "in her Hand a Targett of her Maister's Arms" which was then affixed to a post beneath the Queen's gallery at the upper end of the tiltyard.[27]   However, by the late 1570's and certainly by 1581 shields displaying coats-of-arms seem to have been replaced by shields with imprese.

Although none of the Tudor or Jacobean tournament impresa shields has survived (Figures 3 and 4), we nonetheless know about an extraordinary number of them.   Early in the 1580's, and perhaps before, it became the custom at Whitehall Palace to hang up the impresa shields after each tournament in a special gallery in the palace.   Over the years this collection grew, and one has only to calculate the number of tournaments and the numbers of participants in each to realize that many hundreds of shields must have been presented by the time the last tournaments took place in the early 1620's.   Early on, the collection became a major attraction for visitors taking the guided tours of Whitehall that seem to have been available.   A number of those visitors described the gallery and even wrote down descriptions of some of the imprese they saw there.   A German visitor in 1585, Lupold von Wedel, gave us the first description of the gallery itself.   "We were taken into a long passage," he says, "which on both sides is beautifully decorated with shields and mottoes.   These shields originate from tournaments. . . Everybody who wishes to take part must ask permission; this being granted, he offers the shield to the queen, who orders it to be hung up there."[28]   Fourteen years after von Wedel had seen what eventually became known as The Shield Gallery, Paul Hentzner, another visitor from abroad, said that among the Whitehall treasures that he had seen was a "variety of emblems on paper, cut in the shape of shields, with mottoes, used by the nobility at tilts and tournaments, hung up here for a memorial."[29]   A year later in 1599 Thomas Platter recorded his visit to "a chamber . . . [at Whitehall], hung all round with emblems and mottoes."[30]   Other visitors followed, among them the nineteen-year-old Moravian Baron Waldstein; the young Philip Julius, the Duke of Stettin-Pomerania; the London lawyer John Manningham; and the English emblem writer Henry Peacham. These, together with William Camden, recorded descriptions of a number of the imprese preserved in the gallery at Whitehall. Peacham, who made use of some of the imprese in his *Minerva Britanna*, even appears to have made a collection of the majority of them but was, unfortunately for us, dissuaded from publishing it on account of prohibitive costs. Commenting on the contemporary fashion for imprese, and anxious to point out that the English were capable of holding their own, Peacham remarked in *The Compleat Gentleman* (1622):

> *Emblemes* and *Impresa's* if ingeniously conceipted, are of daintie deuice and much esteeme. The Inuention of the Italian herein is very singular, neither doe our English wits come much behind them, but rather equall them euery way. The best that I haue seene, haue beene the deuises of Tiltings, whereof many are reserued in the priuate Gallery at White Hall, of Sr. *Phillip Sidneie's*, the Earle of *Cumberland*, Sr. *Henry Leigh*, the late Earle of *Essex*, with many others, most of which I once collected with intent to publish them, but the charge disswaded me.[31]

From what we can guess about the probable total number of imprese composed for tournaments, it must be clear that the various descriptions recorded by the visitors just mentioned account for only a small fraction of the great wealth of emblematic material that was originally hung up for all to see.[32] However, there is yet another source. This is the 34-page list of imprese appended to the diary of one of those who accompanied the Landgraf Otto of Hessen-Kassel on his visit to England in the summer of 1611. The document in question, part of a lengthy travel diary, is in the Kassel Landesbibliothek und Murhardsche Bibliothek and is one of four such manuscripts dealing with Landgraf Otto's visit.[33] According to its compiler, a small group of Otto's followers spent an afternoon at Whitehall and managed to copy about half the devices in the gallery.[34] Since the number of imprese listed in the manuscript is just over four hundred, the total number in the gallery when he visited it may well have been about eight hundred. After 1611, of course, the collection would have grown still larger. When the Kassel list is combined with all the previous known sources--and these, it should be noted, are often duplicated by it--the total number of known English tournament imprese turns out to be approximately five hundred and twenty.   In fact the Kassel text is the single largest extant source of information about the English impresa. It is also the largest extant text having to do with English tournaments, and a major addition to the corpus of English Renaissance emblem literature in general.

Yet, despite the abundance of English tournament imprese, in only about a hundred or so instances do we know both their precise or even approximate dates and the names of their original bearers.   As a result it is hopeless in most cases to attempt detailed interpretations.   Our inability to interpret the personal particularities intended by an impresa may not be very significant in the case of some of the early Tudor imprese consisting of compliments by Henry VIII and others to the Queen, whose presence offered the traditional female focus for the knights' devotions and chivalric exploits.   In Elizabeth's reign, however, tournament imprese took on added political significance once she became the object of an elaborate cult which defined her (among other things) as Virgin Queen of the Reformed Church.   Her Accession Day of 17 November developed as a great national holiday in which her virtues, England's delivery from Popish bondage, and the people's subsequent peace and prosperity were celebrated each year with bell-ringing, sermons, bonfires, and a tournament at Whitehall.   This was indeed an occasion for the right kind of personal/political compliments, as in Sir Henry Lee's "Caelumque solumque beavit" [She makes blessed both heaven and earth] but it is clear that the opportunity, like the annual giving of gifts to her each New Year's day, was one that Elizabeth's courtiers learned to exploit in another way.   Whoever presented either Elizabeth or her successor, James I, with the impresa of a fruit tree with the motto "Speramus regalem pluviam" [We hope for royal rain] was obviously doing more than merely complimenting his ruler as the source of all bounty.[35]   Robert Dudley's use much earlier of the "Te stante virebo" impresa from Paradin works in a similar way.   Elizabeth is complimented by being represented as a golden pyramid-like column without whom her subjects (the ivy) cannot flourish.[36]   But Dudley's impresa is probably also a plea that Elizabeth should offer him assistance, though in fact she had just made him a Garter Knight and Master of the Horse.   On a more subtle level, the impresa may hint at something more personal, a tempting idea given what is known about the relationship between Dudley and Elizabeth at this date. A host of further examples in which compliments are mixed with personal pleas could be cited, among them such imprese as "De lumine petimus lumen" [We seek for light in the light] depicting a burning light; or "Dum splendes floreo" [While you shine, I flourish] depicting a rose just below the sun; or "Fatum subscribat Eliza" [Elizabeth writes below my fate] depicting a blank space below the motto; or "Si non sustenatus pereo" [I perish if not held up] depicting vines held up with supports.[37]

When a courtier had been out of favour, an appearance at a tournament, together with a suitable impresa, might well turn the tables in his favour. When Sir Robert Cary appeared at the Windsor tournament in 1593 disguised as a forsaken knight who had vowed solitude, he presented Elizabeth with an extremely expensive gift, but presumably his impresa also conveyed in some fashion his contrition for having earlier displeased the Queen by getting married without her permission. Such a situation would have been well served by the impresa "Dolor meus apertus" [My sorrow is open], although there is now no way of knowing to whom this particular device originally belonged.[38] In 1590 the Earl of Essex, who was as renowned as Sidney for his imprese,[39] faced a similar situation to that of Cary. He had enraged Elizabeth by secretly marrying Sidney's widow. At the tournament in November, he and his train entered as a funeral cortege. George Peele vividly described the dramatic scene in his *Polyhymnia* (1590). Essex, we are told,[40] was

> . . . all in Sable sad,
> Drawn on with cole-blacke Steeds of duskie hue,
> In stately Chariot full of deepe device.

Though Peele interpreted the pageant as an expression of grief for the death of Sidney, those in the know would have understood Essex's need at this particular moment in his career to reconcile himself with Elizabeth. For his impresa on this occasion he may have carried a black shield with the motto "Par nulla figura dolori" [No picture is appropriate to this grief]. This was attributed to Essex by Manningham, Gershow, and Camden, all of whom recorded descriptions of it. Unfortunately, none of them provided a date, so its use in 1590 remains conjectural.

It was his appearance at this tournament that Essex decided to commemorate by having his portrait painted by William Segar. The painting, now in the National Gallery of Ireland, shows Essex dressed and armed in black, presumably as he appeared in the tiltyard at Whitehall when he made his entrance in his chariot drawn by coal black horses and driven by the personified figure of "gloomie Time."[41] Several of those who participated in tournaments decided to have such portraits made of themselves. Essex himself had Nicholas Hilliard do a miniature of him in armour, standing before a tent. On either side of Essex's bases are embroidered within a circle a series of diamonds with the motto "DUM FORMAS MINUIS" [While you shape, you diminish]. On his right sleeve is tied the Queen's glove and in the background a page wearing the Queen's colours of black and white is holding Essex's horse. This portrait, now in a private collection, probably dates from between 1592 and 1596. Very likely it was commissioned to commemorate the Accession Day tournament of 1595 at which Elizabeth gave Essex her glove.[42] Essex's impresa shield for this occasion--a large diamond with the motto "Dum formas minuis"--was hung in the Shield Gallery where John Manningham saw it in 1602, the year of Essex's execution, and its presence there and attribution to Essex is further confirmed in Camden's *Remaines*, in Jonson's *Conversations with Drummond*, and in the Kassel manuscript.[43] Without a confirmed date, it is impossible to be sure about an interpretation, but there appears to be some intended allusion to the bearer's relationship to the Queen. The image of the diamond and the accompanying motto are a reminder, so Camden suggests, that diamonds are always impaired when they are cut. Essex perhaps felt that Elizabeth should recognize his great virtues and accept with them any flaws in his behaviour. The sentiment has more in it of personal pleading than compliment, but this would have been not entirely uncharacteristic of the egocentric Essex.

Several other portraits show their respective subjects in tilting armour and display in some way their imprese. Among them, for example, is Hilliard's famous portrait miniature of the Earl of Cumberland, now in the National Maritime Museum at Greenwich. This probably commemorates the Accession Day tournament of 1590 at which Cumberland succeeded Sir Henry Lee as Queen's Champion. In his cap Cumberland wears the Queen's glove, and his gauntlet lies as a challenge on the ground before him. In his right hand he grasps his tilting lance, and his helmet and second gauntlet lie to his left. Behind him hanging in the tree is his impresa shield on which is depicted the sun, the moon and the earth, and his motto "Hasta Quando" [The spear until such time as]. The meaning of the device seems to be that Cumberland, the new Champion, will serve his sovereign with his lance (hasta) until the sun, the moon and the earth are in eclipse.[44]

Such examples of known tournament imprese as I have cited are obviously only a tiny representative sample of those that have survived, and a full study of English tournament imprese would require a volume for itself. However, before concluding this brief survey it should be pointed out that the tournament impresa did not die with the end of the era of tournaments. As Thomas Blount remarked in 1646 in his translation of Henri Estienne's *The Art of Making Devises*, "Some may object, that. . ., Tournaments, and Masques, (where *Devices* were much in request) are for the most present laid aside, therefore *Devises* are of lesse use. Whereto I answer, that as those Justing or jesting Wars are disused, so have we now an earnest, though much to be lamented Warre, which renders them more usefull then ever, I meane for *Cornets* and *Ensignes*."[45] Blount goes on to give various examples from the Royalists and Parliamentarians, and he further demonstrates the link with the earlier tournament imprese by including four of these latter on his engraved title-page.[46] Even more detailed is John Prestwick's *Respublica* (1787), which describes 237 Parliamentarian imprese used in the Civil War, each exemplifying an art once associated primarily only with what Blount punningly called "jesting Wars." In the 1640's Englishmen may have laid aside the courtly art of encounters at the tilt, but the associated literary art of the impresa clearly remained for a time to exercise the wit and ingenuity of those who wished publicly to state some personal intention or attitude when they rode into combat. Here, waiting for the student of emblem literature, is a rich and abundant source that stretches back to the late fifteenth century and continues until the English Civil War, its existence yet further evidence of the vitality and ubiquity of the English fashion for things emblematic.

74 Alan R. Young

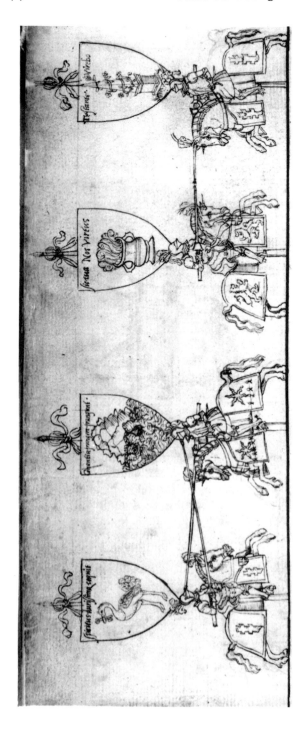

Figure 1
Early Elizabethan tournament imprese. The four imprese belong (from left to right) to Ambrose Dudley, (?) the Earl of Sussex, William Howard, and Robert Dudley. (College of Arms, MS. M. 6, fol. 56b). Reproduced by courtesy of the College of Arms.

Figure 2
Early Elizabethan tournament imprese. The knights may be tentatively identified (from left to right) as Lord Hunsden, Lord Scroop, Lord Windsor, and Lord Darcy. As in Figure 1, the imprese were copies for use in the tournament from printed sources, an unusual practice with regard to English tournament imprese. (College of Arms, MS. M. 6, fol. 57a). Reproduced by courtesy of the College of Arms.

Figure 3
Design by Inigo Jones for an imprese shield with the figures of
Minerva and Chivalry. This was probably for the use of Prince
Henry in the barriers (January 1610). Reproduced by courtesy
of the Devonshire Collection, Chatsworth. Photograph supplied
by the Courtauld Institute of Art, London.

Figure 4
Design by Inigo Jones for an imprese shield, to be carried by a knight or squire dressed à l'antique. The shield has no picture but a scroll has been made to show where the motto would be placed. Reproduced by courtesy of the Devonshire Collection, Chatsworth. Photograph supplied by the Courtauld Institute of Art, London.

NOTES

1. The material in this essay presents a succinct version of a planned chapter on the English tournament impresa to be included in a forthcoming book on the Tudor and Jacobean Tournament.

2. *Remains Concerning Britain*, ed. R. D. Dunn (Toronto, Buffalo and London: University of Toronto Press, 1984), p. 177.

3. *Letter-Book of Gabriel Harvey, A.D. 1573-1580*, ed. Edward John Long Scott (Westminster: Camden Society, 1884), p. 79.

4. John F. Leisher, "Puttenham and *Emblemata*," *Boston University Studies in English*, 1 (Spring 1955), 3.

5. See Lloyd Goldman, "Samuel Daniel's *Delia* and the Emblem Tradition," *Journal of English and Germanic Philology*, 67 (1968), 45-63; and Joseph Kau, "Daniel's *Delia* and the *Imprese* of Bishop Paolo Giovio," *Journal of the Warburg and Courtauld Institutes*, 33 (1970), 325-28.

6. Camden, *Remains*, pp. 178, 182.

7. Sydney Anglo, *The Great Tournament Roll of Westminster* (Oxford: Clarendon, 1968), pp. 33-34.

8. J. Gairdner (ed.), *Letters and Papers Illustrative of the Reigns of Richard III and Henry VII*, Rolls Series Vol. 24 (London: J. Johnson, 1861), I, 396.

9. Ibid., pp, 396, 399.

10. Edward Hall, *The Union of the two noble and illustre Families of Lancastre and Yorke*, ed. Henry Ellis (London, 1809), pp. 511, 591; and *Letters and Papers, Foreign and Domestic, of the Reign of Henry VIII*, ed. J. S. Brewer, J. Gairdner, and R. H. Brodie (London: H.M.S.O., 1862-1920), III ii, p. 1551.

11. Hall, pp. 517-18, 580-81, 611-18, 630-31, 707, 722; and *Letters and Papers, Foreign and Domestic*, II ii, 1516, 1517; III ii, 976; IV ii, 1393.

12. Hall, pp. 630-31.

13. See, for example, Hall's description of King Francis's complex punning impresa (really three imprese in one) that took three days to appear in full.

14. See Sydney Anglo, *Spectacle, Pageantry, and Early Tudor Policy* (Oxford: Clarendon, 1969), pp. 113, 261-80.

15. See, Albert Feuillerat, *Documents Relating to the Revels at Court in the Time of King Edward VI and Queen Mary* (Louvain: Uystpruyst, 1914), pp. 9, 56, 63, 66, 67, 82-84, 188.

16. College of Arms MS. M. 6, fols. 56b-57a.

17. William Segar, *The Booke of Honor and Armes* (London, 1590), p. 94.

18. That a tournament was held on 21 April 1560 has been questioned by Sydney Anglo ("Archives of the English Tournament," *Journal of the Society of Archivists*, 2 no. 4 [1961], 160), but see College of Arms, Partition Book I, fol. 213b.

19. Richard C. McCoy identified the family crests in "From the Tower to the Tiltyard: Robert Dudley's Return to Glory," *The Historical Journal*, 27, no. 2 (1984), 432-33. McCoy believes that the pictures memorialize the Dudleys' achievement in the November 1559 tournament.

20. McCoy (see the above note), is unaware of the origins of the imprese, but the dates of their sources further assist in dating the tournament at which they were used.

21. E. g. "Spes mihi magna tamen" [There is yet great hope for me], accompanied by a picture of a man with a heavy stone attached to his arm (Camden, p. 184; and MS. Hass. 68, fol. 138a). Cf. Alciato, *Emblemata* (Padua, 1621), Emb. 121.

22. E. g. "Fatum inscribat Eliza" [Let Eliza inscribe my fate], inscribed on a blank shield (Camden, p. 186; and MS. Hass. 68, fol. 138a). Cf. Paolo Giovio, *Dialogo dell'Imprese militari et amorose* (Lyons, 1559) p. 120.

23. E.g. "Fata obstant" [The fates stand in the way], accompanied by a picture of a man climbing a spiked wheel that is prevented from turning by a block of stone on a chain (MS. Hass. 68, fol. 127b). Cf. Claude Paradin, *Devises Heroiques* (Lyons, 1557), p. 161.

24. Adam Ottley Papers (National Library of Wales), quoted by Peter Beal, "Poems by Sir Philip Sidney: The Ottley Manuscripts," *The Library*, 5th ser., 33 (1978), 287-88. Beal discusses the probable authorship of the entertainment, pp. 285-89.

25. See Alan R. Young, "Sir Philip Sidney's Tournament Impresas," *Sidney Newsletter*, 6 no. 1 (1985), 6-24.

26. Elena Povoledo, "Le théâtre de tournoi en Italie" in *Le Lieu théâtral à la Renaissance*, ed. Jean Jacquot (Paris: Editions du Centre National de la Recherche Scientifique, 1964), p. 98.

27. British Library MS. Harl. 69, fols. 7a, 28b; Hall, p. 510; *Letters and Papers, Foreign and Domestic*, XV, 300; John Nichols, *Progresses and Public Processions of Queen Elizabeth* (London, 1823), I, 16-17; John Leland, *De Rebus Britannicis Collectanea* (London, 1774), II, 667.

28. Von Wedel, "Journey Through England and Scotland Made by Lupold Von Wedel in the Years 1584 and 1585," *Transactions of the Royal Historical Society*, n.s. 9 (1895), 236. This account appears in a different translation in Victor von Klarwill, *Queen Elizabeth and Some Foreigners* (London: John Lane The Bodley Head, 1928), pp. 331-332.

29. *Travels in England* during the Reign of Queen Elizabeth (London, New York & Melbourne: Cassell, 1889), p. 33: "Emblemata varia papyracea, clypei formam habentia, quibus, adiectis symbolis, nobiles in exercitiis equestribus & gladiatoriis uti sunt soliti, hic memoriae causa suspensa."

30. *Travels in England 1599*, trans. Clare Williams (London: Cape, 1937), p. 164.

31. *The Compleat Gentleman*, p. 199.

32. Shakespeare, too, may have been familiar with the contents of the Shield Gallery (see Alan R. Young, "A Note on the Tournament Impresas in *Pericles*," *Shakespeare Quarterly*, 36 no. 4 [1985], 456).

33. Quarto MS. Hass. 68. The three other manuscripts in the Kassel library are: Octavo MS. Hass. 6; Quarto MS. Hass. 66; Quarto MS. Hass. 67. A transcript of this last is in the British Library (B.L. Add. MSS. 33838). Karl Josef Höltgen has used the Kassel manuscripts to trace connections between Lord Hay's compass impresa and its motto and John Donne's famous conceit of a pair of compasses. Höltgen suggests that the writer of the diary is Johann Georg Dehn-Rotfelser, the adopted son and secretary of the chief Hessian negotiator, Colonel Caspar Widmarckter. See the essay "Donne's 'A Valediction: Forbidding Mourning' and Some Imprese" in Höltgen *Aspects of the Emblem*, (Kassel: Edition Reichenberger, 1986), pp. 67-90.

34. Quarto MS. Hass. 68, fol. 85b: "Kegen 4 uhr abends, sindt unser etliche in den Witehall zu schieff gefahren, und die Emblemata, so daselbst in einem langen gallerey zu sehen, uber die halfte abgeschreiben."

35. Ibid. fol. 139a.

36. For a description of the impresa in the Shield Gallery, rather than the drawing in the College of Arms manuscript, see Quarto MS. Hass. 68, fol. 132a.

37. These are all taken from Quarto MS. Hass. 68, fols. 130b, 131a, 138a, 129a respectively.

38. Ibid. fol. 140a.

39. See, for example, Sir Henry Wotton, *Reliquae Wottonianae]* (1651), p. 21. Wotton also praised Essex's "inventions of entertainment; and above all. . . his darling piece of love, and selflove," this last being Essex's 1595 Accession Day tilt entertainment.

40. *The Life and Minor Works of George Peele*, ed. David H. Horne (New Haven & London: Yale University Press, 1952), I, 235.

41. Ibid., I, 235.

42. Letter from Rowland White to Sir Robert Sidney, 22 Nov. 1595, in Arthur Collins, *Letters and Memorials of State* (London, 1746), I, 362. For a summation of available information on this portrait, see Roy Strong, *Artists of the Tudor Court: The Portrait Miniature Rediscovered 1510-1620* (London: Victoria and Albert Museum, 1983), pp. 136-37.

43. *Diary of John Manningham*, ed. J. Bruce (Westminster: Camden Society, 1868), p. 4; Camden, *Remains*, p. 190; *Ben Jonson*, ed. C. H. Herford and P. Simpson (Oxford: Clarendon, 1947), I, 148; and Quarto MS. Hass. 68, fol. 131a.

44. For a discussion of the work and of other such portraits, see Strong *Artists of the Tudor Court*, pp. 133-38, 142.

45. *The Art of Making Devises* (1648 ed.), sig. A4a.

46. "Sunt quos ignis alit" [There are those whom fire nourishes]; "Post tenebras lucem" [After darkness, light]; "Saepe cadendo" [By constant dropping]; and "Sub judice lis est" [The quarrel is before the judge] (see Quarto MS. Hass. 68, fols. 137a, 132b, 125b, 135b).

UNPUBLISHED AND UNEDITED EMBLEMS BY GEFFREY WHITNEY: FURTHER EVIDENCE OF THE ENGLISH ADAPTATION OF CONTINENTAL TRADITIONS

JOHN MANNING
The Queen's University of Belfast

The Houghton Library manuscript, MS. Typ 14, contains fifteen emblems which do not appear in the printed text of Whitney's *Choice of Emblemes*, published at Leyden in 1586. Although the provenance of the manuscript is uncertain before 1899, when it was offered for sale, it is likely that this was the manuscript which the author presented to Robert Dudley, Earl of Leicester on 28 November, 1585, before the Earl's departure for the Low Countries.[1] The aim of this essay is to make the text of these unpublished emblems available for the first time, and to examine them for the light they throw on the author's habits of emblematic composition, his indebtedness to Continental traditions, and his efforts to adapt these to the tastes and preoccupations of his noble patron, the Earl of Leicester.

Surprisingly, the manuscript has until recently received little attention. Rosemary Freeman in her *English Emblem Books* (1948) makes no mention of it in her bibliography and supposed that the manuscript dedicated to Leicester had disappeared.[2] Franklin Leisher made some use of MS. Typ 14 in his 1952 Ph.D. dissertation, but his treatment of it is disappointingly cursory.[3] An introductory note by Frank Fieler to a 1967 reprint of Henry Green's edition of Whitney contains a description of the manuscript, but such a note could not permit any full discussion of its importance.[4] The most detailed treatment of the manuscript had to wait till 1976, when Mason Tung's very thorough article traced comparisons between the manuscript and the printed *Choice of Emblemes*.[5] There could, of course, be no question that the manuscript had acted as copy text for the printer. The 1586 *Choice of Emblemes* substantially increased the number of emblems, changed the manuscript order, and added extensive shoulder notes and dedications. Tung, however, does show that the manuscript collection did form the core of the printed book, and he investigates some of the changes the author made in adapting his manuscript for publication.[6] However, in treating the manuscript as essentially the first draft of the printed work, Tung misunderstands the fundamental distinction between the manuscript and the book, and depresses the value of the manuscript. In a very real sense the manuscript and the book, in spite of the overlap in their contents, are different works, each with a different audience and function. The manuscript is a private act of fealty between poet and patron; the book is public and general in its appeal. The manuscript was designed to please one man; the book envisages a wider readership. The manuscript reflects the poet's perception of the ideals, ideas, and sentiments which his patron might find congenial; the appeal of the printed book must necessarily be less particular. Where the reader of the manuscript was almost chauvinistically English, the book, issuing as it did from one of the foremost Continental publishing houses, was intended to draw its readership from Europe as well as England. Some of the changes between manuscript and printed book are governed by a subtle decorum, a sense that what is suitable to one is not necessarily appropriate to the other.

If the manuscript itself has received little attention, the unpublished emblems, which form the basis of this essay, have received even less. Of course, Fieler mentioned that certain emblems in the manuscript were omitted from the printed version, and Tung discusses them in so far as their suppression was part of the process of the adaptation of the manuscript for publication.[7] However, there seems little need of special pleading on behalf of the suppressed emblems. They are no better or worse than the printed ones. Three would, in fact, appear to be early drafts of emblems to be found in the printed *Choice*, but the handling of the material differs so radically that they may almost be considered separate compositions. Some are taken from the Continental sources which Whitney most generally favours: Alciati (three emblems), Junius (one emblem), La Perrière (one emblem), Paradin (one emblem).[8] Others derive from English sources, or would appear to be "original" compositions by Whitney. The material does not differ in kind from that which is presented in the printed book. But as long as the manuscript was viewed as a first draft of the book, then the unpublished emblems could be seen only as casualties in the transfer from one medium to another, and deserving less attention than those favoured by inclusion in the end product. But once the separate aims of manuscript and book are grasped, then the suppressed emblems may be seen as worthy of more particular attention. These emblems were rejected from the published work, not because they were deficient in merit, but because they did not fit into the aims of the new project. These suppressed emblems express the nature of the original, more intimate and private communication between poet and patron, and through them we gain some insight into the poet's expectations of his patron's moral and political views, and of his literary taste. In preparing his book of emblems for publication, Whitney, it seems, took some pains not to broach personal, private, patriotic, and political themes which, when exposed on a broad and public stage, might embarrass his patron. Some of the suppressed emblems are aristocratic and elitist in their bias, or tend to praise aggressively expedient policies, or are nationalistic and patriotic in their sentiments, or allude to Leicester's personal achievements and are overtly gratulatory. Others depend on sophisticated literary allusion, and by such means praise famous Englishmen, past and present acquaintances of Leicester's. Such allusiveness might be lost on a wider, Continental audience, for whom in any case the personal point would be missing.

In the following pages I shall transcribe[9] and discuss all of the suppressed emblems, first the "original" compositions, next the first drafts, and lastly the translations.

I. The "Original" Emblems.

No direct source has been discovered for Whitney's fable against rebellion, "Estote subditi principibus" [Be subject to your rulers] on fol. 39^r of the manuscript. The hands turn against the head and, in so doing, bring the whole body to destruction. Just as in the human body the hands should serve the more noble, rational powers, so in the body politic, the emblem argues, the subject should serve the prince. Such obedience is to the welfare of all.

Estote subditi principibus.

[Picture: Man beating his head with his hands.]

> The cheefist parte and honor of the man,
> The head, I meane, that dothe the heaven behoulde,
> Throughe which all artes and sciences wee can,
> Without the which wee are but sencelesse moulde,
> > The handes which were but made to serve his turne,
> > As poettes faine, against it once did spurne,

Regardinge not the mansion of the mynde,
The onelie place where witt and reason dwelles,
Where memorie hir seate is still assign'de,
With hearinge, sight, with taste, and sence that smelles,
    And eeke the toungue with eloquence divine:
    Yit theise not weyd, the stubberne handes repine.

Theie did not wey from whome theire good did growe,
And howe the heade the bodie whole did guyde
But did rebell, and gave it manie a blowe;
Till at the laste theie altogither dyed.
    Let subiectes then in tyme consider this,
    And love theire Prince, in whome theire welfare is.

The emblem subtly alters the circumstances of a classical fable, Menenius' "fable of the belly," which Whitney would have known from Plutarch or Livy.[10] Where the classical fable emphasized the mutual dependence of all parts, Whitney stressed the superiority of the noble and exalted head, which he connects with the god-like powers of reason and "eloquence divine." By contrast, the hands are menial and, in their rebellion, are characterized as brutish and senseless. Furthermore, the subjection of these lower orders is divinely ordained by creation: the hands "are made" to serve the head. Whitney thus inculcates an aristocratic and elitist position that would be bound to appeal to his patron, who might readily identify himself with "the cheefist parte," "honor," "the onelie place where witt and reason dwelles," and with "eloquence divine." Such equations would flatter the patron, who could not but agree with the general political sentiments contained in the emblem. Such particular allusion may have been sufficient cause for the emblem not to appear in the printed book. However, the changed circumstances between the time the manuscript was presented to the patron and the appearance of the book might have given Whitney pause had he thought of including this emblem in the published work. On his arrival in the Netherlands, Leicester was offered the Governor-Generalship of the Province, and, against his precise orders from the Queen, he accepted it. In such a context the emblem, "Estote subditi principibus," might look more like a reproach than an enunciation of sound political principles. There were many who would be prepared to see it as the former.

In the emblem on fol. 53ʳ, "In logum et foelicissimum statum illustrissimi comitis Leicestrensis" [On the estate and condition of the right honourable Earl of Leicester] Whitney praises the achievement of his patron, as a man who has achieved mastery over fortune and is sustained in his achievements by God himself. The symbolism and iconography are thoroughly traditional: the wheel of Fortune, the laurel branch as a sign of victory. But Whitney has brought it to bear on the particular praise of his patron.

In logum et foelicissimum statum illustrissimi
comitis Leicestrensis.

[Picture: Man holding laurel branch, sitting on Fortune's wheel, teadied by the hand of God stretched from a cloud.]

The varyinge Dame that turnes the totteringe wheele,
To whome the woorld hathe longe ascribed power
To lifte men vp, where theie all pleasures feele,
To throwe them downe, where all theire sweete is sower,
  Whose woorshippes longe in euerie coaste was ryfe
  Eauen as the guide and Goddesse of this lyfe.

Yit here, behoulde, hir Deitie is dassh'de,
And shee subdude, and captiue vnto man:
And nowe, all those that seru'd hir be abassh'd,
And do confesse, that fortune nothinge can,
  But onelie god defendes the mightees seates,
  And houldes them vp in spyte of envies threates.

This emblem perfectly illustrates one of the fundamental differences between the manuscript and the printed book. In the manuscript such direct praise of the patron is fit and appropriate; in the printed book it would be out of place. The Folger Library possesses a variant issue of the *Choice of Emblemes*, which shows that Whitney did at an early stage of printing think of including this emblem in his published work, though under a different motto, "Fato, non fortuna" (By God's will, not by fortune).[11] Such a change from particular gratulation to more general moral reflection indicates the different decorum that pertains respectively to manuscript and printed book. In the Folger copy this emblem appears on p. 109, but Whitney appears to have changed his mind about its inclusion after only a few sheets had been printed. The worsening fortunes of Leicester's campaign in the Low Countries during the Spring of 1585/86, the quarrels between the commanders in the field, the criticism from home of the handling of the campaign, and suspicions of Leicester's competence served only to emphasize the inappropriateness of the manuscript emblem. Fortune's power was certainly not "dassh'de," Leicester was not securely placed in the "mightees seates," "envies threates" were far from silenced and still had power to harm. To publish the original emblem in these circumstances would have been insensitive and could only have caused embarrassment.

Whitney's emblematic technique gains considerable strength and pithiness from traditional proverbial sources in his "Sæpe, sub vili panno latet sapientia" [Often beneath a poor man's cloak wisdom lies hidden] on fol. 60ᵛ of the manuscript.

Sæpe, sub vili panno latet sapientia.

[Picture: Men fallen into stream.]

Wee ought not to dispise the men wee silent see:
    For oftentymes, if theie be tryde, theie wise and woorthie
                                                            be.
    The streame dothe smoothlie runne within the deepist
                                                            place,
    And deepe, and reachinge wittes, oftetymes, are cloak'de
                                                with soaber grace.

The motto of the emblem elegantly varies a famous line by the comic poet Cæcilius Statius, which Cicero quotes in the *Tusculan Disputations*: "Sæpe est etiam sub palliolo sordido sapientia."

In its Ciceronian context[12] this is meant as a comfort against the burden of poverty, particularly as suffered by the learned, but more usually it was proverbially applied to the concealment of knowledge in strange disguise. That Whitney means it in this latter sense is confirmed by his application of a parallel English proverb in the third line of his epigram: "The stream doth smoothlie runne within the deepist place."[13] Whitney cross-references the motto, picture, and verse in such a way that the one cannot be understood without the others. The "streame" of the third line picks up the visual motif in the emblem's *pictura*, while the last line echoes the motto: "sapi-

entia" becomes "deepe, and reaching wittes," and the "vilis pannus"
is transformed to the verb "cloak'de." The epigram also conceals
an allusion to a manuscript poem by one of Leicester's retinue,
Sir Edward Dyer, which Whitney may have expected his patron
to recognize:

> Wher waters smothest ronne, ther deepest are the foords,
>
> . . .
>
> The firmest fayth is fownd in fewest woordes.[14]

By means of such an allusion Whitney indicates the wider literary
circle who have enjoyed his patron's patronage and identifies
Leicester with such "deepe and reaching wittes" who can appreciate concealed wisdom in such trifles[15] as the poet offers.

The emblem takes up themes mentioned in other manuscript
emblems: honour, worthiness, wisdom, and eloquence. But its
preoccupation with silent wisdom was something that occupied
many emblematists. Alciati's "Silentium" was later translated by
Whitney and included in the printed *Choice*.[16] In fact, the
whole science of emblematics was placed under the tutelage of
Harpocrates and Angerona, the deities of silence.[17] Whitney
takes up this traditional preoccupation with some originality, and
uses the quasi-enigmatic quality of proverbial utterances and
allusiveness to cloak truth in such "pleasing obscurity" as the
Continental theorists, Junius and Sambucus, advocated.[18] Perhaps
we might allow Whitney even greater wit in suppressing the
emblem than might at first be apparent. There had always been
an implicit contradiction in the activity of publishing that which
was intended to be secretly mysterious. In refusing to print his
emblem on silence, Whitney retains it as a private communication
between poet and judicious patron. In such a way he endorses
the principle, "ut saepe summa ingenia in occulto latent" [how
often it is that the greatest devises are shrouded in obscurity].
Such wit alludes to the principle set out in the first line of the
epigram, that "wee ought not to dispise the men wee silent see."

Whitney also writes in praise of eloquence in the emblem
"Facunda senectus" [An eloquent old age] on fol. 75ᵛ of the
manuscript. The symbolism of the swan that sings most sweetly
before its death is traditional.[19]

Facunda senectus.

[Picture: An old man and a swan.]

> The snowishe swanne, when that his ende is neare,
> Dothe yeelde his noates, and sweetelie tune his songe.
> Which shewes, when men with snowishe heades appeare,
> Then are theie wise, and eloquent of toungue.
>   For, reverende age is still the cheefist grounde,
>   Which makes our witte and sugred speeche abounde.

This topic was handled frequently in emblem books of the period: the *Hieroglyphica* of Horapollo provides the symbol, and it can be found in Valeriano and Barthélemy Aneau's *Picta poesis*.[20] The reason why it might have been considered more appropriate for a collection privately presented to a patron, rather than a printed book, might be found in Erasmus' handling of the proverb, "Cygnea cantio" [Swan-song]. Erasmus there refers to his epigram dedicated to his patron, William Warham, Archbishop of Canterbury, "that universal Maecenas of studies, never to be praised enough."[21] The private dedication of this emblem to Leicester within the collection is Whitney's allusive tribute to his Maecenas in the same symbolic key.

The symbolism of the crows in the emblem "Poenitentia sera" [Late repentance] on fol. 85^v of the manuscript derives from less learned sources.

Poenitentia sera.

[Picture: Man and crows, who cry "Cras".]

> The beste of all offendes, so proane *is man <is> to sinne:
> Yit all, repentaunce do defer, and loathe are to beginne.
> The yungue do headlonge runne, and will not see theire
>   crime:
> The oulde perswade them selues of lyfe, and will repent in
>   tyme.
> Cras, cras, the crowe dothe crye, which noate mankynde
>   dothe chuse:
> But when too morrowe commes, theie still theire cras againe
>   do vse.
> But lett them, while theie maie, repent and stande in feare,

And thinke, howe Atropos to daie perhappes theire thredd
maie sheare.

The crow is an attribute of Hope in Alciati, "In simulacrum Spei"
[On the image of Hope]. Whitney, however, draws his symbolism
more directly from the popular iconography of Sebastian Brant's
Das Narrenschiff, where the thirty-first chapter, "Vom Auf-
shubsuchen," is prefaced by the picture of a fool, surrounded by
crows singing, "Cras."[22] The theme was, it seems, a congenial
one to Leicester. One of the few allegorical paintings the Earl
possessed was of Occasion and Repentance.[23]

The theme is continued in more classical vein in another
emblem, "Fortuna vitrea" [Brittle fortune] on fol. 97[r] of the
manuscript.

Fortuna vitrea.

[Picture: Chariot with man cutting another's throat.]

Truste not to fortunes smyles, shee Tullie did promoate,
And made him longe in Rome to rule, at lengthe shee cutt
his throate.

The emblem is a good illustration of one of Whitney's
favoured techniques of emblematic composition, in which he
causes historical material to become the subject of general moral
reflection. In the Preface, "To the Reader," added in 1586,
Whitney, following the Continental theorists Mignault and Sambucus, distinguished three kinds of emblems, "*Historicall, Naturall,
and Morall*," and yet he affirms that the "*Morall* is the chiefe of
the three, and the other two may be in some sorte drawen into
this head."[24] This manuscript emblem shows how history might
be put to the service of morality. The motto allusively sets out
the general issue. Whitney would have expected his learned
reader to complete the last half of the proverb from Publilius
Syrus' *Sententiae*, from which he draws the phrase, "Fortuna
vitrea": "Fortuna vitrea est: tum cum splendet frangitur" [Fortune
is made of glass: just at the moment she shines, she breaks].[25]
The particular circumstances from history set out in the epigram
illustrate precisely those general principles outlined in the motto.
The manuscript shoulder notes emphasize the events described,
drawn as they are from "Plutarch: in vita Tulij," that is, Plu-

tarch's Life of Tullius Cimber, which Whitney probably knew in
the Latin translation by Xylander.   The truth of the proverbial
wisdom is reinforced by the truth of history and rendered inesca-
pable by the authority of the historian.   The emblem gains
strength from its allusive pithiness and makes some demands
upon its reader.   However, it was probably suppressed out of
tact, rather than because of its difficulty.   Leicester's current
progress in the Netherlands may have been all too sufficient
illustration of the brittleness of Fortune.   Like the emblem on
fol. 53^r, "Fortuna vitrea" may well have been a casualty of the
changed circumstances between the time when the manuscript
was presented, and the publication of the book.

No source has been traced for the emblem, "Infamia" [De-
traction], which is found on the same folium as "Vitrea fortuna":

Infamia.

[Picture: Man slain by darts of reproach.]

Omnibus amissis famam seruare memento

Though all thinges els thou loose, remember fame to save,
If not, reproache shall plague the here, and wounde the in
thy grave.

The emblem picks up the general concern with honour that runs
through the manuscript collection.   This topic would obviously be
appropriate to the preoccupations of a noble patron.

The last of the "original" emblems, on fol. 98^r of the manuscript, adapts and translates a Latin epigram by the English
courtier and humanist, Walter Haddon:

[Picture: Portrait painter.]

Quid facis ah demens? cur ora fugacia pingis?
Aut nouus, aut nullus, cras tibi vultus erit.

What mean'st thou foolisshe man thy fadinge forme to graue?
Thie fauour, either newe or none, tomorrowe shalt thou
have.

The shoulder note, "Gualter Haddonus," acknowledges the source
of the Latin epigram.[26]   The quotation shows some patriotic

pride in English cultural achievement, for Haddon was one of the most celebrated Latin epigrammists of the age. Whitney presses this poem into emblematic service by adding to it the drawing of a portrait painter. The omission of any motto should remind us that many emblematists of the sixteenth century considered the epigram as the basis of the emblem. Any notion of the emblem conforming to a strict tripartite structure of motto, picture and verse was something that only later hardened into orthodoxy.[27]

II. The Early Drafts.

Three emblems, "Celsa potestatis species," "Furius Camillus," and "Dissimulatio", would appear to be earlier drafts of those that appeared in the *Choice* of 1586. In all cases one might prefer Whitney's first thoughts to his later revised versions. On fol. 90[v] appears "Celsa potestatis species" [A noble image of a great man]:

Celsa potestatis species.

[Picture: A lion rampant bearing a sword.]

This forme engrauen was in noble Pompeis ringe,
When he in Ægipte was betraide by Ptolemeus kinge.
By which, his prowes greate, and valiaunt mynde appeares,
Which, with his heade, when Caesar sawe, he wass'de the
same with teares.

In the printed text the emblem appears on p. 116. Motto and *pictura*, from Claude Paradin, *Heroica Symbola*, are identical, but in the 1586 version the verse has been expanded to eighteen lines.

When *Pompey* great, with fortune longe was bleste,
And did subdue his foes, by lande, and sea,
And conquestes great obtained in the Easte,
And *Parthians*, and *Arabians*, made obaye,
And seas, and Iles, did in subiection bringe,
Whose name with feare, did throughe *Ivdæa* ringe.

And had restor'de kinge *Masinissas* righte,
And ouercame *Sertorivs* with his power:
And made the Kinge of *Pontvs* knowe his mighte.
Yet, at the lengthe, hee had his haplesse hower:
  For ouercome by *Cæsar*, fled for aide,
  To *Ægypte* lande; wherein hee was betrai'd.

Within whose ringe, this forme aboue was wroughte,
Whereby, his force, and noble minde appeares;
Which, with his head to *Cæsar* being broughte,
For inwarde griefe, hee wash'd the same with teares,
  And in a fire with odours, and perfumes:
  This princes head with mourning hee consumes.

The manuscript is closer to Whitney's symbolic source;[28] the printed version merely fills in historical circumstances from classical historians, Cornelius Nepos and Appian,[29] which do little more than parade Whitney's knowledge and put the uninformed general reader in possession of background information. In the manuscript emblem Whitney could depend on his reader knowing who Pompey was and what he did. The manuscript also contains a different and more favourable interpretation of the image: "prowes greate, and valiaunt mynde" as opposed to "force, and noble minde" in the printed version. Furthermore, the manuscript emblem concerns "noble" Pompey, as opposed to "*Pompey* great" in the 1586 version. We might here detect a slight change in the author's expectations of the class of his reader: the manuscript seems to suppose a shared nobility between the reader and that of the emblem's subject, the printed version implies some inferiority of the reader as compared to the "great" Pompey. Apart from the scribal error in the last line, we might well prefer the manuscript's brevity and succinctness to the long-winded nature of the printed version.

Similar changes were made in transferring the emblem on fol. 95[r], "Furius Camillus," to the printed version, where it appears on p. 112 under the motto, "Habet et bellum suas leges" [Even war has its laws].

Furius Camillus.

[Picture: Boys beating schoolmaster back to the town.]

Loe here Camillus facte deservinge praise for aie,
When that the schoolemaister deuis'd Phalicia to betraie,
Which more his fame increaste then winninge of the towne:
A mirror for all Martiall wightes that do desire renoume.

In the 1586 version the epigram is considerably expanded:

Camillvs then, that did repulse the Gaules,
And vnto Rome her former state did giue:
When that her foes made spoile within her waules,
Lo here, amongst his actes that still shall liue.
 I made my choice, of this example rare,
 That shall for aye his noble minde declare.

Wherefore, in briefe then this his woorthie parte
What time he did besiege *Faleria* stronge:
A scoolemaster, that bare a *Ivdas* harte,
Vnto the place where he was fostred longe,
 Ofte walk'd abrode with schollers that hee toughte,
 Whiche cloke hee vsde, so that no harme was thoughte.

At lengthe, with sonnes of all the best, and moste,
Of noble peares, that kepte the towne by mighte:
Hee made his walke into the Romane hoste,
And, when hee came before *Camillvs* sighte,
 Quoth hee, my Lorde, lo these thy prisoners bee,
 Which beinge kepte, *Faleria* yeeldes to thee.

Whereat, a while this noble captaine stay'd,
And pondering well the straungenes of the cause:
Vnto his frendes, this in effecte hee say'd.
Thoughe warres bee ill, yet good mens warres haue lawes,
 And it behooues a Generall good to gaine
 With valiaunt actes, and not with treacherous traine.

With that, he caus'de this *Sinon* to bee stripte,
And whippes, and roddes, vnto the schollers gaue:
Whome, backe againe, into the toune they whipte,
Which facte, once knowne vnto their fathers graue:
 With ioyfull hartes, they yeelded vp their Toune:
 An acte moste rare, and glasse of true renoume.

The brevity of the manuscript emblem depends on its allusiveness. Where the printed version narrates, the manuscript assumes the reader's prior knowledge of the circumstances, merely referring in the shoulder notes to the classical authorities Valerius Maximus, Livy, and Plutarch.[30]   Where the printed emblem describes in detail the events taking place in the emblem's *pictura*,[31] the beating of the bound schoolmaster back to the town, the manuscript can depend on the reader's recognition of the event.   The author merely directs the reader's attention to it by means of a rhetorical gesture, "Loe here. . . ."   The printed text heavily labours the moral, repeating it in the motto, and several times within the verses; the manuscript makes the point once and depends upon its reader's acute sensitivity to questions of honour and renown, which are frequent pre-occupations of the manuscript, to register its importance.

"Dissimulatio" [Dissembling] on fol. 91[r] of the manuscript was the basis of the verses on Hypocrisy on p. 226 of the printed book.   The manuscript takes its *pictura* from the sixth emblem of Guillaume de la Perrière's *Theatre des bons engins*.[32]

Dissimulatio.

[Picture: Masks.]

> A face deform'd, a visarde faire dothe hyde,
> That none can see his vglie shape within.
> To hypocrites the same maie be applied,
> With outwarde shewes who all theire credit winne.
> Theie zealouse seeme, yit haue no fruite at all,
> But be as coulde as painted fier on walle.

Since Plantin never printed La Perrière there was no block to hand which Whitney could employ, and he made one block, from Paradin's *Heroica symbola*[33] serve for two emblems in the printed text.   In so doing he changed the motto to "Ferè simile, in Hypocritas" [Much the same, on Hypocrites].   Possibly Whitney may have turned these circumstances forced upon him in publication to witty advantage by making the double service of one block reflect the doubleness of Hypocrisy.   The changed motto takes up the third line of the epigram of both the manuscript and printed versions:

To hypocrites the same may be applied.

The printed text also changes the last couplet of the manuscript:

> Yet giue no heate, but like a painted fire;
> And, all their zeale, is: as the times require.

This change would seem to have been a result of the slight change in subject: time-serving may be seen as the mark of the hypocrite, while fruitless ingratitude is the sign of the dissembler.

III. The Translated Emblems.

Whitney draws no more than the *pictura* from La Perrière in the last emblem. Neither the manuscript nor the printed verses owe anything to the French text. Elsewhere, however, the manuscript emblems draw heavily on the text and commentaries of Continental emblem books.

"Improba foemina" [A wicked woman] on fol. 48[r] of the manuscript takes its illustration from Hadrianus Junius' *Emblemata*, number 38.[34]

Foemina improba.

[Picture: The female viper biting off the head of the male in copulation.]

> The wanton wyfe, whose love is all for luste,
> Not still dothe lyke hir husbande <for> to imbrace,
> But thinkes it longe, vntill againe shee muste
> An other have, for to possesse his place.
>   And often tymes shee dothe procure his ende,
>   When moste shee smyles, and love dothe moste pretende.
>
> The vypers loe, when theie ingendringe be,
> The shee suffis'de, deprives the male of life
> By bytinge of his heade, as here wee see.
> Which is compar'de vnto a wicked wyfe;
>   Which monsters vile, if anie where theie breede,
>   I wisshe theie mighte the poisned vipers feede.

Whitney's verses are loosely based on Junius' Latin, considerably
expand the original four lines, and heavily underline the outrage
that the English poet feels against such behaviour.   Where Junius
contrasts the changed behaviour before sexual satisfaction and
after, Whitney particularly emphasizes the abuse committed against
marriage.   Whitney may have suppressed this emblem, because of
his sensitivity towards his patron's reputation.   Leicester's first
wife had died in suspicious circumstances, and he had remarried,
but the scandal was never wholly forgotten.[35]
    Whitney's most favoured source is Alciati, and he treats him
with a good deal of freedom.   The marginal gloss, "Alciatus,"
that appears beside the Latin couplet, which Whitney translates
for his emblem, "Forma bonum fragile" [Beauty is a perishable
commodity] on fol. 72[v], points not to the author of the emblem,
but to the book from which Whitney took the lines.

                        Forma bonum fragile.

[Picture: Lais gives a looking glass to Venus.]

    Lais, beinge oulde, giveth hir glasse to Venus with theise
                                                    wordes.
Alciatus. At mihi nullus in hoc vsus, quia cernere talem
        Qualis sum nolo, qualis eram nequeo.
        In age thus Lais saied, nowe Venus take my glasse
        I will not see me as I am, I cannot as I was.

                        An other thereof.
        Loe betwie howe it fades, and witherith like the grasse,
        I maie well see me as I am, but neuer as I was.

The Latin couplet is not by Alciati, but Ausonius.[36]   It was
Alciati's commentator, Claude Mignault, who quoted the ancient
poet in the annotation on Alciati's emblem 74, "Tumulus mere-
tricis" [The tomb of a harlot].[37]   To these verses Whitney provides his own illustration and adds a motto, from Ovid's *Ars
amatoria*.[38]   The theme of the emblem is one of the main preoccupations of the manuscript collection and it might be compared
with the emblem of the portrait painter on fol. 98[r].   Nevertheless,
the allusiveness of the emblem may have been sufficient to
exclude it from the printed collection, whose bias, we have seen,
tends to be less sophisticated and more popular.

To his translation of Alciati's emblem, "Potentia amoris" [The power of love], which was to appear on p. 182 of the printed collection, fol. 74^v of the manuscript adds "The description of loue by Marullus and Augerianus".

Potentia amoris.

[Picture: Cupid holds flowers in one hand, and a fish in the other.]

The description of loue by Marullus and Augerianus.

What wighte arte thou declare? Cupido is my name:
Somme saie that Mars did me begette on Venus pierlesse
Dame.
Where was thou borne sweete boie? In pleasaunte Paphos ile.
What tyme?   In gallant monthe of Maie, when Flora moste
dothe smile.
Why doste thou naked goe? I simple am and plaine:
And perfect love will still be seene, and cloakes are worne
in vaine.
Whie dost *thou seeme a chielde, and passist Nestors age?
Because, I children make of those that are seveare and sage.
How happes that fethered winges, thy shoulders do adorne?
Inconstancie did give me them as soone as I was borne.
Whie arte thou reau'de of sight? Hereby a sorte I tutche,
That with immoderate luste are blynde, by lykinge me to
mutche.
Who goe before the stille? Slothe, idlenesse, and sleepe,
And drunkennesse, and fowle excesse, do alwaies with me
keepe.
Who followeth streight at hande?   Contention, hate, and
stryfe,
With slaunder, shame, and ielousie, the cankers of this lyfe.
What makes the leane?   My greefe, my watchinge, and my
care.
What is thy meate?   Sweete lookes, and smyles, and sport-
inge is my faire.
What haste thou still in stoare?   Deepe sighes, and flooddes
of teares,
And evermore a tremblinge harte besette with doubtfull
feares.

[fol. 75^r]

What meanes thy dubble dartes?   The goulden one dothe
                                                    wounde,
The leade darte driues love awaie, and makes them hole
                                                    and sounde.
Why is thy mother saied, of sea hir forme to haue?
It shewes, the hartes of them that loue, are tossed like the
                                                    wave.
And be theise partes in the? Cupido then adue:
A thousande *tymes I coumpte him bleste, thy force that
                                                    neuer knewe.

Whitney has based this on the poems quoted in Mignault's notes
to Alciati's emblem 113, "In statuam amoris" [On the statue of
love].[39]   "Augerianus" is, in fact, the neo-latin poet, Angerianus,
but Whitney has followed the misprint in Mignault's commentary.
Whitney depends not on a separate edition of these poets, but
on his edition of Alciati.[40]   Whitney, however, has blended two
separate poems by two authors into one: the first seventeen
lines are loosely based on Marullus, the last eight on Angerianus.[41]   Whitney has pointed his translation much more adverse-
ly against love than either of the originals.   In fact he turns
the usual symbolism of love's golden and leaden darts on its
head.[42]   In Whitney's view the leaden dart, because it drives
love away, is more favourable than the wounding golden dart.
Such wit may have been considered too sophisticated for the
printed Choice, which tends to rehearse a traditional iconography.
       Whitney copies the illustration to Alciati's emblem 10,
"Foedera" [Alliances], the lyre and the music book, to form a
generous compliment to the English musician, Robert Johnson, in
his "Musicæ modernæ, laus" [The praise of modern music].

[fol. 87^v]

                    Musicæ modernæ, laus.

[Picture: Lute and music book.]

       When that Apollo harde the musicque of theise daies,
       And knewe howe manie for theire skill, deserved iustlie
                                                    praise,
       He left his chaire of state, and laide his lute away,

As one abash'd, in English courte, his auncient stuffe to
plaie.
And hyed vnto the skyes somme fyner pointes to frame:
And in the meane, for cunninge stoppes, gaue Johnsonne all
the fame.

The function of the emblem's *pictura* has been changed. Where
Alciati used the lyre as a hieroglyph of concord,[43] Whitney
makes it a more literal-minded representation of the art in which
Johnson excels. Although Johnson went on to gain fame as the
composer of music to Shakespeare's *The Tempest*, perhaps his
reputation at this time, while known to Leicester,[44] would not
have been sufficient for his inclusion in a Continental publication.

The manuscript emblems show Whitney as a more sophisticated emblematist than we might at times suspect from his printed
Choice. We also glimpse, in his suppression of some emblems,
some tact and sensitivity to his patron's reputation.

Part of the rhetorical training of the humanist poet was,
of course, in the practice of imitation, wherein the best authors
in a particular genre were chosen as models and served as the
basis of fresh compositions. Whitney's choice of Continental
models, Alciati, Junius, Paradin, and La Perrière, for seven of
his emblems was soundly based, and one that would not have
surprised his contemporaries.[45] In only two cases can Whitney
actually be said to translate. In the emblem taken from Paradin,
Whitney follows the Latin closely and, as a result, produces an
emblem whose succinctness contemporary theorists would have
found preferable to the more long-winded effort printed in 1586.
When emblematists referred to their work as "crammed," they
thought of it as consisting of pregnant brevity,[46] rather than as
stuffed with diffuse and circumstantial details, such as those
which encumber the printed version of "Celsa potestatis species."
In the other translation, from Junius, Whitney depends upon the
Continental model for motto, *pictura*, and verse, but shifts the
emphasis to a stronger tone of moral censoriousness than can be
found in the original. Elsewhere, Whitney's practice of imitation
is freer and bolder, and exhibits his mastery of the two aspects
of imitation: "dissimilis materiei similis tractatio" [the similar
treatment of dissimilar matter], and "similis materiei dissimilis
tractatio" [the dissimilar treatment of similar matter].[47] Of this
last we might consider Whitney's treatment of La Perrière where
the same *pictura* forms the basis of a different epigram on a

similar theme, and Whitney's adaptation of the *pictura* from
Alciati's "Foedera" for particular gratulatory purposes. Such
particularity is, we have seen, one of the distinguishing features
of this manuscript collection. Elsewhere Mignault's notes provide
Whitney with the stimulus to fresh emblematic composition on
parallel themes of love and fading beauty. Such exercises as
the verses on the power of love and on Lais donating her mirror
to Venus show Whitney's attempts to produce a similar treatment
of dissimilar material in an attempt to rival Alciati himself.
Whitney's freedom and independence in treating his Continental
sources in these manuscript emblems shows that the English poet
was prepared to regard the Europeans as his guides rather than
his masters in emblematic composition.

NOTES

1. The dedication is undated in the ms. The dating is derived from the printed text.

2. Rosemary Freeman, *English Emblem Books* (1948; London: Chatto and Windus, 1967), p. 66. Freeman's treatment of emblematic manuscripts is most unreliable.

3. John Franklin Leisher, "Geoffrey Whitney's *A Choice of Emblemes* and Its Relation to the Emblematic Vogue in Tudor England," dissertation, Harvard University, 1952, published by Garland (New York and London, 1987) in the series "Harvard Dissertations in American and English Literature."

4. Frank B. Fieler, "Introduction" (1966) to *A Choice of Emblemes by Geffrey Whitney (1548-1603)*, ed. Henry Green (1866; New York: Benjamin Blom, 1967).

5. "Whitney's *A Choice of Emblemes* Revisited: A Comparative Study of the Manuscript and the Printed Versions," *Studies in Bibliography*, 29 (1976), 32-101.

6. "This essay . . . will concern itself with . . . 1. source, 2. motto, 3. woodcut, 4. verse, 5. annotation, and 6. "newly devised" emblems. In each area the manuscript version will be compared with the printed version in order to disclose the process by which one is converted into the other" (Tung, 34-35).

7. Fieler, p. xi; Tung, 41-42.

8. These proportions are comparable to the figures given by Tung (41) for the sources of the emblems in the ms and the printed text.

9. In the transcriptions of the following poems orthography and punctuation follow the ms. throughout. Contractions have been silently expanded, and the use of long "s" has been normalized. Deleted words have been recorded within pointed brackets, added words flagged with an asterisk, and the foliation of the Houghton Library manuscript, when not indicated in the text of the essay, is in square brackets. The description of pictorial matter within square brackets, and the translations, are my own. Quotation from the ms is by permission of the Houghton Library.

10. Livy, *Historiae*, II, xxxii-xxxiii: Plutarch, *Life of Coriolanus*.

11. Leisher, 399f.

12. III, xxiii, 56f.

13. A contemporary English source, George Pettie's translation of *The Civile Conversation of M. Steeven Guazzo*, mentions

the similar proverb, "where the ryver is deepest, it runneth quietest," as applied to the learned (1581; London and New York: Constable and Co. Ltd, 1925), p. 222. See Morris Palmer Tilley, *A Dictionary of the Proverbs in England in the Sixteenth and Seventeenth Centuries* (Ann Arbor: University of Michigan Press, 1950), W123.

14. *The Life and Lyrics of Sir Edward Dyer*, Ralph M. Sargent (1935; Oxford: Clarendon Press, 1968), pp. 197 and 210f. For Whitney's tribute to Dyer in *A Choice of Emblemes*, see pp. 196f.

15. The motto possibly plays on such a meaning of *vilis* = "of trifling value" (Charlton T. Lewis and Charles Short, *A Latin Dictionary* [Oxford: Clarendon Press, 1879], s.v. *vilis* II A). Emblem theorists frequently saw the activity of the emblematist as consisting of the concealing of profound truth beneath the trifling and the nugatory.

16. Alciati, Emblem 11; Whitney, *Choice*, pp. 60f. Tung, 36, suggests that this emblem was to be found on a missing leaf of the ms. preceding fo. 44^r.

17. On this tradition, see Edgar Wind, *Pagan Mysteries in the Renaissance*, rev. and enl. edn. (Harmondsworth: Penguin in association with Faber, 1967), pp. 12f. and n. 40.

18. Hadrianus Junius, *Emblemata* (Antwerp: C. Plantin, 1565), p. 65; J. Sambucus, "De Emblemate," in *Emblemata* (Antwerp: C. Plantin, 1564), sig. A$_2$^{r}.

19. See Tilley, S1028. See also Plato, *Phaedo* 84E-85B.

20. Horapollo, *Hieroglyphica* (1505; Rome, 1606), II, 37; Valeriano, *Hieroglyphica* (1556; Venice, 1604), Lib. 23, caps. 1 and 2; Barthélemy Aneau, *Picta Poesis* (Lyons, 1552), p. 28.

21. *Collected Works of Erasmus*, vol. 31, *Adages*, tr. Margaret Mann Phillips (Toronto: University of Toronto Press, 1982), pp. 195-196 (i.e. I, ii, 55).

22. On the symbolism of the crow, see Dora and Erwin Panofsky, *Pandora's Box: The Changing Aspects of a Mythical Symbol*, rev. with additions (1956; Princeton: Princeton University Press, 1962), pp. 27-33.

23. John Buxton, *Elizabethan Taste* (London: Macmillan, 1963), p. 101.

24. *Choice*, sig. **$_4$^{r}. See also Claude Mignault (Claudius Minos), "Syntagma de Symbolis" in A. Alciati, *Emblemata elucidata* . . . *Claudii Minois Commentariis* (1574; Lyons, 1614), p. 10; J.

Sambucus, "De Emblemate" in *Emblemata* (1564; Antwerp. 1584), sig. A$_2$^{r}.

25. Publilius Syrus, *Sententiae*, ed. Otto Friedrich (Berlin: Theobald Grieben, 1880), p. 44, l. 189.

26. W. Haddon, *Poemata*, ed. T. Hatcher (London, 1567), p. 114: "In effigiem svam."

27. For a discussion of this point, see Hessel Miedema, "The Term *Emblema* in Alciati," *Journal of the Warburg and Courtauld Institutes*, 31 (1968), 234-50.

28. C. Paradin, *Symbola Heroica* (Antwerp, 1562), p. 86.

29. Noted in the shoulder notes to the emblem.

30. "Valer. li.i. cap. 5; Idem. li. 5. cap.3; Liuius deca. i. li. 5.6; Plutarch: in vita Camil."

31. Derived from an engraving by Jost Amman in Plutarch, *Parallela Vitae* (Frankfurt, 1580), fo. 42^v, as noted by Tung, 98.

32. (Paris, 1539), sig. B$_3$^{v}. Some earlier editions did not contain woodcuts.

33. The original illustration, which Plantin's edition copies, appeared in G. Simeoni, *Le sententiose imprese* (Lyons, 1559), p. 23.

34. (Antwerp. 1565), p. 44:
Cum ruit in venerem, blanditur Echidna marito,
    Mox satura insertum præscidit ore caput.
Improba palpatur, tentigine feruida coniunx;
    Continuò letum poscit anhela viri.
[When she rushes into the sexual act, the viper carresses the male; as soon as she has had her fill of him she bites off his head, which he had placed in her mouth. When burning with lust the shameless wife flatters; but straightaway the panting one kills her husband.]

35. Leicester was "infamed by his wife's death," his rival at court, Cecil, wrote. See *The Compact Edition of the Dictionary of National Biography*, 2 vols (Oxford: Oxford University Press, 1975), i, 582. Leicester had been viciously libelled in the anonymous *The Copie of a Leter, Wryten by a Master of Arte of Cambridge* (Paris, 1584), and in *La Vie abominable de Lecestre Machiaueliste* (Paris, 1585). In the same year Julius Briegerus, *Flores Caluinistici*, printed at Milan, contained similar libelous attacks. The tradition continued after Leicester's death: see *Thomas Rogers: Leicester's Ghost*, ed. Franklin B. Williams, Jr. (Chicago: University of Chicago Press, 1972).

36. *Epigrammata Ausonii de diversis rebus*, "LXV. De Laide dicante Veneri speculum suum," in *Ausonius*, vol. ii (London and Cambridge, Mass.: Heinemann, 1921), 194.

37. Alciati, ed. cit., p. 279.

38. II, 113.

39. "Potentia amoris" is Alciati's emblem 106.

40. Alciati, *ed. cit.*, pp. 396f. The misprint occurs from the beginning in Mignault's commentary. The poems were first quoted in Mignault's commentary in the Antwerp, 1573 edn of Alciati's *Emblemata*, and the error is repeated in Antwerp, 1574, Antwerp, 1577, Antwerp, 1581, and is still to be found in the Lyons, 1614 edn. Michael Tarchaniota Marullus, *Hymni et epigrammata* appeared at Florence in 1497; the *Erotopaignion* of Hieronymus Angerianus was published at Florence in 1512, and republished at Naples in 1520. An edition of the poems of Marullus, Angerianus, and Secundus was published in 1595, but the fact that Whitney refers to "Augerianus" would suggest his dependence on Mignault's commentary.

41. Whitney, 1.5 = Marullus, 1.3; Whitney, 1.7 = Marullus, 1.4; Whitney, 1.8 = Marullus, 1.4; Whitney, 1.9 = Marullus, 1.5; Whitney, 1.10 = Marullus, 1.5, and Angerianus, 1.7; Whitney, 1.11 = Marullus, 1.7; Whitney, 1.12 = Marullus, 1.7; Whitney, 11.13-14 = Marullus, 1.9; Whitney, 1.15 = Marullus, 1.10; Whitney, 1.17 = Marullus, 1.8; Whitney, 1.18 = Angerianus, 1.13; Whitney, 1.21 = Angerianus, 1.4: "cur stant in dextera spicula?" but the reply in Whitney differs from his source; Whitney, 1.23 = Angerianus, 1.17; Whitney, 1.24 = Angerianus, 1.18.

42. Ovid, *Metamorphoses* I, 468 - 475.

43. Valeriano, Lib. XLVII, cap.1.

44. Johnson supplied the music for the lavish entertainment for the Queen which Leicester gave at Kenilworth. His inclusion in the manuscript would have particular relevance for Leicester and would recall his musical, as well as his literary patronage.

45. The list is similar to, if not identical with, the lists of Continental emblematists given by Whitney's contemporaries: Gabriel Harvey cites "Jouios and Rassellis Emblemes in Italian, Paradines in Frenche. . ." (*Letter-Book of Gabriel Harvey, A.D. 1573-1580*, ed. Edward John Long Scott, Camden Society Publications, n.s. XXXIII (Westminster: Camden Society, 1884), pp. 78-79); Abraham Fraunce lists Sambucus, Beza, Aneau, Reusner, Faernus, Junius, and Alciati by name (*Insignium, Armorum, Emblematum, et Symbolorum. . . explicatio* (London, 1588), sig. N2[r]; while

Whitney himself lists Reusner, Junius, Sambucus, Alciati, La Perrière, and Bocchi in his epistle to the Reader in the printed *Choice* of 1586.

46. The phrase, "oratio referta" (crammed speech), is Claude Mignault's: see his "Syntagma de symbolis" in A. Alciati, *Emblemata, Elucidata doctissimis Claudii Minois commentariis* (1573: Lyons, 1614), p. 15. Barthélemy Aneau in his preface to his translation of Alciati describes the succint style of the emblem as "en briefue parolle concluans tresample sentence" [containing great meaning in few words] (*Les emblemes d'Alciat* [Lyons, 1549], p. 11).

47. Roger Ascham, *The Scholemaster* (1570), in G. Gregory Smith (ed.) *Elizabethan Critical Essays*, vol. 1 (Oxford: Clarendon Press, 1904), 8. The English translation is my own.

FROM PERSONIFICATIONS TO EMBLEMS: A STUDY OF PEACHAM'S USE OF RIPA'S *ICONOLOGIA* IN *MINERVA BRITANNA*

MASON TUNG
University of Idaho

My purpose in this essay is to present Ripa's *Iconologia* as a major source of Peacham's *Minerva Britanna* and to analyze his manner of using this source.[1] In the process I hope to show that Peacham, in borrowing thirty-one personifications from Ripa either merely translates the Italian originals into English verses or transforms some of them into bona fide emblems. But first, a brief description of Ripa and his *Iconologia*.

Born in Perugia of humble origin, Cesare Ripa (1560-1623), whose real name was Giovanni Campani, worked in Rome as a chef and later as the chief butler at the court of Cardinal Antonio Maria Salviati. While at this court he began in his spare time to compile the *Iconologia*, the publication of which in 1593 won for him the admiration of Duke Charles Emmanuel of Savoy, who conferred upon him the Order of Sts. Mauritius and Lazarus. Thenceforth Ripa was always referred to as "cavaliere," or knight. The second edition of *Iconologia*, without illustrations like the first, was published in Milan in 1602, followed by the third edition in Rome in 1603, this time illustrated with woodcuts based on the designs of Giuseppe Cesari, Cavaliere d'Arpino.[2]

Since the popularity and the long-lasting influence of Ripa's *Iconologia* parallel those of Alciati's *Emblemata*, it may be instructive to compare and contrast briefly these two most important compilations, affecting as they did most literary expressions and artistic activities of the Renaissance. Both underwent numerous editions during their authors' lifetime and in the centuries following their deaths. Both were translated into French, Spanish, Dutch, and German. Alciati's *Emblemata*, written originally in Latin, had, before the appearance of the two Alciati volumes of the *Index Emblematicus* (Toronto: University of Toronto Press) in 1985, not been published in an English translation, and Ripa's *Iconologia*, written originally in Italian, is not known to have been translated into Latin.[3] Both works were edited and commented on by a number of scholars during and after their authors' lifetime. The *Emblemata* was edited and commented on by Aneau, Stockhammer, Sanchez, Mignault, López, Pignorius, and Thuilius, and the *Iconologia*, by Pietro Paolo Tozzi (the publisher of Alciati's Padua editions), Giovanni Zaratino Castellini, Jean

Baudoin, and Abbot Cesare Orlandi.[4] One interesting difference is in their expansions. Although both authors expanded their original works to a certain number before they died, Alciati's *Emblemata* remained unchanged in its total of 211 emblems,[5] whereas Ripa's number of entries continued to increase after his death. Castellini, for instance, increased the number of allegories by "several hundred" and Orlandi increased the total number "to over a thousand."[6] Consequently, some late eighteenth-century editions even dropped Ripa's name from their titles. For instance, George Richardson's 1777-79 two-volume edition is entitled *Iconology or, A Collection of Emblematic Figures*, and Jean-Baptiste Boudard's 1759 three-part edition calls itself *Iconologie tirée de diverse Auteurs*, even though many of its 630 illu-strations are faithful renderings of unillustrated entries in the early editions of Ripa.[7] Other editions do mention Ripa but along with Castellini, Valeriano, and Horapollo.[8]

Another difference is in the time of their appearance. Alciati originated the emblem genre in 1531, whereas Ripa's *Iconologia* appeared in 1593 when Alciati's *Emblemata* had already reached the peak of its popularity. Consequently, although both drew their subject matters from the same sources--namely, natural history, fable, proverbial lore, medals and coins, heraldry, mythology, classical and medieval commonplaces--Ripa was also indebted to Alciati's emblems, quoting from them no fewer than twenty-six times (see n. 14 below). Thus, purported to be a source book for emblems and imprese, Ripa's work itself came under the influence of Alciati; as a result, Ripa rendered some of his descriptions in the emblematic way. However, *Iconologia* is not an emblem book, and this is the major difference between the two works, a difference that was gradually being ignored and finally set aside by the translators and redactors of Ripa's work, as seen in the changes made in its titles.

The 1593 title, *Iconologia*, is initially explained by Ripa in its subtitle as "overo Descrittione dell'Imagini universali" [or Descriptions of universal Images], and in the 1603 title as "overo Descrittione di diverse Imagini" [or Descriptions of diverse Images].[9] Beginning with the 1611 title, these images are specified as to their nature: "Descriptions of Images of Human Virtues, Vices, Affections, & Passions, of Celestial Bodies, and of the World and Its Parts."[10] Along with this change come the rewordings of the announced usefulness of the work. The titles of 1593 and 1603 state that the work is "not only useful but necessary to poets, painters, and sculptors for representing human virtues, vices, affections and passions," whereas those of 1611 and 1618 claim much more: the compilation is "necessary to orators, preachers, poets, makers of emblems and imprese, devising apparatus of nuptials, funerals, and triumphs, etc."[11]   Perhaps it is the mentioning of emblems and imprese in these later titles that caused the word *emblem* to creep into titles of translated editions and blur thereby the clear distinction originally maintained by Ripa himself.   After all, it would be redundant to consider *Iconologia* an emblem collection when it is designed to be a source for making emblems.   Nevertheless, the blurring began with the French translation by Jean Baudoin, whose title reads: *Iconologie ou, Explication nouvelle de plusieurs images, emblèmes, et autres figures Hyerogliphiques des Vertues, des Vices, des Arts, etc* (Paris, 1644).   In German and Dutch editions, the words *Sinnbilder* and *Zinnebeelden* appear in their titles.   The 1709 English translation is entitled *Iconologia, or, Morall Emblems by Caesar Ripa*, and Richardson's subtitle, already cited, calls the work "A Collection of Emblematical Figures."   The 1866 Spanish translation published in the new world is entitled: *Iconologia o tratado de allegorias y emblemas.*   But nothing is more blatant than the 1698 two-volume French edition printed in Amsterdam, which proudly announces as its title: *Iconologie ou la science des emblèmes.*[12]

Strictly speaking, *Iconologia* is not an emblem collection by the simple fact that most of its images are personifications of abstract ideas explained by their symbolic attributes in discursive prose.   Missing are the mottoes and their metaphorical relations to the pictures.   It is true that there are a few personifications with mottoes, which thus resemble emblems.   For instance, the image of FORTVNA has the inscription of "Fortunae suae quisque faber" [Each man forges his own fortune] (Ripa, p. 182).   Or that of AMICITIA [Friendship] (Ripa, p. 15) is explained with the help of three mottoes: HIEMS, AESTAS [Winter and Summer], LONGE, ET PROPER [Far and Near], and MORS, ET VITA [Death and Life].   Although Peacham modeled his emblem "Amicitiae effigies" [Portrait of Friendship] (p. 181) not after the picture in Ripa but rather after that in *Mikrokosmos*,[13] he did summarize the moral of true friendship in the second sestet of his verse as follows:

Vpon his skirt, stoode LIFE and DEATH below,
To testifie in life and death his loue,
That farre and neere, with open heart do show,
Nor place, nor space, true frendship should remoue:
    Winter and sommer, whatsoever came,
    In faire or foule, we should be still the same.

The last line of Peacham's verse states a universal moral that true friendship never changes, making his emblem more nearly true to form than the description in Ripa.   Perhaps the best way to refine the distinction between a true emblem and the emblem-like personification in Ripa is to refer to Ripa's use of Alciati among his descriptions of AMICITIA.[14]   The young maiden, pictured in Ripa as representing friendship, is embracing a dead elm tree which is encircled by a green vine.   Alciati's emblem (no. 159) consists of just these two trees with the motto, "Amicitia etiam post mortem durans" [Friendship enduring even after death]. The metaphorical relation between the motto and the picture is that just as the green vine is supported by the dead elm so a true friend will support his friend even after death.   Unlike both Alciati and Peacham, Ripa neither applies the mottoes in his personification to a universal moral nor sums up the metaphorical relation between his picture and the mottoes.   In short, Ripa's AMICITIA, though more emblem-like than most of his other personifications, lacks the succinct moral application and the brevity of wit required of the emblem.   Moreover, compared with Alciati's emblem, Peacham's is less perfect because he, like Ripa, uses a descriptive title, "Amicitiae effigies."   By using the title instead of a motto, Peacham deprives his emblem of the necessary metaphorical relation which is essential to a bona fide emblem.[15] With descriptive titles, the veiling effect of the motto is lost; consequently, there will be less of an enigma which teases the mind in order to give the moral inculcation its maximum impact upon solving the riddle.   Thus, emblems with mottoes are as a rule superior in quality to those simply with titles.[16]

    The point I am belaboring here is important to the analysis of how Peacham uses Ripa.   For if *Iconologia* is not an emblem book, then many of Peacham's close borrowings from Ripa will not be genuine emblems either but poetic renderings of personifications.[17]   On the other hand, if he substitutes mottoes for Ripa's titles and explicates the metaphorical relations between mottoes and pictures, then he has changed his non-emblematic models into more nearly perfect emblems. Obviously it is imperative that any attempt at analyzing Peacham's manner of using his source must include this consideration. Also indispensable is the examination of unillustrated entries in Ripa which outnumbered by seven to one the illustrated ones.[18] This is so because Peacham did not borrow only from the illustrated personifications. As a matter of fact, seven out of those fourteen emblems which I have identified in the list below are based on Ripa's text alone. (In the list the capital letters in square brackets following Peacham's mottoes represent the initials of last names of [F]reeman, [Y]oung, and [T]ung, indicating who identified each emblem. When two initials occupy the same brackets, the second one adopts in total or in part the identification made by the first and includes it in his total count. The page numbers in square brackets following Ripa's titles represent those of the 1611 edition. I also divide the closeness of Peacham's modeling into three classes: "A" signifies close copying in both text and picture; "B," copying with deviations, and "C," remote or doubtful modeling.)

List of Attributions

Peacham	Ripa	
1 5 Philautia [T]	416 PRVDENZA [441]	B
2 7 Cuique & nemini [T]	149 Fede Christiana [161]	C
3 21 Gloria Principum [Y]	190 GLORIA DE'PRENCIPI [205]	A
4 22 Ragione di Stato [Y]	426f RAGIONE DI STATO [453]	B
5 25 Foelicitas publicae [FY]	155 FELICITA' PVBLICA [166]	A
6 26 Doctrina [FY]	[113] DOTTRINA [128][19]	A
7 35 Est hac almus honor [FT]	511 VIRTV [541]	+
	142 FAMA [154]	B
8 36 Virtus Romana [T]	507 VIRTV HEROICA [538]	B
9 41 Vicinorum amicitia [T]	81 Concordia [91]	B
10 46 Paenitentia [FY]	388 PENITENZA [413]	B
11 47 Dolus [Y]	229 INGANNO [248]	A
12 58 Pulchritudo foeminea [T]	42f BELLEZZA FEMINILE [48f]	A
13 93 Temperantia [T]	481 TEMPERANZA [509]	B
14 126 Melancholia [FY]	79 MALENCONICO [89]	B
15 127 Sanguis [FY]	77 SANGUIGNO [86]	A
16 128 Cholera [FY]	75 COLLERICO [84]	A
17 129 Phlegma [FY]	78 FLEMMATICO [87]	B
18 132 Matrimonium [FY]	306 MATRIMONIO [327]	A

19	134	Veritas [FY]	500	VERITA [529]	A
20	141	Eternitas [FY]	140	ETERNITA [152]	A
21	143	Sic audaces fortuna [T]	24f	ARDIRE MAGNANIMO [27]	A
22	146	Icon Peccati [Y]	383	PECCATO [408]	A
23	147	Inconstantia [FY]	225	INCOSTANZA [244]	A
24	149	Levitas [FY]	48f	CAPRICCIO [55f]	A
25	151	Somniorum Dea [T]	464	Sonno [492]	C
26	153	Sors [FY]	465f	SORTE [494]	A
27	170	Zelus in Deum [T]	101f	DESIDERIO DI DIO [116]	A
28	177	Hinc super haec, Musa [T]	349	VRANIA [371]	B
29	195	Nec in vna sede morantur [T]	171	Forza d'Amore [184]	B
30	198	Personam non animum [T]	134	ESILIA [145]	+
			200	HIPPOCRESIA [217]	C
31	206	Aula [T]	93f	CORTE [107f]	B

Peacham evidently used the 1603 edition of Ripa as his model. This can be conclusively shown through a comparison of Peacham's wooducts with their corresponding models in both the 1603 and the 1611 editions of Ripa. The woodcuts of the 1603 edition are the work of an unknown artist whose skill in drawing is superior to those of Peacham and of the copyist for the 1611 edition (who modeled after those of the 1603 edition). The superiority is clearly visible in the aesthetic quality of his designs, his attention to anatomical details, and his use of cross-hatchings. Accordingly, in modeling after the 1603 cuts, both Peacham and the 1611 copyist, whose artistry is no better than Peacham's, are sometimes forced to make changes, resulting in inferior copies. At other times both would modify their models either to be more faithful to Ripa's text, or to achieve a kind of independence. For example, "Doctrina" [Learning] (Peacham, p. 26) shows Peacham closely following the 1603 model in every detail, whereas the 1611 copyist chooses to draw the lady's hair short instead of the long, flowing, over-the-shoulder hair as in the 1603 model (the same is true of the model for "Veritas" [Truth], Peacham, p. 134) and to add a lion behind the seated lady, a detail not in his model nor in Ripa's text (see Figures 1, 2, & 3). The 1611 copyist's penchant for adding details on his own can also be seen in the model for "Icon Peccati" [Image of Sin] (Peacham, p. 146), where he gives snaky hair to the blind young man. In the model for "Sanguis" [Sanguine] (Peacham, p. 127), the 1611 copyist pictures the goat eating a bunch of grapes on the ground behind the lute-playing young man, whereas the 1603 artist shows the grapes in the mouth of a goat standing erect. Though following the 1603, Peacham, however, omits the music stand to the right of the young man and adds a floral garland to his head, a detail called for in the text but ignored by the other two artists (see Figures 4, 5, & 6). Similarly, the 1611 copyist restores a textual detail by adding a serpent trodden under the feet of the young man to the 1603 model for "Matrimonium" [Matrimony] (Peacham, p. 132), which Peacham, as remarked by Young (p. 52 & n. 41), has drawn in reverse. From these examples it would appear that Peacham's models had to be those in the 1603 edition; in four other emblems, the evidence to support this contention is conclusive. In "Gloria Principum" [Glory of Princes] (Peacham, p. 21), the square base on which stand both the pyramid and the lady's left foot is missing in 1611, and in "Sic audaces fortuna" [Thus daring fortune] (Peacham, p. 143), the fully armored arm of Lysimachus is, in 1611, clothed in an ordinary sleeve. In both "Dolus" [Deceit] (Peacham, p. 47) and "Cholera" [Choleric] (Peacham, p. 128), the 1611 versions differ so drastically from both 1603 and Peacham that no more elaboration is necessary (see Figures 7-9 & 10-12). It must be pointed out, however, that to the model for "Dolus" (Figure 7) the 1611 copyist adds the fish hooks, the flower, and the serpent on the basis of one of the three un- illustrated descriptions of INGANNO [Deceit] ("nella mano destra tenga molti hami, & nella sinistra vn masso di fiori, dal quale esca vn serpe," p. 229) [in his right hand he holds many hooks, and in his left a bundle of flowers, from which a serpent emerges] and the goatskin coat and the fish in a net (Figure 9) on that of another ("Huomo coperto da vna pelle di capra. . . In mano tenga vna rete, con alcuni sarghi pesci" p. 229) [A man covered with a goatskin. . . holds in hand a net with some fish]). In this manner he produced from three separate accounts a composite drawing which differs pictorially from his model in 1603 yet remains true to Ripa's texts, a common practice utilized by all other artists and by Peacham himself.

So far we have mentioned nine out of a total of twenty-one emblems that are modeled after the 1603 woodcuts. All nine are close modelings: Peacham, pp. 21, 26, 47, 127, 128, 132, 134, 143 and 146 (classed as A in the list above). In what follows, we will, from the remaining twelve, describe five in more detail (Peacham, pp. 22, 35, 46, 126, and 129) because of their greater divergences in modeling (classed as B). Among the seven which base their pictures exclusively upon Ripa's text, we will examine

six (Peacham, pp. 36, 41, 58, 177, 195, and 206) to see how Peacham models his emblems after textual sources alone. The seventh
(Peacham, p. 151) is one of the four emblems (along with those
on pp. 5, 7, 93) which have manuscript predecessors and are based
initially on the text of King James I's *Basilikon Doron* (see Young,
pp. 38-42). They are, however, indebted to Ripa in one way or
another and their analysis will conclude this essay.

   Although pictorial divergences are few in "Ragione di Stato"
[Reason of State] (Peacham, p. 22), they are noteworthy. Unlike
his model in mainly three details, the armed man (no longer a
lady), representing reason of state, strikes the poppies with the
wand in his right hand instead of pointing at them, and puts behind his hip his left hand instead of patting with it the lion's
head, and the lion raises its left front paw instead of its right.
The reason Peacham changes the gender of "Ragione di Stato" and
of the personal pronouns in his text may lie in the fact that he
dedicated this emblem to Sir Julius Caesar, who was one of those
sitting "at sterne of state." Other changes have been noted by
Young (p. 53). More significant is the change made in the text.
As in the example of "Amicitiae effigies" (see above), Peacham
summarizes the moral application of his personification in the
first stanza of his three-sestet poem before enumerating individual pictorial attributes:

> WHO sits at sterne of Common wealth, and state
> Of's chardge and office heere may take a view,
> And see what daungers howerly must amate,
> His ATLAS-burden, and what cares accrew
>   At once, so that he had enough to beare,
>   Though HERCVLES, or BRIAREVS he were.

In doing this Peacham has changed his non-emblematic model in
Ripa into a more emblem-like creation, although it is far from
perfect.

   Peacham is not afraid to add new details to his pictures as
we have seen in "Sanguis," one of the four humors. In "Phlegma"
[Phlegmatic] (Peacham, p. 129), he places the old man, seated on
a square stone block, next to an outdoor fireplace, a detail not
in Ripa's text but present in his own ". . . in the Chimney slee-
pes." The modification is even greater in "Melancholia" [Melan-
choly] (Peacham, p. 126) where Peacham changes the figure in his
model from a standing into a seated position (Figure 14). His

melancholy man--whose mouth is still bound like that in Ripa, in his right hand the same "sealed Purse," and his right foot still on the cube "fixt vpon the ground"--now sits on a long bench, an open book in his lap instead of in his left arm, an owl perches at one end of the bench instead of a partridge on his head as in Ripa (Figures 13 & 15) and a cat not in Ripa sits at the other end. This group is surrounded by four large trees, representing "a wood, devoid of companie," and Peacham adds more local colors by naming the owl and the cat "Madge the Owle, and melancholly Pusse." These changes amply attest to Peacham's inventiveness and independence in creating his own details. In "Paenitentia" [Penitence] (Peacham, p. 46), the 1603 model shows the lady standing, with a scourge in her right hand and a fish in her left (Figure 17). Keeping these details unchanged, Peacham has his lady seated in front of a fountain (Figure 16); this detail may have been inspired by an unillustrated description from Ripa, "stia à sedere in luogo solitario sopra vna pietra, donde esca vn fonte" [is sitting in a solitary place on a rock from which flows a fountain] (p. 388). These four emblems, despite their pictorial variations, are not genuine emblems but poetic renderings of personfications of Ripa.

Virtue on the right, in Peacham p. 35, is pictorially based in the main on Ripa (Freeman, p. 80), but Fame on the left, which is unillustrated in Ripa, is drawn from the text alone. Ripa's VIRTV' is winged, a brilliant sun on her chest, a long staff in her right hand, and in her left a laurel wreath (Figure 21). In Peacham's design, Fame and Virtue holding between them a scroll with the motto "Est hac almus honor" [Thus honor is refreshed], which is an anagram of Thomas Chalonerus to whom the emblem is dedicated.[20] Three quarters turned toward the viewer, Peacham's Virtue supports the scroll in the middle with her right hand extending out from her body and holds in her left hand a long staff against her shoulder. The wings have been removed, and the laurel wreath has been placed on her head. Facing her at left is Fame, winged, holding the left end of the scroll in her right hand and blowing the trumpet held in her left hand (Figure 20). Ripa's unillustrated FAMA has the wings and the trumpet: "hauerà due grand'ali" [has two large wings] and "nella destra mano terrà vna tromba" [in the right hand holds a trumpet].[21] In this manner an emblem has truly been "Newly devised," as Peacham claims in the subtitle of *Minerva Britanna*. Moreover, in combining two of Ripa's personifications and in giving

the anagrammatic motto to his picture, Peacham succeeds in creating a new emblem that satisfied the demands of a perfect specimen.   The turning of Sir Thomas Chaloner's name into an anagram
and making it the motto may not require the keenest of wits, but
the motto does achieve the encomium intended as seen in the
verse: "HEERE Virtue standes, and doth impart a scroule, / To
living fame, to publish farre and neere: / The man whose name,
she did within   enroule."   These and other lines in the sestet
unfold a story which tells that Virtue, out of envy of Chaloner's
"worth," "fame," and "memorie," kept his name enrolled, "And kept
to view, vnseene this many yeare."   So why does Virtue now wish
to use Fame to broadcast Chaloner's name?   Peacham answers the
question in the second sestet:

> But since she sees, the Muse is left forlorne,
> And fortune fawning, on the worthles wight,
> And eke her selfe, not cherisht as beforne.
> She bringes Moecenas once againe to light:
>   The man (if any else) a frend to Artes,
>   And good rewarder, of all best desertes.

Comparing Chaloner to Maecenas is certainly not very original.
However, it is precisely the very use of worn-out commonplace
in a new light that constitutes wit.   Gombrich rightly reiterates
the point in *Symbolic Images*: "it is precisely the task of what the
Renaissance called 'wit' to find the apt but unexpected application" (p. 163).   The metaphorical relation between the motto and
the picture is made clear by the second sestet.   Just as Virtue--
regretting her earlier envy of Chaloner and prompted now by the
world's neglect of the Muse, worthy men, and herself--decides to
make his name known through Fame, so Peacham wishes to exalt
Sir Thomas's Maecenas-like goodness as a patron of the arts by
inventing this emblem of Virtue and Fame displaying on a scroll
Chaloner's name in an anagrammatic motto which identifies his
virtue "Thus honor is refreshed."   In using the anagram, Peacham's wit lies in saying not that the motto fits the man but
that the motto is the man because it spells the man's name.
        One of the seven emblems which base their pictures exclu-
sively on Ripa's text, "Virtus Romana et antiqua" [Roman and
Ancient Virtue] (Peacham, p. 36) depicts Hercules standing; in his
extended right hand (although the text says left, see below) are
three golden apples, and with his left hand he supports a tall

mace which stands on its long stem next to him (Figure 19). In the 1603 edition, the unillustrated VIRTV' HEROICA [Heroic Virtue] is the third one on p. 507, whereas the 1611 has a wood-cut on p. 538 whose design is quite different, not only in having the apples in the left hand but also in standing the knotty club on its head (Figure 18). Having drawn his picture, Peacham expands several parts of Ripa's text in his two-sestet poem. From Ripa's first statement, "SI troua in Roma, cioè in Campidoglio vna statua di metallo indorata d'Ercole. . ." come the first four lines:

> THVS HERCVLES, the Romanes did devise,
> And in their Temples, him a place assignd:
> To represent vnto the peoples eies,
> The image of, th'Heroique virtuous mind:

The next phrase deals with the three golden apples and their significance, "& con la sinistra mano tiene tre pomi d'oro portati da gli horti Esperidi, i quali significano le tre vrtù [sic] eroiche ad Ercole attribuite." This is rendered as

> Within whose hand, three apples are of gold,
> The same which from th'Hesperides he fetcht,
> These are the three Heroique vertues old, . . .

Then in the margin Peacham lists in English the three virtues, reversing Ripa's order of the second and the third: 1. Moderation of anger--"La prima, è la moderatione dell'Ira"; 2. Contempt of pleasure--"L'altra, è il generoso sprezzamento delle delitie, & de i piaceri"; 3. Abstinence from covetousness--"La seconda, la temperanza dell'Auaritia."[22] For the significance of the lion skin and the club, which is not explained in this particular account in Ripa's text, Peacham selects what he wants from the unillustrated account preceding this one. "La spoglia de Leone in Ercole ci dimostra la generosità, & fortezza dell'animo" becomes "The Lions skinne, about his shoulders stretcht, / Notes fortitude. . . ," and the lengthy explication of the knots on the club as representing the difficult path to virtue--"la via della virtù quantuncunque ardua, & di grandissima difficultà"--is simplified into "his Clubbe the crabbed paine, / To braue atcheiuements, ere we can attaine." In designing this particular emblem on a familiar subject, Peacham drew his picture from one unillustrated text and made a composite text of his own from more than one account in Ripa. Far from being a bona fide emblem, this description of "antique and Roman virtue" does contain a universal moral in the last two lines of the first sestet, Virtue "who like ALCIDES, to her lasting praise, / In action still, delightes to spend her dayes."

The clue to finding the basis in Ripa for "Vicinorum amicitia" [Friendship of neighbors] (Peacham, p. 41) is rather indirect. Having discovered Peacham's heavy dependence upon Ripa in the second book of *The Gentleman's Exercise* (see n. 21 above), I checked to see how closely Peacham had translated Ripa's "Concordia." First the Italian version: "Donna, che nella destra mano tiene vn pomo granato, & nella sinistra vn mazzo di mortella, e si fabrica tal maniera, secondo il detto di Pierio Valeriano, con l'autorità di Democrito, dicendo, che la mortella, & i pomi granati s'amano tanto, che se bene le radici di dette piante sono poste alquanto lontane l'vna dall'altra, si auuicinano nondi-meno, & s'intrecciano insieme" (p. 81), which Peacham renders as follows: "*Concord. Pierius Valerianus* out of *Democritus* would haue *Concord* like a faire Virgin holding in one hand a pomgranate, in the other a bundle of Mirtle, for such is the nature of these trees, that if they bee planted, though a good space one from the other, they will meet, and with twining one embrace the other" (*The Gentleman's Exercise*, p. 112 [misprinted as 116]). Mentioning neither Ripa nor Valeriano nor Democritus, Peacham includes only the nature of these two trees in the first sestet on p. 41 of *Minerva Britanna*.

> SVCH frendly league, by nature is they say;
> Betwixt the Mirtle, and Pomegranate tree,
> Who, if not planted over-farre away,
> They seeke each others mutuall amitie:
>   By open signes of Frendship, till at last,
>   They one another haue with armes embrac't.

The moral application and the metaphorical relation between the motto and the picture explained in the second sestet make this a true emblem:

> Which doth declare, how neighbours should vnite
> Themselues together, in all frendly loue;
> And not like Tyrants, excercise [sic] their spight,
> On one another, when no cause doth moue:
>   But letting quarrels, and old grudges cease,

Be reconcild, to liue, and die, in peace.

A greater dependence on Ripa's text is seen in the next emblem. For his title, "Pulchritudo foeminea" [Feminine Beauty] (p. 58), Peacham simply translates Ripa's BELLEZZA FEMINILE. For the first four and a half lines of his text, he renders Ripa's "DONNA ignuda, con vna ghirlanda di gigli, & ligustri in testa, in vna mano haurà vn dardo, nell'altra vn specchio, porgendolo in fuori, senza specchiarsi dentro, sederà sopra vn drago molto feroce" (p. 42) into

A VIRGIN naked, on a Dragon sits,
One hand out-stretch'd, a christall glasse doth show:
The other beares a dart, that deadly hits;
Vpon her head, a garland white as snow,
Of* print and Lillies. . . .

The asterisk refers in the margin to "Alba ligustra cadunt. . . which is taken from Virgil's second *Eclogue* by Ripa: "Alba ligustra cadunt, vaccinia nigra leguntur" (p. 43) [The white privets fall, the dark hyacinths are culled! -- tr. H. R. Fairclough, LCL]. In the second stanza Peacham picks and chooses phrases here and there to explicate each item in the picture also according to Ripa's text. Below Peacham's verse are two Latin distichs which the marginal notes indicate as from "Ovid: 2. de Arte amandi" and "idem." Although the second two lines are indeed from *The Art of Loving*, quoted in Ripa, the first two lines are really from Ovid's *Tristia* (3. 7. 37-8). As to why Peacham made a mistake like this, it is impossible to venture a guess. In any event, besides relying heavily upon Ripa's text for his own verse, the end verse, as well as for the marginal annotations, Peacham has drawn his picture after the Italian text also, not without a certain degree of realism, especially in the ferocity of the dragon, inspired perhaps by the Italian "vn drago molto feroce" [a very ferocious dragon] (Figure 22). On the other hand, in spite of closely modeling the picture after Ripa's text, it is still a poetic rendering of BELLEZZA FEMINILE, nothing more.

In contrast, "Hinc super haec, Musa" [Muse, henceforth more than this] (Peacham, p. 177), which is the anagram of Peacham's own name in Latin, uses Ripa's VRANIA text only slightly for both picture and text. "HAVERA' vna ghirlanda di lucenti stelle" [has a garland of bright stars] becomes a group of stars in the sky at

which the lady points with a staff; "sarà vestita di azurro" [is
dressed in an azure robe] shows in the lady's dress decorated with
stars; and "hauerà in mano vn globo rappresentante le sfere
celesti" [has in her hand a globe representing the celestial sphere]
is the only detail materialized in her right hand (Figure 23). With
a crescent moon to her right, the lady is standing on the bank
of a lake which Peacham mentions in his text, "Let muddy Lake,
delight the sensuall thought, / Loath thou the earth, and lift
they selfe aloft." This is the only reference to the explication
in Ripa's text that Urania means heaven, "che è l'istesso che il
Cielo."[23]   The second stanza of Peacham's verse is a personal ad-
monition (rendering this emblem more of an impresa), urging himself not to be discouraged by the arduous task of emblem making:

> Repent not (though) my time so idlely spent,
> The cunning'st Artist ere he can, (We see)
> Some rarest Modell bring to his Intent,
> Much heweth off in Superfluitie:
>   And many a pretious hower, I know is lost,
>   Ere ought is wrought to countervaile the cost.

Perhaps this "ought" is wrought in "Nec in vna sede moran-
tur" [Not contained in one place] (Peacham, p. 195), which is
based on two of Ripa's entries on love, which in turn may be
influenced by Alciati. Ripa's illustrated FORZA D'AMORE [Force
of Love], picturing a winged Cupid with a floral wreath in one
hand and fish in the other, is based on Alciati's "In statuam
Amoris" [About Love's statue], no. 113. The unillustrated *Forza
d'Amore* [Force of love] is also based on Alciati's "Vis amoris"
[Force of love], no. 107. Now, Peacham's drawing is partially
based on this second text of Ripa. His Cupid has Ripa's "l'ali
alle spalle, con l'arco, & le saette in mano, & con la faretra al
fianco" [wings over the shoulders, with bow and arrows in hand
and with the quiver by his side]. But, instead of Ripa's Cupid
raising his left hand towards the sky and drawing down flaming
arrows. Peacham's Cupid raises his left hand to hold a crown
over his own head. Peacham's text appears to be entirely his
own, exalting the power of love in the first sestet and asking
Cupid to persuade his "sweet saint" to love him in the second
sestet. Because of this personal application, this use of a love
motif is in the nature of an amorous impresa rather than an
emblem.

Finally, both Freeman (p. 80) and Young (p. 147, n. 42) regard Peacham's last emblem "Aula" (p. 206) as deriving from Ripa (pp. 147f.). The "apparent" clue is in the first two lines of the second sestet of Peacham's verse: "A Ladie faire, is FAVOVR feign'd to be, / Whose youthfull Cheeke, doth beare a louely blush," and opposite the second line in the margin is the note: "*Caesare Ripa in Iconologia*." On pp. 147 and 148 are two unillustrated descriptions of *Fauore*. The first describes a cheerful youth (not a fair lady), winged and naked, blindfolded and standing on a wheel; the second depicts an armed youth (again not a fair lady) with a large shield on which is a picture of Arion being rescued by a dolphin. So Peacham does not seem to have based his "Aula" on these youths. His note only suggests, and nothing more, that Ripa does treat the personification of favor which the two youths represent but which the fair lady "feign'd to be." The "real" clue is in the title "Aula," courtiers, and there is an unillustrated description of the traits of courtiers in Ripa under *Corte* (pp. 93-95). There, some, though by no means all, of the courtiers' traits are found: Peacham's "A Ladie faire" is in Ripa's "Donna giouine," "a knot of guilded hookes" in "de gli ami legati," "on her feete she weares / Lead-shoes" in "ne piedi hauerà le scarpe di piombo," and "a paire of Stocks" in "vn paro di ceppi di oro." On p. 207 Peacham glosses "Stocks" with the marginal note: "Aureas compedes. *Alciatus*," referring the reader to Alciati's "In aulicos" [About courtiers] (no. 86). Peacham has switched gold from the stocks to the hooks, and he wants the reader to know that he knew that stocks in both Ripa and Alciati were supposed to be golden. In addition, the "Holywater brush" which the lady holds in her hand along with the "knot of guilded hookes" and the "fawning Spaniel" lying at her feet are not in Ripa's *Corte* (see Figure 26). The hooks could be based on Ripa's *Inganno* [Deceit] (p. 249) and the dog on Ripa's *Adulatione* [Flattery] (p. 7). Thus, this emblem is a composite modeled in large part after Ripa's *Corte* with other traits from other Ripa personifications. Despite its lack of a motto, this emblem is more nearly true to form by summarizing its moral in the first stanza of its verse.

Similarly, in "Personam non animam" [Person not mind] (p. 198), Peacham casts his net widely to make a composite emblem from several entries of Ripa's HIPPOCRESIA (Figure 24), but the only pictorial detail used is the rosary in the left hand of Peacham's pilgrim-like old man (Figure 25). The staff in his right hand may be taken from Ripa's ESILIO, the exile, whose staff resembles that in Peacham, and St. James's seashell on the exile's lapel appears on the hat of Peacham's hypocrite.   In the first stanza of Peacham's verse, there are snatches of phrases from Ripa's hypocrite: "A feigned Zeale of Sanctitie within" from "vna fintione, di bontà, & santità" (p. 199 [misprinted as 195]) or "And humblest habits, but a false disguise, / To cloke their hate, or hidden villanies" from the second description "Il vestimento. . . dimostra. . . l'opera di coloro, i quali con parole, & attione d'hippocresia cuoprono la sottigliezza della malitia interna" (p. 201).   These scattered resemblances and echoes, however, are insufficient either to claim Ripa as a definite source or to rule out the possibility that Peacham might have found a model elsewhere for this particular emblem.

"Philautia" [Self-love] (Peacham, p. 5), with three manuscipt predecessors, is partially indebted to Ripa's PRVDENZA [Prudence] (p. 416).   The partial model in Ripa depicts a helmeted lady with two faces like Janus, holding in her right hand an arrow wound around by a remora and a mirror in her left; behind her on the ground sits a stag with large antlers.   This illustrated prudence is preceded and followed by unillustrated ones.   The one preceding it is very close to Peacham's design.   It shows a lady who, also with faces like Janus, looks into a mirror and has a serpent wound around her arm.   The one following it consists of a lady, without the Janus-like faces, holding in her left hand a skull and in her right a serpent.   Peacham conflates all three descriptions, retaining the mirror but transferring it to the right hand and keeping the serpent wound around the left arm.   The suprising, and ironic, adaptation of prudence to depict self-love is the result of Peacham's witty invention.   His wit here is particularly daring because he refers the reader in a marginal note to Alciati's "Philautia" (no. 69) which is represented by the traditional Narcissus and is quoted by Ripa in "Amor di se stesso" [Self-love] (p. 19). As a symbol of evil the serpent is related to original sin, in this case the flattering self-love.   Moreover, the mirror now stands for blindness as the result of pride, "Know how in Pride Selfe-loue doth most surpasse, / And still is in her Imperfections   blind." Thus, Peacham converts the traditional attributes of prudence-- serpent of wisdom and mirror of self-knowledge--into those of sin and blindness.   Yet, the emblem is of inferior quality in that it lacks a motto and a moral application.   It resembles too much Ripa's typical description of a personification, even though its two-sestet text in the format of questions and answers between an interlocutor and Philautia is indebted to that in Alciati's "In occasionem," [About Occasion] (no. 121).

"Cuique et nemini" [Each one and no one] (Peacham, p. 7) also has three manuscript predecessors. The woodcut portrays Faith as a lady who stands behind a St. Anthony cross, her left arm and hand rest on its horizontal bar, and her outstretched right hand holds an open book. A possible source could be Ripa's unillustrated "Fede Christiana" [Christian Faith] (p. 149) which mentions the cross and the open book, but they are both held in Faith's right hand. If Peacham indeed borrows these two items from Ripa for his own purposes, he has converted Ripa's personification into a more nearly genuine emblem by using the motto "Cuique et nemini" and explaining its relation to the picture. "My hope is heauen, the crosse on earth my rest," Peacham has Faith explain, "The foode that feedes me is my Saviours bloud." He should perhaps have used the word *"word"* instead of *"bloud"* to be represented by the open book, but it would not have rhymed with *"good"* in the fourth line. Relating to the motto, Peacham gives her more declarations in the second sestet:

> Nor Heresie, nor Schisme, I doe maintaine,
> But as CHRIST's coate so my beliefe is one,
> I hate all fancies forg'd of humane braine,
> I let contention and vaine strifes alone.

Similarly, "Somniorum Dea" (Peacham, p. 151), with its two manuscript precedents, is somewhat indebted to Ripa. The goddess of false dreams, *Brysus*, is by no means a Renaissance commonplace;[24] therefore, Peacham feels it necessary to document his source. He traces it to Frischlinus' commentary on Persius.[25] The picture shows a lady standing sideways; her right hand holds a flower vase upside down, emptying a large quantity of worldly goods such as crowns, scepters, and jewels, to which the index finger of her left hand points. Where could Peacham find a source for his picture? Perhaps it is in Ripa's *Sonno*, an unillustrated account of the winged god of dreams: "VN Giouane con l'ali alle spalle, che con la destra mano tenghi vn Cornucopia, onde esca fumo, sarà languido, con due vesti, vna bianco di sopra, che cuopra sino alla cintura, & l'altra di sotto nera, & lunga; nella sinistra mano terrà vna verga" [A youth, with wings on his shoulders, holds in his right hand a cornucopia which emits smoke; he appears languid, wearing two gowns--a white one above which reaches down to the waist, the other underneath long and black; he holds a wand in his left hand] (p. 464). If Peacham indeed borrows from Ripa, he changes the cornucopia into the flower vase but retains the two gowns. In changing the winged *Sonno* into the goddess *Brysus*, Peacham perhaps intends to puzzle his contemporary readers, however knowledgeable they might be, who would have to track down Peacham's sources both in the text and in the picture with some effort and consequently to admire the agility of his inventiveness and wit. The moral application in the second sestet makes this a good emblem, though far from being a perfect specimen.

In "Temperantia" [Temperance] (Peacham, p. 93), with only one manuscript predecessor, one would expect Peacham to model his picture closely after that in Ripa's TEMPERANZA (p. 481). There are, however, only two things Peacham's drawing has in common with Ripa's: the standing lady and the bridle. Ripa's lady holds the bridle in her right hand, grasping the bit with her fingers, while the end of the cords is seized in her left hand along with the stay of a clock; there is, moreover, an elephant standing behind her. However, the shape of the bridle in Peacham is altered. Although still dangling from the end of the rope, the bridle's other end is now in her right hand, and in her left hand she holds an empty "golden cup." Why did Peacham consciously deviate from Ripa? The answer seems to lie in the passage from *Basilikon Doron* (2.84): "Make Temperance the queene of all other virtues within you," writes James I to his son Henry, "I meane not by the vulgar interpretation of Temperance, which onely consistes in gustu and Tactu, by the moderating of these twoo [sic] senses but I meane of that wise moderation that first commaunding your self, shall shall [sic] as a Queene commaund all the affections and passions of your mind." The sestets in Peacham refer to the bridle and the cup:

HEERE *Temperance* I stand, of virtues, Queene,
Who moderate all humane vaine desires,
Wherefore a bridle in my hand is seene,
To curbe affection, that too farre aspires:
   I'th other hand, that golden cup doth show,
   Vnto excesse I am a deadly foe.

For when to lustes, I loosely let the raine,

And yeeld to each suggesting appetite,
Man to his ruine, headlong runnes amaine,
To frendes great greife, and enimies delight:
    No conquest doubtles, may with that compare,
    Of our affectes, when we the victors are.

The first sentence in the *Basilikon Doron* passage, "Make Temperance the queene of all other virtues," becomes the first line above, and the last part, "that wise moderation that first commaunding your self, shall shall as a Queene commaund all the affections and passions of your mind," appears as the last two lines of the second sestet. But what influence does King James's distinguishing between his wise moderation and "the vulgar interpretation of Temperance, which onely consistes in gustu and Tactu" have on Peacham's emblem? Interestingly enough, the senses of taste and touch are mentioned in an unillustrated account of temperance in Ripa. In explicating the significance of the bridle, Ripa writes: "Il freno dichiara, che deue esser la temperanza principalmente adoperata nel gusto, & nel tatto, l'vno de quali solo si partecipa per la bocca, & l'altro è steso per tutto il corpo" [the rein declares that temperance ought to be used principally in taste and touch, the one is confined to the mouth, the other extends over all the body] (p. 480). Could King James possibly have reacted against Ripa's popular interpretation? Being a scholar himself, James could certainly have gleaned this information from other sources (as the margin in *Basilikon Doron* notes Aristotle's *Politics* and Cicero's *De inventione*); still it is a fascinating idea that the king might have seen a copy of the 1603 Ripa too. Especially, neither the manuscript version of *Basilikon Doron* (British Library, MS Royal 18. B. XV) written in Scots--between 1594 when the prince was born and 1599--by the king through an amanuensis nor the privately printed edition in 1599 by Robert Waldegrave contains this phrase "by the moderating of these two senses in gustu and Tactu." It appears for the first time in the 1603 edition of *Basilikon Doron*. In its place, the manuscript has "in the moderate using of meate & drinke" which is followed in the 1599 edition. In any event, what is important to stress here is the fact that the king's emphasis upon self-control over the "affections and passions" of the mind might have compelled Peacham to play down the taste and touch aspects in Ripa and to select other elements among the one illustrated and four other unillustrated accounts of temperance to make his

point.   Thus, from the illustrated account he borrows "col freno
in vna mano per dimostrare l'offitio della temperanza, che è di
rafrenare, & moderare gl'appetiti dell'animo" [with a rein in one
hand to demonstrate the office of temperance which is to restrain
and moderate the appetites of the mind] (p. 481) for his third and
fourth lines of the first sestet (quoted above).   The golden cup
in the next two lines has no parallel in Ripa; the nearest thing
may be the last unillustrated account in which this phrase occurs:
"nella sinistra vn vaso di acqua" [in left a water   vase] (p. 482).
Although the water pot may be similar to the golden cup, the use
for which the water pot, held in her right hand, is intended, i.e.,
to temper the red-hot pincers by plunging them into the water,
makes it not only an unlikely source but also unsuitable   for
Peacham's purposes.   The last two lines in the second sestet may
find a parallel in another of Ripa's unillustrated accounts of
temperance.   This lady holds in her right hand a palm branch
which stands for victory (p. 480).   Peacham's last phrase, "when
we the victors are" as has been noted above, comes from *Basilikon
Doron*: "that first commaunding your self, shall. . . commaund all
the affections and passions of your mind."   The sense of a peer-
less victory might very well suggest to Peacham the palm.   In-
cidentally, the moralizing in the second sestet makes his emblem
of good quality inspite of its lacking a motto.   In short, given the
distinction insisted upon by King James, Peacham attempts in his
picture to present as different an image from that in Ripa as he
can;   nevertheless, he knows Ripa's accounts too well to resist
picking up elements from Ripa that suit his purposes.
      This is, in fact, true of all these four emblems that are
initially based on *Basilikon Doron*.   Although in varying degrees
they may be indebted to one or more of Ripa's descriptions,
whether illustrated or not, they all maintain an uniqueness all
their own.   The reason for this integrity lies in Peacham's desire
for preferment by presenting his manuscript emblem books to King
James or to Prince Henry.   According to Young (pp. 38-41), the
first one (Bodleian Library, MS. Rawlinson poetry 146), intended
for Prince Henry, was unfinished and never presented to its
dedicatee; the second one (British Library, MS. Harleian 6855,
Art. 13), or a clean copy of it, was presented to King James on
the occasion of his assuming the title of "King of Great Britain"
in 1603; and the third one (British Library, MS. Royal 12 A LXVI),
known and cherished for its colored drawings, was presented to
Prince Henry shortly after his investiture as the Prince of Wales.

Naturally, whether it is for the king or for the prince, the manuscript emblem books must be distinguished by their uniqueness and
singularity. It simply would not do for either the king or the
prince to discover that some of the drawings were close copies
or derivations of other well-known iconologies or emblem books.
Consequently, each manuscript emblem not only illustrates one of
King James's pieces of royal advice to his son, but also constitutes
a rare and original invention by Peacham.[26] Even if some of
them are indebted to sources other than the text of *Basilikon
Doron*, as we have seen in the case of Ripa's influence, the
emblems would still present a new look, or would be considered
"newly devised."[27] It is for this reason that few of those manuscript emblems reused in *Minerva Britanna* are close copies of
other sources.

   In summary, Peacham modeled a total of thirty-one emblems
in *Minerva Britanna* after Ripa's *Iconologia*: nineteen after both
picture and text, seven after text only, four after partial picture
but mainly text (Peacham, pp. 5, 7, 35, 198), and one after partial text but mainly picture (Peacham, p. 93). By any standards,
Ripa must be considered a major source of *Minerva Britanna*. In
terms of closeness of modeling, there are sixteen class A, twelve
class B, and three class C emblems. However, closeness of modeling generally but not always indicates Peacham's intention of
simply translating Ripa into English as we will now attempt to
set forth. Whenever Peacham closely copies both picture and text
from Ripa, his emblems are but poetic renderings of *Iconologia*
(see n17 above). Occupying the middle ground between just translating Ripa's personifications into English and transforming them
into nearly true emblems are six emblems that have titles instead
of mottoes but have provided moral summations in their verses.
Of these (Peacham, pp. 22, 36, 93, 132, 151, and 206) one is of
class A, four of class B, and one of class C. But when he
replaces Ripa's titles with mottoes and explicates the metaphorical relations between the mottoes and the pictures, these emblems do reach certain degrees of perfection, as seen in Peacham,
pp. 7, 35, 41, 143, 177, 195, and 198. Of these one again is of
class A, four of class B, and two of C. Thus, while it is true
that better than half of the thirty-one borrowings from Ripa are
nothing more than poetic renderings, it is not always true that
they are of the closest modelings. As we have seen, there are
four class B emblems among them. Among the middle group and
that of more nearly perfect emblems, there are specimens of all

three classes. Moreover, even among those more nearly true emblems some are technically imprese (e.g., personal impresa in
Peacham, p. 177 and amorous impresa in Peacham, p. 195), attes-
ting to the veracity of the subtitle of *Minerva   Britanna*: "OR A
GARDEN OF HOEROICAL Deuises, furnished, and adorned with
Emblemes and *Impresa's* of sundry   natures, Newly devised, *moralized*, and *published*." It is for this reason that the study of
Peacham's manner of using his sources (besides Ripa, there are
such other major sources as Camerarius, Alciati, Typotius, *Mikrokosmos*, Heraldry, Aesop's fables) is challenging by virtue of its
variety and unpredictability. But it is from his transformation of
Ripa's personifications into more nearly perfect emblems that we
most appreciate his inventiveness and wit, his agility in providing variety and in making new applications of commonplace and
traditional motifs, as well as in his ability of turning borrowed
materials to suit his own purposes.

Figure 1
DOTTRINA, Ripa, *Iconologia* (1603), p. 113.

Figure 2
Doctrina, Peacham, *Minerva Britanna* (1612), p. 26.

Figure 3
DOTTRINA, Ripa, *Iconologia* (1611), p. 128.

Figure 4
SANGVIGNO, Ripa, *Iconologia* (1603), p. 77.

Figure 5
Sanguis, Peacham, *Minerva Britanna* (1612), p. 127.

Figure 6
SANGVIGNO, Ripa, *Iconologia* (1611), p. 86.

Figure 7
INGANNO, Ripa, *Iconologia* (1603), p. 229.

Figure 8
Dolus, Peacham, *Minerva Britanna* (1612), p. 47.

Figure 9
INGANNO, Ripa, *Iconologia* (1611), p. 248.

Figure 10
COLLERICO, Ripa, *Iconologia* (1603), p. 75.

Figure 11
Cholera, Peacham, *Minerva Britanna* (1612), p. 128.

Figure 12
COLLERICO, Ripa, *Iconologia* (1611), p. 84.

Figure 13
MALENCONICO, Ripa, *Iconologia* (1603), p. 79.

Figure 14
Melancholia, Peacham, *Minerva Britanna* (1612), p. 126.

Mason Tung

Figure 15
MALENCONICO, Ripa, *Iconologia* (1611), p. 89.

Figure 16
Poenitentia, Peacham, *Minerva Britanna* (1612), p. 46.

Figure 17
PENITENZA, Ripa, *Iconologia* (1603), p. 388.

Figure 18
VIRTV' HEROICA, Ripa, *Iconologia* (1611), p. 538.

Figure 19
Virtus Romana, Peacham, *Minerva Britanna* (1612), p. 36.

Figure 20
Est hac almus honor, Peacham, *Minerva Britanna* (1612), p. 35.

Figure 21
VIRTV', Ripa, *Iconologia* (1603), p. 511.

Figure 22
Pulchritudo, Peacham, *Minerva Britanna* (1612), p. 58.

Figure 23
Hinc super haec, musa, Peacham, *Minerva Britanna* (1612), p. 177.

Figure 24
HIPPOCRESIA, Ripa, *Iconologia* (1603), p. 200.

Figure 25
Personam non animam, Peacham, *Minerva Britanna*
(1612), p. 198.

Figure 26
Aula, Peacham, *Minerva Britanna* (1612), p. 206.

NOTES

1. For previous attributions by Rosemary Freeman (in her *English Emblem Books* [London: Chatto & Windus, 1948], pp. 79-82) and by Alan Young (in his *Henry Peacham* [Boston: Twayne, 1979], n. 42, p. 53), see the "List of Attributions" below.

2. See Edward A. Maser, ed. *Cesare Ripa: Baroque and Rococo Pictorial Imagery: the 1758-60 Hertel Edition of Ripa's "Iconologia" with 200 Engraved Illustrations* (New York: Dover Publications, 1971), "Introduction," pp. vii-xvii. Maser bases the biographical information on Erna Mandowsky's *Untersuchungen zur Iconologie des Cesare Ripa* (Hamburg: H. Proctor, 1934), also published in Italian as *Ricerche intorno all'Iconologia di Cesare Ripa* (Florence: L. S. Olschki, 1939), and as the article "Ricerche intorno all'Iconologia di Cesare Ripa," in *La Bibliofilia*, Anno XLI (1939), XLI, Florence, 1940, pp. 7-27, 111-124, 204-35, 279326. For a bibliographical description of various editions and translations of Ripa, see Mario Praz, *Studies in Seventeenth-Century Imagery* (Rome: Edizione di Storia e Letteratura, 1964), pp. 472-75. Recent studies on Ripa are the following: E. Mâle, *L'art religieux après le Concile de Trente* (Paris: A. Colin, 1932) (on influence of Ripa, pp. 383ff.). Jacques Saulnier, "Allegorique et Symbolisme," *Livre et ses amis* [Paris] 15 (1947), 7-11 (6 illus. from *Iconologia*). Allan H. Gilbert, *The Symbolic Persons in the Masques of Ben Jonson* (Durham: Duke University Press, 1948). Arie Zijderveld, "Cesar Ripa's *Iconologia* in ons land," *Oud-Holland*, 64 (1949), 113-28, 184-92 (20 illus.). L. D. Ettlinger, "The Pictorial Source of Ripa's 'Historia,'" *Journal of the Warburg and Courtauld Institutes*, 13 (1950), 322-23. K. L. Selig, "The Spanish Translation of Cesare Ripa's *Iconologia*," *Italica* [Menasha, Wisc.], 28 (1951), 254-56 and "A Note on Ripa's *Iconologia*," *Italica*, 29 (1952), 108-109. William R. Crelly, *The Painting of Simon Vouet*, (New Haven: Yale University Press, 1962). Katharine Fremantle, "Themes from Ripa and Rubens in the Royal Palace of Amsterdam," *Burlington Magazine*, 103 (1961), 258-61 (11 illus.). A. Hope, "Notes on British Art: Cesare Ripa's Iconology & the Neo-classical Movement," *Apollo* [London], 86 (1967), 1-4. Latest interest in Ripa may be seen in the following studies: Joseph Rosenblum, "Why an Ass? Cesare Ripa's *Iconologia* as a Source for Bottom's Translation," *Shakespeare Quarterly*, 32 (1981), 357-59 and G. Savarese & A. Gareffi, *La letterature delle immagini nel Cinquecento* (Roma:

Bulzoni, 1980), which deals with Giovio, Tasso, and Bruno along with Ripa.

3. The only Latin rendering, not of Ripa's text but of the *fatti* or historical applications of the allegory, is by Johann Georg Hertel (n. 2 above), who translated the German inscription and couplet to each engraving into the scholarly language; see Maser, p. xiv. Henry Green, in *Andrea Alciati and His Emblem Books* (London, 1872), has observed that "it is not certain whether England ever down to 1871 possessed an English version" of Alciati (p. 57) and the translation in progress in 1872 by Rev. G. S. Cautley (no. 179 of Green's bibliography) remained unpublished. See also Green, no. 137 which is a manuscript version in English of ninety-one emblems copied from the 1608 Antwerp edition (no. 133), the only unpublished, partial English translation of Alciati. This manuscript, Karl Josef Höltgen informs me, survives in private ownership.

4. Praz, p. 473 and Maser, p. xi.

5. This number was established by Alciati himself in the 1550 Lyons edition, the year he died. In restoring the offensive emblem no. 85, expurgated since it first appeared in the 1546 Venice edition (Green, no. 28), the 1621 Padua edition (Green, no. 152) has 212 emblems.

6. Maser, p. xi.

7. As one example among many, Boudard translated and illustrated the first of two unillustrated entries under Ripa's *Abondoza Maritim*. Ripa's Italian reads: "Cerere si rappresenta con le spighe nella destra mano stesa sopra la prora d'vna naue, & a piedi vi sarà vna misura di grano con le spighe dentro come l'altra di sopra," which Boudard renders into French fairly closely: "Ceres assise sur la proue d'un vaisseau, caracterise ce sujet. Elle tient d'une main un bouquet de chanvre avec ses fuilles, & de l'autre un rameau de genet sur lequel sont attachés plusieurs cocons de vers à soye; & elle s'appuye sur une mesure pleine de grains, qui se rependent" (I.2). Although Boudard mentions Ripa neither in his title nor in his "Raisonnement Necessaire a L'Intelligence de L'Iconologia" (a2-a8ᵛ), he returns to Ripa's early editions (1603-1611) frequently. The 1603 edition has recently been reprinted by Georg Olms Verlag (1984) with an introduction by Erna Mandowsky.

8. For instance, the 1743-50 three-part Dutch edition mentions in its title "uit de oirsprongklyke Schriften van Cezar Ripa,

Zaratino Kastellini, Pierus Valerianus, Horus Apollo en andere" (Praz, p. 474).

9. Like the words *impresa* and *emblem* iconology undergoes various changes in meaning, especially in the hands of modern critics. Ripa obviously meant the term as he had defined it: namely, as the description of images. Boudard, whose "Raisonnement" (n7 above) is closely translated by Richardson (though the latter never mentions the former's name), defines iconology as "the Art of personifying the Passions, Arts, Sciences, Dispositions of the Mind, Virtues, Vices" (Richardson, *Iconology*, 1779, Vol. 1, "An Introductory Discourse Upon the Science of Iconology," p. i). In Erwin Panofsky's definition, Ripa's iconology becomes iconography (Maser, p. vii). According to Panofsky, there are three strata in distinguishing the subject matter of meaning of a work of art. The first stratum consists of "primary or natural meanings" identified by pure forms which carry "primary or natural meanings" or artistic motifs. "An enumeration of these motifs would be a pre-iconographical description of the work of art" (*Meaning in the Visual Arts; papers in and on art history* [Garden City, N.Y.: Doubleday, 1955], p. 28). The next stratum consists of "secondary or conventional subject matter" in which artistic motifs are connected with themes or concepts. " Motifs thus recognized as carriers of a secondary or conventional meaning may be called images. . . stories and allegories," and "the identification of such images, stories and allegories is the domain of what is normally referred to as 'iconography'" (p. 29). "Iconography is, therefore, a description and classification of images much as ethnography is a description and classification of human races" (p. 31). It is with this sense that Ripa's *Iconologia* fits. As a matter of fact, Jean Seznec considers Ripa as an iconographer (*The Survival of the Pagan Gods*, translated by Barbara F. Sessions [New York: Harper, 1961], "Index," p. 370). Panofsky himself later considers *Iconologia* as the "Bible of Renaissance and Baroque iconography," in *Problems in Titian Mostly Iconographic* (New York: New York University Press, 1969), p. 60. Iconology concerns itself with the third stratum, the "intrinsic meaning or content." It takes iconography a step further towards interpretation and synthesis. "For as the suffix "graphy" denotes something descriptive, so does the suffix "logy" denotes something interpretive. So I conceive of iconology as an iconography turned interpretive and thus becoming an integral part of the study of art" (p. 32). E. H. Gombrich defines iconography as the "identification

of text illustrated in a given religious or secular picture," and iconology as "the reconstruction of a programme rather than the identification of a particular text" (*Symbolic Images; Studies in the art of the renaissance* [London: Phaidon Press, 1972], p. 6). I realize that I may be doing a grave injustice to Panofsky in thus oversimplifying, if not misrepresenting, his text. But my simple purpose here is to suggest the probable existence of a limited affinity betweeen Ripa's method in *Iconologia* identified as iconography and the emblematic method in say Alciati or Peacham, which may be identified as iconology in just this respect. Whereas Ripa's descriptions of images require or demand no interpretation, bona fide emblems like iconology do, in order to reveal the intrinsic meaning which is hidden in the metaphorical relation between the emblem's motto and picture. For further illustration of this point, see the discussion on Ripa's AMICITIA below.

10. "DESCRITTIONE D'IMAGINI DELLE VIRTU', / Vitij, Affetti, Passioni humane, Corpi celesti, / Mondo e sue parti."

11. "Opera non meno utile, che necessaria à Poeti, Pittori, & Scultori, per rappresentare le virtù, vitij, affetti, & passioni humane," "Fatica necessaria ad Oratori, Predicatori, Poeti, Formatori d'Emblemi, & d'Imprese, Scultori, Pittori, Dissegnatori, Rappresentatori, Architetti, & Diuisatori d'Apparati" or "Per inventar Concetti, Emblemi, ed Imprese. Per divisare qualsivoglia apparato Nuttiale, Funerale, Trionfale."

12. Praz, pp. 473-5.

13. *Mikrokosmos Parvus Mundus.* (Colophon) Extant Antverpiae apud Gerardum de Iode, 1579. For fuller bibliographical infor-mation see Praz, pp. 427f. The 1579 edition is listed under Laurentius Haechtanus and the 1619 edition under Jacob de Zetter by Henkel and Schöne in their *Handbuch* (Stuttgart: Metzler, 1967), p. LVI.

14. In the 1603 edition, there are altogether five entries: the first, which is the only one illustrated, shows the maiden with the three mottoes and embracing the dead elm encircled with vine (see below); the second and the fifth (entitled "Friendship without Advantage") are unrelated to Alciati, but the third depicts the three Graces, which is emblem no. 162 of Alciati's *Emblemata* and the fourth is emblem no. 160, "Mutuum auxiliam" [Mutual help], of a blind man carrying a lame man on his shoulder (Ripa quotes Alciati's tetrastich in Italian). Even more significant is the fact that there are only four entries under "Amicitia" in

Alciati, nos. 159-162, yet Ripa incorporates three of them among
his five descriptions.   The only one that Ripa chooses not to use
is no. 161, "Auxilium numquam deficiens" [Help never lacking], telling of Myrtilius' shield, which assists him both during battle on
the ground and carrying him to escape over the sea.

15. The relation between an emblem and a metaphor should
be familiar to emblem students by now.   It is emphasized by most
Renaissance theorists of emblem and impresa and reviewed by
recent emblem critics, especially by Peter M. Daly in his many
publications.   The most cogent summary, however, is by Yves
Giraud, who, writing in a "Proposition" that clarifies the whole
issue of defining and analyzing what an emblem is, states: "Le
processus emblématique repose sur. . . un trope d'analogie (méta-
phore) se fondant sur une particularité de forme, une propriété,
une qualité, un caractère, qui se voit conférer une valeur symboli-
que (la balance représentant le juge ou la justice)" [The emblematic method is based on the trope of analogy (metaphor), groun-
ding itself in a particularity of form, a propriety, a quality, a
character, which confers a symbolic value (the balance representing the judge or justice)].   Quoting from Du Marsais, he continues: "'L'Emblème et la devise sont des métaphores, c'està-dire
des signes qui portent à la connaissance d'autres choses que celles
qu'ils montrent à nos yeus'" [Emblem and impresa are metaphors,
that is to say, of signs which convey the knowledge of other
things by what they display to our eyes] (L'Emblème à la Renaissance [Paris: Société d'édition d'enseignement supérieur, 1982], p.
11).

16. It is a widely held misconception that every emblem in
a collection such as Alciati's or Peacham's is like every other
emblem, perfect.   This simply is not so.   On the contrary, most
emblems in any collection vary greatly in quality.   This is even
true of Alciati because nearly half of his 211 emblems have titles
instead of mottoes.

17. There are eighteen poetic renderings of Ripa: fourteen
under class A (Peacham, pp. 21, 25, 26, 47, 58, 127, 128, 134, 141,
146, 147, 149, 153, & 170) and four under class B (Peacham, pp.
5, 46, 126, 129).   See the "List of Attributions" below.   A typical
example of merely converting Ripa into English is "Doctrina"
(Peacham, p. 26) whose picture is a faithful copy of Ripa, p. [113]
(figs. 1, 2, 3 & n. 19 below) and whose two-sestet verse is but a
poetic rendering of Ripa's text.

18. Among the bibliographical descriptions of the various editions of Ripa, the total number of entries both illustrated and unillustrated is seldom specified. Accordingly, it is difficult to know the true total when it is said that such and such an editor increased the number by several hundred or such and such an editor expanded the total to over a thousand (see n. 6 above). By actual count, the 1603 edition contains 1065 entries and exactly 151 of which are illustrated. The 1611 has 201 illustrations out of a total of 1058, resulting in an improved ratio of 5.26 to 1. In this light, the claim that the great Perugia edition edited by Orlandi expanded the total number to over a thousand is meaningless, because the same is true of the totals in both the 1603 and the 1611 editions. It would be most helpful, therefore, if any future bibliography of Ripa were to include statistics of total entries vis-à-vis illustrated ones.

19. Page [113] in the 1603 edition of Ripa is a conjectured number because all numbers after 109 have been misnumbered. I owe this information to Janet L. Thomason of the Department of Rare Books of the Duke University Library. "If you count forwards [from 109]," she writes, "the page number would be [113]. If you count backwards, the page number would be [117]; however there are no missing pages according to the signature count. Technically, it should be p. [113] or Signature H1 recto."

20. Peacham wss fond of anagrams and obviously proud of his skill in constructing them. There are fifteen emblems in *Minerva Britanna* that have anagrammatic mottoes; a few of them are based on William Camden's *Remains concerning Britain* (1605), even though Peacham openly acknowledged Camden as his source only once.

21. See *The Gentleman's Exercise or Graphice* (1612), p. 117 [misprint for 113], where Peacham briefly translates the entry from Ripa: "A lady clad in a thinne and light Garment, open to the middle thigh, that she might runne the faster, two exceeding large wings, her garments embroydered with eies and eares, blowing of a trumpet, as shee is described by the Poet Virgill." This translation of Ripa is part of Peacham's attempt to use Ripa to teach the art of drawing and limning.

22. In *The Gentleman's Exercise*, however, Peacham follows Ripa exactly: "In the Capitol in Rome he was framed in a goodly stature guilt al ouer, in his hand three golden Apples designing the three Heroicall vertues, which are 1. Moderation of Anger, 2. Temperance in Coouetousnesse, 3. The despising of pleasures."

23. Peacham's direction in *The Gentleman's Exercise* is as follows: "Let Vrania bee showne in a robe of Azure, imitating the Heaven vpon her head a Coronet of bright starres, in her hand a globe representing the celestiall spheres. Her name imports as much as heauenly, for it is her office to describe heauen, as the spheres, Vrania coeli motus scrutatur et Astra" (p. 127 [misprinted 129]).

24. A probable source for Brysus may be found in Lilio Giraldi's *Historiae Deorum* (1560), Syntagma IV, 305.12: "Brizo dea apud Graecos existimata, quae uaticinijs per somnia praeesse credebatur, etc" [Worshipped among the Greeks, Goddess Brysus was believed to be prophetic through dreams]. The editio princeps has the title of *De Deis Gentium Varia* (Basil, 1548), where the title of Syntagma is "DE MERCVRIO, IRIDE, SOMNO, INSOMNIIS," p. 433A.

25. The commentator is Nicodemus Frischlini (1547-1590), who edited Persius's *Satires* (Basil, 1582 and Frankfurt, 1587, 1596). Peacham refers to Persius's *Satires* three times in *Minerva Britanna*: on p. 67 from l.7, on p. 137 from l.113, and on p. 151 138-41.

26. It appears that Freeman came to the same conclusion: "For the personifications in the manuscripts of *Basilikon Doron*, however, he [Peacham] has either relied upon his own resources or looked to the older emblem books. *Gula* comes from Alciati, but none of the other appears in any of the books which Peacham declares himself to have known" (p. 80).

27. Referring to Peacham's putting a spit in Gula's hand (see note above) and his borrowing other details from sources besides Ripa, Young emphasizes that "Peacham's witty composite here is his own contribution. As in so many of the emblems in his *Basilicon Doron* collections, he works from recognizable formulae but these he modifies to fit the very special context provided by his initial inspiration" (p. 43).

I wish to thank the American Council of Learned Societies for a fellowship that made possible my research on Peacham and emblematics.

WENCESLAUS HOLLAR, THE LONDON BOOK TRADE, AND TWO UNIDENTIFIED ENGLISH EMBLEM BOOKS

ALAN R. YOUNG
Acadia University

The comparative sparsity of English emblem books during the sixteenth and seventeenth centuries has been attributed in part to the state of the English book production industry.[1] To produce the pictures that provided one of the most characteristic --and certainly one of the most attractive--features of an emblem book, the services of a skilled engraver, etcher, or woodblock maker were essential, as were the preliminary services of an artist to provide the initial drawings, for those who made blocks or copperplates were not necessarily designers themselves.[2] Yet, it is clear that although woodcut illustrations and even copperplate engravings were to be found in English books during the sixteenth century, there did not develop in England anything like the number of highly skilled illustrators who supplied book and print sellers with material on the Continent. Henry Peacham, the English emblematist, pointed this out in his *Art of Drawing* in 1606 when he remarked upon the lack of graphic skill among English craftsmen: "rare the perfection of it amongst vs, euery man may perceiue, when scarce England can afoord vs a perfect penman or good cutter."[3] As is well known, the dearth of native craftsmen encouraged a number of Continental craftsmen to take up residence in England or work there for a period; however, their presence did not substantially alleviate the shortage of English-born illustrators during the latter part of the sixteenth and the early decades of the seventeenth centuries, a shortage which inevitably placed the would-be-author or printer of an emblem book at a considerable disadvantage.[4]

Though risking an oversimplification, one can argue that for English booksellers generally and for would-be-authors of emblem books in particular the solution to the lack of a good source of woodblocks and engraved plates meant that either the attractions of pictorial illustration had to be done without, or the necessary blocks or plates had to be imported. This latter alternative posed problems of its own regarding emblem books, however, since either the author's verses would then have to be adapted to the picture, or the author would be faced with the difficult task of providing elaborate but clear instructions in writing to a craftsman whom he might never see. Printers in England already regularly imported type, paper, type ornaments, and decorated initial letters, but expensive blocks or plates that might only be suitable for one book were another matter, especially if the process of getting them in the first place was going to involve complex negotiations between the author of the texts and the person responsible for the woodblocks or copper plates.

Expense was always a major factor in the production of any illustrated book, but an emblem book with an illustration per page was probably an especially daunting prospect for most English printers.   The high expenses involved in producing an emblem book are commented upon by Henry Peacham in his preface "To the Reader" in *Minerva Britanna* (1612) and in the later *The Compleat Gentleman* (1622), in which he mentions that he once collected material for a further emblem book but subsequently abandoned the project due to the high costs involved.[5] Forty years later, Thomas Fuller pointed out that part of the reason for high expenses where engravings were concerned was that it was not just a matter of paying for a designer, for the copper to make the plates (plates were sold by weight), and for the labour of the engraver: "Cuts are Cuts," he remarked, "as I have found by dear Experience.   Besides, when they are *done*, they are not *done*, the working them off at the *Rowling Presse* being as expensive as the *Graving* them; both which will mount our Book to an unreasonable price."[6]

The subsequent high cost of producing an emblem book, whether it contained woodcuts or copperplate engravings, was understandably passed on to the consumer.   Peacham's *Minerva Britanna*, Heywood's *The Hierarchie of the Blessed Angels* (1635), and Wither's *A Collection of Emblemes* (1635) were all sold for prices well above those for the average unillustrated book, and in fact it appears that any illustrated book during the first half of the seventeenth century was generally priced 75% to 100% higher than other books made up of the same number of sheets.[7] On the other hand, it should be noted that in Antwerp Christopher Plantin quickly grasped the fact that if an illustrated work appeared in multiple editions, the initially high capital costs could to some extent be recouped.   In calculating the cost for the first edition of Sambucus' *Emblemata* in 1564, for example, he noted that illustration costs need only be entered in the account books once as the wood-blocks would henceforth be available for further editions.[8]   English emblem book publishers either did not realize this (something that hardly seems likely) or the emblem books themselves did not sell sufficiently well to justify further editions, except, of course, in the case of certain books by such authors as Quarles, Drexel, Jenner, and Harvey.

None the less, the fact remains that if new (as opposed to used and worn) copperplates were involved, expenses could be especially high. The plates for Quarles's *Emblems* and *Hierogly-phics*, for example, cost him over £120, or so he claimed.[9] Indeed, it is known that the cost of producing and printing the copperplates of a number of seventeenth- and eighteenth-century books equalled the production costs for the remainder of the book.[10] The expenditure of the Plantin-Moretus house on illustrations during the first decade of the seventeenth century, though not of course to be taken too strictly as an indication of English experience, is worth citing at this point, since it is known that during this period Moretus' expenditure on illustrations was equal to about 25% of the printing-house wage bill.[11] However, the pattern, as far as the individual books of that press are concerned, was set quite early. In 1564 Plantin's accounts recorded that 1,250 copies of Sambucus' emblem book had been printed. Production costs worked out at about 6 stuivers per copy. Of the total cost of 372 florins and 5 1/2 stuivers, the cost of the designs and actual cutting of the woodcuts (drawing and cutting) amounted to 260 fl. 3 1/2 st.[12]

As one examines the earlier English emblem books, the various responses of their authors and printers to the problems of finding designers and engravers and of coping with the economics of producing an emblem book are clear. Andrew Willet omitted pictures altogether from his *Sacrorum emblematum centuria una* (?1591-92) and was content to publish what he referred to as "naked" emblems. A similar decision appears to have been made by Samuel Daniel and/or Simon Waterson, his printer, when the former's translation of Giovio's *Dialogo dell'imprese militari et amorose* was published in 1585. Likewise Abraham Fraunce's *Insignium, Armorum, Emblematum, Hieroglyphicorum, et Symbolorum* (1588) was devoid of pictures. Geffrey Whitney, however, adopted a different approach and published his *A Choice of Emblemes* (1586) in Leyden from Francis Raphelengius' branch of Christopher Plantin's printing house. Whitney could have chosen no more ample source for illustrative blocks,[13] since the Plantin house in Antwerp had already published numerous emblem books and was able to supply Whitney with a variety of blocks previously used in the works of Alciati (1577), Paradin, Sambucus, Faernus, and Hadrianus Junius. Faced with such riches, Whitney

employed 207 of Plantin's "used" blocks, had twenty-five new
blocks made to copy *picturae* from printed books by La Perrière,
Aneau, and de Montenay for which Plantin did not have the
blocks, and had a further fifteen blocks made of "newly devised"
emblems.[14]

    Yet another approach appears to have been adopted by Henry
Peacham, a keen amateur artist who composed at least four
manuscript emblem books for which he himself drew his own
illustrations.[15]   Possibly, he also produced his own woodblocks
for *Minerva Britanna* in 1612.[16]   Such an approach was highly
unusual, since (to judge from Castiglione's pleas in his *Cortegiano*
and Peacham's in *The Art of Drawing* and the later *Graphice*) a
strong prejudice against the practice of the graphic arts persisted.
The kind of educated humanist likely to compose an emblem
book was unlikely to be able to draw (let alone carve wood),
though the existence of a number of illustrated manuscript emblem
books shows there were exceptions as far as drawing is concerned.[17]   George Wither, on the other hand, acquired his plates
abroad but had his *A Collection of Emblems, Ancient and Moderne*
printed in London in 1635.   As he explained in his preface "To
the Reader," he began to compose his emblems in about 1615 when
he first obtained a copy of Gabriel Rollenhagen's *Nucleus emblematum selectissimorum* (Utrecht, 1611? and 1613) and, retaining
the engravings by Crispin van de Passe, added his own text to
accompany some of them.   At the time his friends had been
delighted by these and had urged him to "Moralize the rest."
This he "condiscended unto" but at the time, he says, "the Copper
Prints (which are now gotten) could not be procured out of
Holland, upon any resonable Conditions."[18]   Unfortunately, it is
not clear from Wither's reference to "Copper Prints" whether he
is referring to engravings printed in Holland to which he then
added texts in England or whether he actually bought the plates
themselves.   Perhaps it does not make a great deal of difference,
especially since engravings and letterpress had to be printed on
separate presses, although the normal procedure when engravings
were to be accompanied by letterpress was for the latter to be
printed first.[19]

    One further means of obtaining the necessary expensive
blocks or plates for an emblem book was that involved in the
production of the anonymous H. G.'s *The Mirrour of Maiestie*,
printed by William Jones in 1618.[20]   According to Ludovico
Petrucci, an Italian poet, soldier of fortune, and refugee from

the Inquisition, who came to England in 1610, he (Petrucci) once spent five years and £150 on the blocks of his emblems and other preparatory work for his *Apologia:* "cinq(ue) Ani d'tempo co il costo mio di 150 lire sterline insculture di emblemi & figure con altre necessarie spese, in vn'opera ho'consummati."[21]   However, when the book was half printed and half in manuscript, he was unjustly imprisoned,[22] so that the book appeared in 1619 in an incomplete form and only after a long delay.   The incomplete state of Petrucci's planned book was due to the piracy of his emblems.   Indeed, he considered that his whole miserable situation was due, not only to the machinations of Papists, but the malice of booksellers and printers: "non pure per segreta inteligenza di Papisti son stato fin qui da i librarj, et stampatori procrastinato, truffato, sualigiato, battuto, incarcerato, lacerato, caluniato et infamato; ma. . . da incognito Authore secretamente parte degli Emblemi miej in Inglese conversi, & senza buona licenza (a mio gran danno) sotto falso pretesto stampati, diuersamente dedicati, et presentati furono."[23]

As Martin Smith has convincingly shown, the "incognito Authore", who Petrucci felt had so villainously defrauded him of his investment in emblem blocks and had translated each *descriptio* into English, was the anonymous H. G.   The financial victors in this affair appear to have been H. G. and the printer of *The Mirrour of Maiestie*, William Jones, who obtained their emblem blocks at someone else's expense.   The unfortunate Petrucci, meanwhile, remained in the Fleet prison where it appears he probably died.   Of the planned emblems that had cost him so much to prepare, only a single printed sheet (signed "A") appeared under his name in the *Apologia*.   For the remainder, we must turn to the pages of H. G.'s book, an example of how high costs appear to have tempted one emblem book author and/or his printer into piracy and fraud.

This variety of responses to the problem in England of supplying the pictures for emblem books remained characteristic during the early decades of the seventeenth century.   One emblem book, Thomas Heywood's *Pleasant Dialogues and Drammas* (1637), a translation of Jacob Cats's *Maechden-Plicht*, contained forty-five emblem texts but no accompanying pictures.   Another translation by Heywood, *The Hierarchie of the Blessed Angels* (1635), contained nine emblems from the 51 in Cats's *Proteus* and none of these was illustrated, although Heywood (or his printer Adam Islip) added nine emblematic engravings and an emblematic title-page as if in part to make up for the loss.   Two emblem books, Drexel's *The Christian Zodiack* (1633) and Henry Hawkins's *Partheneia Sacra* (1633), were published abroad in Rouen, the former without pictures and the latter with engravings by a Flemish engraver (P. van Langeren).   Other works, among them the translation of La Perrière by Thomas Combe, and Robert Farley's much later *Kalendarium Humanae Vitae* (1638) and *Lychnocausia* (1638), were fully illustrated with woodcuts, but Farley's use of an engraved title-page for the earlier of his works and his incorporation of one engraved emblem among his 57 woodcuts in his later work suggests, I suspect, a dissatisfaction with the woodcut.   This is hardly surprising in view of the impact that both Wither's and Quarles's emblem books, with their copious use of engravings, appear to have had in 1635,[24] and it is even less surprising given the general decline in woodcutting for the purpose of book illustration in England as early as the late sixteenth century and the corresponding shift of taste in favour of line-engravings in copper.[25]   In 1636 the time was more than ripe in England   for the appearance of skilled engravers, resident if not native, to provide authors of emblem books with the kind of artistic partnership that had long been a familiar feature of Continental emblem books.   William Marshall (see Note 18) was one of the craftsmen who fulfilled this need.   The highly skilled Bohemian etcher, Wenceslaus Hollar, who arrived in England late in 1636, was another.   Before Hollar left England in 1644, he had provided etchings for two emblem books, neither of which, I believe, has been identified in any bibliography of English emblem books.   The first was an edition of Jeremias Drexel's *Zodiacus Christianus* that was published in London in 1643 in an English translation entitled *The Christians Zodiake*, and the second was a version of Van Veen's *Quinti Horatii Flacci Emblemata* entitled *Emblemata Nova* and published in London at some time between 1641 and 1644.

　　　Born in Prague in 1607, Hollar was trained as an artist and etcher, first in Bohemia, then in Stuttgart (1627-28), Strasburg (1629-30) and Frankfurt (1631-32).   In this last city he joined the workshop of Matthew Merian, one of the greatest topographical draughtsmen of the day and a friend of Jacques Callot.[26]   Two years later in about 1633, Hollar moved to Cologne and the workshop of Abraham Hogenberg.   While in Cologne, Hollar attracted the interest of Thomas Howard, Earl of Arundel, who was there in May 1636 while on a diplomatic mission from Charles

I to the Emperor Frederick II at Vienna. Arundel was not only
the premier peer and Earl Marshal of England, but a man of
wide-ranging talents with a consuming passion for the visual
arts. He had been a patron of Inigo Jones, had been instrumental
in bringing Van Dyke to England, had attempted to persuade
Rubens to come, had patronised Daniel Mytens, and possessed
the first collection of classical sculpture in England, the influence
of which upon artistic taste was considerable. In addition Arundel possessed the great collection of drawings by Leonardo da
Vinci now at Windsor, and paintings by such masters as Titian,
Giorgione, Veronese, Tintoretto, Raphael, Dürer, Holbein, and
Van Dyck.[27]

In bringing Hollar to England, Arundel may have been
attracted by the novelty of Hollar's skills since etching (in
contrast to engraving) was virtually unknown in England at that
date. Possibly, too, he planned to have Hollar produce etchings
of the works in his collections and thereby, as with John Selden's
earlier *Marmora arundelliana* (1628), make them more widely
known to the growing circle in England and Europe of those who
appreciated such fine things. But in fact only four etchings by
Hollar of this kind (they are marked "ex collectione Arundeliana")
are extant for the period he spent at Arundel House.[28] Clearly
Hollar was under no great pressure to produce etchings of the
collection, and this is verified by the fact that between 1637
and 1642 Hollar's work consisted chiefly of drawings and etchings
of London, costume studies, maps, portraits, title-pages, and
occasional records of important contemporary events such as the
trial and execution of the Earl of Strafford. To this list may
be added the fruits of his partnership with the emblematist
Henry Peacham, together with the two emblem books that will be
discussed shortly.

Hollar appears to have met Peacham soon after his arrival
at Arundel House.[29] Peacham may also have been under the
patronage of Arundel at the time, but unfortunately there is no
clear proof of this, despite the assertions of a number of scholars
in the past.[30] All that is known for sure is that Peacham became
acquainted with Arundel's son, William Howard, in 1620, that
two years later Peacham dedicated his *The Compleat Gentleman*
to William Howard, having (if we may believe him) originally
written the work for the young boy's private use,[31] and that in
his third edition of *The Compleat Gentleman* (1634) Peacham
included a new chapter "Of Antiquities" dealing with sculpture,

inscriptions and coins, in which he praised Arundel "with much reverence" for his "noble Patronage of Arts and ancient learning."[32]

No matter how they may have met, Hollar the etcher and Peacham the poet subsequently worked together to produce eight works.[33]   Three of these were highly emblematic in character-- the prefatory emblem for Peacham's *The Valley of Varietie* (1638), the broadside emblem "En Surculus Arbor" (1641), and "The World is Ruled and Governed by Opinion" (?1641).   Each demonstrates the skillfully contrived relationship between picture and verbal text essential to the construction of an emblem.   Nothing in Hollar's earlier work quite anticipates these compositions, and we may conclude that it was Peacham who awakened in Hollar an awareness of the possibilities offered to the skilled etcher by the emblem form.   The examples of Quarles's and Wither's respective successes may also have motivated Hollar to try his hand at an emblem book, since, with the outbreak of the Civil War and the departure from England of the Earl of Arundel for Antwerp in February 1642, Hollar suddenly found himself having to earn his keep by making sales of his work to publishers and printsellers,[34] something that appears greatly to have increased his production prior to his own departure for Antwerp in 1644.[35]

Among the works that can be assigned to Hollar between 1642 and 1644 are his title-page and twelve engraved emblems for an English translation of Jeremias Drexel's *Zodiacus Christianus*.   The original of Drexel's work was published in Munich in 1618 (with further editions there in 1619, 1622, 1624, 1625, 1628, 1629, 1630, 1631, 1632) and included an engraved title-page and twelve engraved emblems by Raphael Sadeler (?1560-1628).[36] Another edition appeared in Cologne in 1632 with versions of the engravings by Sadeler.[37]   It was the engravings of this latter edition (or the same ones used in a new Cologne edition in 1634), perhaps familiar to Hollar from the period he himself spent in Cologne, that he copied (with some exceptions to be noted in a moment) when he provided the title-page and etched emblems for *The Christians Zodiake* in 1643.   This book appeared in a second edition in 1647, printed "for / Samuel Browne" (no place of publication is stated, the address on Hollar's title-page having been altered but not by him) and in London by William Willson (Hollar's title-page again having been changed but not by him). Emblem scholars, however, have as yet not noted the earlier 1643 edition,[38] no doubt because no complete copy appears to have survived. However, the 1643 title-page exists (Figure 1), stating that the work was printed in London "for Sa= / muell Broun & are to bee sold / at the Signe of the White Ly= / on & Ball in St Paules Church= / yard. 1643."[39]

Samuel Brown was a printer with strong Royalist sympathies who seems initially to have specialized in translated works. The same year that is recorded on Hollar's title-page, Brown left England and set up shop in The Hague where he was to publish various Royalist works, among them the *Eikon Basilike* (1649), but, unlike Hollar, he remained a self-exile until the Restoration. The fact that there is no surviving text for the 1643 edition of *The Christians Zodiake* raises the question, of course, as to whether Brown left London without printing it, leaving Hollar with a set of engravings (complete with title-page) that were not used until he too had left England. In 1647 Samuel Brown, as already mentioned, published a second edition of *The Christians Zodiake*. Presumably Brown was able, for a time at least, to maintain some kind of contact with the English market. That there really was a 1643 edition is, however, something that cannot be assumed without qualification, a point that should be borne in mind in reading what follows.

The author of *Zodiacus Christianus* was Jeremias Drexel (1581-1638), a German Jesuit, and, for the last twenty-three years of his life, preacher to the Court of Kurfürst Maximilian at Munich. He was one of the most widely-read and published authors of works of private devotion during the Counter Reformation. A number of his works appear to have been surprisingly popular among non-Catholics, and in England copies of his writings were regularly offered for sale in booksellers' catalogues, and they are also mentioned in auction sale catalogues and the published catalogues of private libraries.[40] Not only were Drexel's works familiar in England in their original Latin texts, but there were both English translations published abroad for import into England and translations printed secretly in England. Most English translations, however, were by Anglicans or Non-Conformists and were published quite openly in England, even receiving on occasion the official imprimaturs of the Bishop of London.[41]

Drexel's *Zodiacus christianus, seu signa 12 divinae prae-destinationis una cum 12 symbolis quibus signa illa adumbrantur a Raphaele Sadelero imaginibus ex ornatus et venum propositus* provides its readers with twelve emblematic "signs." These are not the familiar ones of the astrological zodiac but appropriately

Christian ones--a candle, a skull, a golden pyx, an altar, a rose
bush with thorns, a figtree, a balsam tree, a cypress tree, two
spears and an olive wreath, a scourge and rods, an anchor, and
a lute. Each is accompanied by a motto, a Biblical quotation,
and an explanatory exegesis designed to assist readers in their
religious meditations.

The earliest English translation of Drexel's *Zodiacus Christi-*
anus was published by the Rouen bookseller John Le Cousturier,
an active producer of Roman Catholic books for the English
market.[42]   It was the Cousturier translation that was used,
together with Hollar's etchings, for the first edition of *Zodiacus*
Christianus to be printed in England.[43]   The Cousturier edition
contains no illustrations other than an engraved title-page depicting God the King between the arms of a pair of compasses, the
points of which touch two columns (Figure 14).   Around each
column are six mottoes (twelve in all) that signify each of the
twelve signs to be discussed in the twelve sections of the book.
These mottoes also function as the mottoes for the emblems that
precede each section and that are carefully described in a preface
so that the reader, even without any illustrations, can perceive
their full intent.   In the London edition the etched subscriptio
for each emblem is a Biblical quotation that also provides the
basis for Drexel's extended letter press devotional meditation,
the prefatory emblem being intended to act, as is so frequently
the case in such works, as an aid to the memory.[44]

In neither the Cousturier nor the London edition is the
English translator identified, but whereas the Rouen edition is
an essentially Catholic product, the English work, by means of
several changes in the text, is to all intents and purposes quite
acceptably "Protestant," a distinction followed, as will be noted,
in Hollar's etchings.   Thus, for example, whereas the prefatory
Cousturier description of the tenth emblem on "Detestation of our
passed sinnes" refers in its Biblical quotation to Revelations for
the need to "doew pennance," the London text uses the phrase
"unlesse thou doe repent," and in the text itself all such uses of
the word "pennance" are replaced by "repentance."[45]   Out of similar concern for Protestant sensibilities, the text for the third
emblem (on "Frequenting the Sacraments") in the London version
omits all references to the sacrament of confession.

Hollar's accompanying etchings begin with a title-page
based, not on the Cologne title-page as one might have expected,
but on that of Cousturier, so presumably he had both editions

available to him (Figures 1 and 14). He retains the two column motif, but omits the potentially controversial image of God the King, replacing it with the tetragrammaton, encircled with rays not clouds. Although naming the original author, he omits the title "Father" and any reference to the Society of Jesus. Thereafter in his ten succeeding emblems Hollar follows the Cologne illustrations, using a slightly larger format.[46] There are, however, two places where he departs radically from his Cologne model in order to remain consistent with the accompanying text. In Emblem 3 ("Frequenting of ye Sacrament"), Hollar omits any subscriptio (the original was on the topic of the Eucharist) and completely changes his illustration (Figure 4). Instead of presenting an altar and a pyx surrounded by depictions of human souls, Hollar provides an altar upon which are a loaf of bread, two covered chalices and two wine jugs. Behind on the wall are the Ten Commandments. Instead of the motto "Frequens Sacramentorum confessionis et communionis usus," he has only the singular "Frequenting of ye Sacrament." Where the Cologne engraving had emphasized the divine mystery of the sacrament, in keeping perhaps with the concept of transubstantiation, Hollar presents a simple "still-life" of bread and wine and so avoids any overt allusion to Catholic doctrine. His omission of any reference to the sacrament of confession is clearly from a similar concern not to offend Protestant readers.

Hollar's other main departure from his Cologne original occurs with Emblem 10 "Detestation of Sins past" (Figure 11). Instead of depicting the traditional instruments of penance (a scourge and rods),[47] Hollar shows a barefooted old man dragging a large cross, thereby mirroring his text's insistence upon the need to repent while one's sins are still young, since their burden becomes greater with age while "true and sincere repentance, doth not only expiate us from our passed sins, but also preserves us from future ones."[48]

At about the same time that Hollar provided the etchings for *The Christians Zodiake*, he also prepared the plates for another set of emblems: "Emblemata Noua / Omne tulit punctum qui miscuit vtile dulci / W: Hollar Bohemus / Aquaforti Expressit / London / Prirted [sic] and sould by Ro: Walton and Tho: / Hawkins at the west end of paules / ouer ag the Catt." The dating of this work is somewhat complex. Presumably Robert Walton, one of the most important seventeenth-century London print sellers, acquired Hollar's plates before the latter left England in

1644, and, since there is no indication that Walton was active as a printseller before 1641, the work is probably best dated between 1641 and 1644.   At some time before 1646 the plates were then acquired and reissued by the London printseller Peter Stent, who added cross-hatching to parts of the title-page and also altered it to read "P: Stent at the / Crowne in Gilts=pur street nere / New=gate."   At the head of the title-page whoever did the alterations also added a small crown, within which are two palm branches, a rather unexpected pro-royalist gesture for someone working in London at the time.[49]   In addition the etcher added "P. Stent Excudit" to the emblems, several of which (with Stent's name erased) were then later used in other works in 1646 and 1651, as will be discussed in a moment.[50]   Although complete certainty is not possible, it thus looks very much as though the plates for *Emblemata Nova*, like those for *The Christians Zodiake*, were a product of Hollar's difficult years between 1642 and 1644 when he was suddenly without the support of the Earl of Arundel.

If Hollar's *Emblemata Nova* was in fact part of a deliberate attempt on his part to seek commercial success, its subject was well-chosen, for Hollar's original was Otto van Veen's *Quinti Horatii Flacci Emblemata*.   First published in Antwerp in 1607, Van Veen's work, like his *Amorum Emblemata* (1608), appeared in numerous polyglot editions throughout Europe during the seventeenth century, a testament to its widespread popularity.   Hitherto it has always been assumed by students of emblem literature that there was no English edition of the *Quinti Horatii Flacci Emblemata* in the seventeenth century; however, the *Emblemata Nova* proves otherwise.

Just who should be credited with this highly abbreviated English version of Van Veen's work is unclear.   Though the title-page names Hollar as the producer of the etchings and Robert Walton and Thomas Hawkins as printers and sellers, the title-page is not in fact the work of Hollar himself.   It is crudely drawn and on stylistic grounds alone can be rejected as his.   More telling, however, is the fact that its script is recognizably not Hollar's.   In addition the title-page, though it names the etcher, makes no mention of who was responsible for selecting the texts. It seems most unlikely that it could have been Hollar himself, the remainder of whose work shows no such literary bent (witness his mutually advantageous collaborations with Henry Peacham). The matter is further complicated by the fact that the mottoes and texts for each emblem have also not been etched by Hollar himself.[51]   References to "Hollar" in the following discussion of *Emblemata Nova* must therefore be understood in a number of instances to include his anonymous collaborator.

Van Veen's *Quinti Horatii Flacci Emblemata* contained 103 full-page engravings by members of Van Veen's studio--Cornelis Boel, Cornelis Galle, and Pieter de Jode I.   Facing each picture is a motto, beneath which is a quotation (sometimes more than one) from Horace.   This is followed by a prose quotation in Latin (perhaps by Van Veen himself) that assists in the interpretation of the emblem.   The three most familiar parts of the emblem--inscriptio, pictura, subscriptio--are thus all present.   In addition Van Veen included appropriate verses in French and in Dutch.[52]   Clearly he hoped to find a wide market, and it was this that seems to have led him in the second edition of his moralized Horace, published in Antwerp in 1612, to include verses in French, Italian, Spanish and Dutch.

From a comparison of Hollar's text with that of the 1607 and 1612 Antwerp editions, it is clear that the English selection of ten of the Van Veen emblems is based on the 1612 version.[53] Hollar's etchings are in reverse, his normal practice when copying non-topographical material and they are slightly smaller in format. Due perhaps to the size of the plates used, the anonymous etcher (a pupil of Hollar's?) who added the script sometimes placed the motto above the picture and sometimes below.   Only a brief text (always in Latin) is copied from the letterpress page of the original that faces each engraving, and in several cases the text has been placed on a separate plate altogether,[54] which raises the possibility that Hollar's plates were not originally designed to include any text, perhaps because the original plan was to accompany the etchings with text in letterpress.   Usually the text chosen to accompany Hollar's etching is a key quotation from Horace central to the meaning of the emblem and functioning as a subscriptio.   However, in two instances the quotations are chosen from one of the other authors quoted by Van Veen,[55] and in two instances they come from the interpretive prose passage, provided (I assume) by Van Veen.[56]   For one emblem, however, Van Veen's motto and text have both been ignored.   Whereas the 1607 and 1612 editions use the motto "Quo plus sunt potae, plus sitiuntur aquae" [The more they drink, the more they thirst], the Hollar etching is headed by the motto "Principijs Obsta" [I resist beginnings], a substitution perhaps made because of a lack of space.   The two-line text accompanying Hollar's etching of the dropsical man who persists in drinking is quite new and I have been unable to find any source for it, though it retains the general sense of the emblem (see the scroll held by the doctor in the picture) that avarice is akin to dropsy in that it is fed by a compulsive desire for the very thing that makes it worse.

Although etchings provide a less hardy form of reproduction than engravings, Hollar's *Emblemata Nova* had a comparatively long life. The plates having been acquired, as already mentioned, by Peter Stent in about 1646,[57] some were subsequently altered and used in other works. To provide a frontispiece for John Wilkinson's religious tract *The Sealed Fountaine Open to the Faithfull, and their Seed, Or, A Short Treatise, Shewing That Some Infants are in a State of Grace, and Capable of the Seales, and Others Not. Being the Chief Point, Wherein the Separatists Doe Blame the Anabaptists* (1646), Hollar's emblem on moderation "Quod satis est cui contingit nihil amplius optat" [Because he is satisfied with what is available he wishes for nothing more] was adapted by the erasure of Stent's imprint ("P. Stent Excudit") and of the dolphin's head and the central support of the fountain in the picture (Figure 20). The original motto and text were retained. In its original form the emblem concerned the distinction between the wise man who drinks at a fountain and the foolish and greedy man who drowns because he tries to drink in a river. For Wilkinson, however, it provides an apt gloss upon the central topic of his book, which concerns a controversy over baptism and the Doctrine of the Elect, as the full title of the work makes clear.

In the same year, and somewhat ironically given Hollar's pronounced royalist sympathies, the plate for Hollar's emblem on "Innocentia vbique tuta" [Innocence is safe everywhere] was used as a vignette on a broadside entitled *The Watchmans Warning-peece, Or, Parliament Souldiers Prediction* (1646) (Figure 23). The text of the broadside urges that the Parliamentary armies should not yet lay down their arms since there is still work to be done. Each of the two accompanying poems in English provides an alternate subscriptio designed to appeal to those with pro-Parliamentary sympathies. Hollar's plate is altered slightly by the additon of the word "Reason" across the chest of the central male figure, who, accompanied by a lamb to signify innocence, confronts a dragon, a leopard and a snake. Each of these last three is now labelled with a "P", the dragon being the Pope, the leopard his priests, and the snake "An Antichristian

Presbyter." Since the motto and text appear already to have been on a separate plate, presumably Stent lent (or sold) only Hollar's contribution to the original emblem.

Five years later the plate just described was used again opposite page 235 of Thomas Hobbes's *Philosophicall Rudiments Concerning Government and Society* (1651). The head of the central figure was altered to that of Charles I and the word "Reason" and the three "Ps" were erased. Below the plate in letterpress was added the original poem that was formerly on a separate plate. However, no motto was included. Other illustrations were also included in this book. There was a crudely engraved frontispiece by Robert Vaughan showing the personified figures of Religion, Dominion, and Society, but opposite page 1 appeared Hollar's emblem on the rejection of wealth "Quis diues? Qui nil cupit" [Who is rich? He who covets nothing] (Figure 27). Some attempt was made to erase Stent's imprint and the top of the plate was cut so as to exclude the motto. However, otherwise the emblem remained unchanged, showing Minerva, her foot upon the ball of Fortune, crowning a man holding a club, his left foot upon three putti, one with a bow and arrow (Cupid?), one with a money-bag (Avarice?), and one reaching for a crown. To the left are various persons offering the man regalia. Facing page 73, Hobbe's publisher included Hollar's emblem on the sword of Damocles "Mortis Formido" [I fear death] (Figure 21). The original separate plate with the text was not used, but the poem (without the motto) was retained in letterpress below the picture of Damocles, who sits at a table set for a meal, with a sword hanging over his head, watched by King Dionysius.

No special significance appears intended by the inclusion of any of the Hollar emblems in Hobbe's book. Unlike the frontispiece engraving by Robert Vaughan, they offer no direct comment on the book's contents and serve only as visual attractions for the reader, suitably serious in their moral tenor.

Two years after the publication of Hobbe's book, Stent advertised Hollar's *Emblemata Nova* ("Plates of Mr Hollars work. [. . .] 9 Plates of Embleames") and four years after that in 1662, he was still able to supply the etchings as another of his advertisements suggests ("Ten Plats, Hollar's Emblems").[58] At Stent's death in 1665, the plates passed to John Overton (fl. 1665-1707), who issued them with a revised title-page: "Prirted [sic] and sould by Iohn Overton at the / White horse Without Newgate." (Figure 17) In his catalogue of 1673, they are listed as "Ten plats, Hollar's Emblems,"[59] but thereafter they appear to have disappeared from publishers' lists, though this could not have been, as Pennington has suggested,[60] because the taste for such works had disappeared, since in 1721 Van Veen's *Quinti Horatii Flacci Emblemata* underwent a magnificent revival in England when the 1646 plates by Pierre Daret (faithful copies in reverse of Van Veen) were used to accompany Thomas Manington Gibb's folio English translation, entitled *The Doctrine of Morality; or a view of human life according to the Stoic Philosophy* (London, 1721), a work that was re-issued in 1726 with the title *Moral Virtue delineated in one hundred and three short lectures.*[61]

The preceding discussion has, I hope, served to make three points. First, it is clear that the study of emblem books needs to be undertaken with an eye to the complexities of printing history, which in this instance explains Hollar's presence in England and the reasons why he may have been tempted to turn to the emblem book as one possible source of income following the loss of his patron. Secondly, two additional items must be added to the relatively short list of English emblem books, these two works having the special distinction of having been illustrated with etchings by one of the finest artists of the period. Thirdly, there is in all that has been said above the inherent lesson that the study of emblem literature cannot be confined to libraries. By their very nature, works such as Hollar's *Emblemata Nova* and the 1643 title-page of *The Christians Zodiake* have found their way into print collections rather than book collections. Other such works (one has only to read Stent's advertisements to see this) await like "discovery."

Figure 1

Title-page by Wenceslaus Hollar for Drexel's *The Christians Zodiake* (London, 1643). The twelve mottoes on the columns correspond to the twelve sections ("signes") of the book, each of which is prefaced by an emblem etched by Hollar. (Hollar Collection, Thomas Fisher Rare Book Library, University of Toronto, P 183). Reproduced by courtesy of The University of Toronto.

Figure 2
The Christians Zodiake, Emblem 1.   Etching by Hollar. (Depart-
ment of Prints and Drawings, British Museum, P 184).
Reproduced by courtesy of The British Museum.

Figure 3
The Christians Zodiake, Emblem 2. Etching by Hollar.
(Department of Prints and Drawings, British Museum, P 185).
Reproduced by courtesy of The British Museum.

Figure 4
The Christians Zodiake, Emblem 3.   Etching by Hollar. Hollar
diverged from the original design for this emblem in order to
satisfy Protestant sensibilities. (Hollar Collection, Thomas Fisher
Rare Book Library, University of Toronto, P 186).   Reproduced
by courtesy of the University of Toronto.

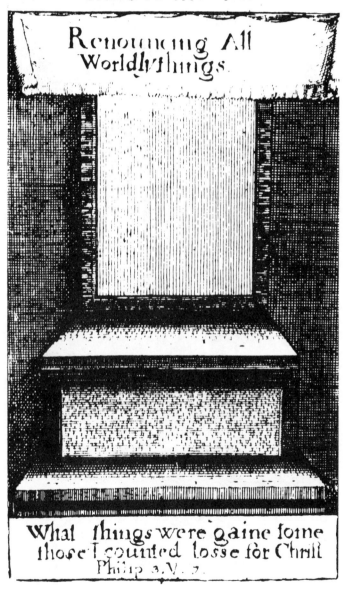

Figure 5
The Christians Zodiake, Emblem 4. Etching by Hollar. (Department of Prints and Drawings, British Museum, P 187). Reproduced by courtesy of The British Museum.

Figure 6
The Christians Zodiake, Emblem 5.   Etching   by   Hollar.
(Department of Prints and Drawings, British Museum, P 188).
Reproduced by courtesy of The British Museum.

Figure 7
The Christians Zodiake, Emblem 6.   Etching by Hollar.
(Department of Prints and Drawings, British Museum, P 189).
Reproduced by courtesy of The British Museum.

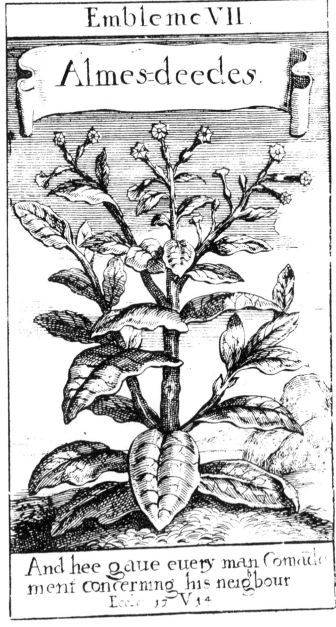

Figure 8
The Christians Zodiake, Emblem 7.   Etching   by   Hollar.
(Department of Prints and Drawings, British Museum, P 190).
Reproduced by courtesy of The British Museum.

Figure 9
The Christians Zodiake, Emblem 8. Etching by Hollar. (Department of Prints and Drawings, British Museum, P 191). Reproduced by courtesy of The British Museum.

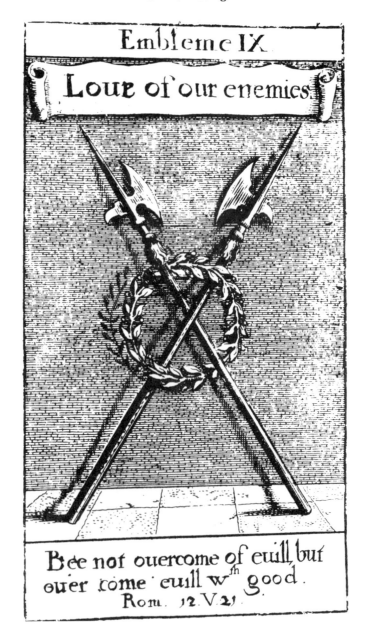

Figure 10
The Christians Zodiake, Emblem 9.   Etching   by   Hollar.
(Department of Prints and Drawings, British Museum, P 192).
Reproduced by courtesy of The British Museum.

Figure 11
The Christians Zodiake, Emblem 10.   Etching   by   Hollar.
(Department of Prints and Drawings, British Museum, P 193).
Reproduced by courtesy of The British Museum.

Figure 12
The Christians Zodiake, Emblem 11.   Etching by Hollar. (Department   of   Prints   and   Drawings,   British   Museum,   P   194).
Reproduced by courtesy of The British Museum.

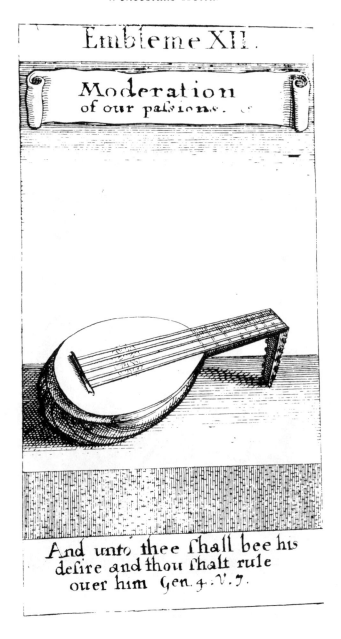

Figure 13
The Christians Zodiake, Emblem 12. Etching by Hollar. (Department of Prints and Drawings, British Museum, P 195). Reproduced by courtesy of The British Museum.

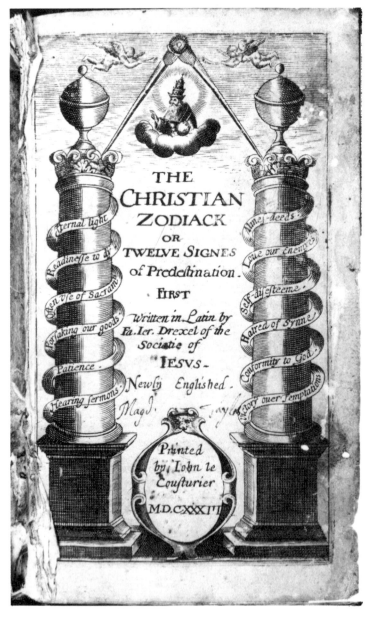

Figure 14
The engraved title-page for *The Christian Zodiack* (Rouen, 1633), Hollar's model for *The Christians Zodiake* (see Figure 13). (British Library, C 111. d. 23). Reproduced by courtesy of The British Library.

Figure 15
Title-page for Wenceslaus Hollar's *Emblemata Nova* (London, ?1641-44). (Hollar Collection, Thomas Fisher Rare Book Library, University of Toronto, P 446 i). Reproduced by courtesy of the University of Toronto.

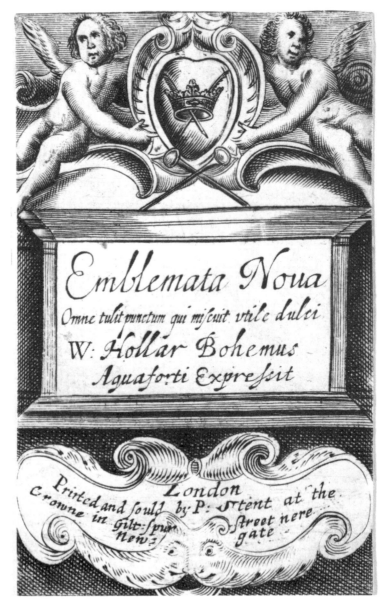

Figure 16
Revised title-page with Peter Stent's imprint for Hollar's *Emblemata Nova* (London, c. 1646). (Department of Prints and Drawings, British Museum, P 446 ii). Reproduced by courtesy of The British Museum.

Figure 17
Revised title-page with John Overton's imprint for Hollar's *Emblemata Nova* (London, 1665). (Department of Prints and Drawings, British Museum, P 446 iii). Reproduced by courtesy of The British Museum.

Incipiendvm Aliquando.

dimidivm facti qui cæpit habet, sapere aude
Incipe, viuendi qui recte prorogat horam
Rusticus expectat dum defluat amnis, at ille
Labitur et, Labetur, in omne volubilis æuum

Figure 18
Hollar's emblem "Incipiendvm Aliquando" [Finally beginning] in
Emblemata Nova. In the background a man leads his oxen to
the plough, while another lays the first course of bricks for a
wall. (Hollar Collection, Thomas Fisher Rare Book Library,
University of Toronto, P 447). Reproduced by courtesy of the
Univesity of Toronto.

Fructus laboris gloria

Adolescens Bacchum et Venerem fugiens, recta ad honoris
Et quietis metam tendit, dum vigilat currit, et
Cæli ac fortuna jniurias inuicto fert animo

Figure 19
Hollar's emblem "Fructus laboris gloria" [The fruit of work is
success] in *Emblemata Nova*. Venus, Bacchus and Cupid watch a
boy run away from them along a bowling alley towards the sun
and three cones with balls on top. From the side two winds
blow at the child. (Hollar Collection, Thomas Fisher Rare Book
Library, University of Toronto, P 448). Reproduced by courtesy
of the University of Toronto.

Quod satis est cui contingit nihil amplius optat .

Multa petentibus

Desunt multa; bene est, cui deus obtulit
Parca, quod satis est, manu .

Figure 20
Hollar's emblem "Quod satis est cui contingit nihil amplius optat"
[Because he is content with what he has, he desires nothing
further] in *Emblemata Nova.* A bearded man fills his cup with
water at a fountain with a dolphin's head. Behind him, a man
who has tried to fill his from a river has fallen in. (Hollar
Collection, Thomas Fisher Rare Book Library, University of
Toronto, P 449). Reproduced by courtesy of the University of
Toronto.

Mortis Formido

Quis quamne regno gaudet? o fallax bonum
Quantum malorum fronte quam blanda tegis
Necesse est vt multos timeat, quem multi timent
Auro venenum bibitus: expertus loquor.

Figure 21
Hollar's emblem "Mortis Formido" [I fear death] in *Emblemata
Nova*. Damocles, as sword suspended above his head, feasts at a
table. On the left stands a harpist and on the right, seated, is
King Dionysius. (Hollar Collection, Thomas Fisher Rare Book
Library, University of Toronto, P 450). Reproduced by courtesy
of the University of Toronto.

In medio consistit virtus.

Est modus in rebus, sunt certi deniqȝ fines
Quos vltra citraqȝ nequit consistere rectum,

Figure 22
Hollar's emblem "In medio consistit virtue" [Virtue consists in moderation] in *Emblemata Nova*. Liberality stands at the centre, holding a cornucopia and a mirror. To her left Prodigality throws coins away over her head. To her right Avarice stands with a hoard of coins in a sack. Above Icarus, having flown to near the sun falls towards the sea, while his father Daedalus continues his flight at a lower altitude. (Hollar Collection, Thomas Fisher Rare Book Library, University of Toronto, P 451). Reproduced by courtesy of the University of Toronto.

Innocentia vbique tuta

Integer vita scelerisq3 purus | Siue per Syrtes jter aestuosas
non eget Mauri jaculis nec arcu | Siue facturus per jnhospitalem
nec venenatic grauida sagittis | Caucasum vel quae loca fabulosus
Fusce pharetra | Lambit Hidaspis

Figure 23
Hollar's emblem "Inoccentia vbique tuta" [Innocence is safe everywhere" in *Emblemata Nova*. A man and a lamb walk past weapons under a tree toward a dragon, a leopard, and a snake. In the background is a wolf (?dog). (Hollar Collection, Thomas Fisher Rare Book Library, University of Toronto, P 452). Reproduced by courtesy of the University of Toronto.

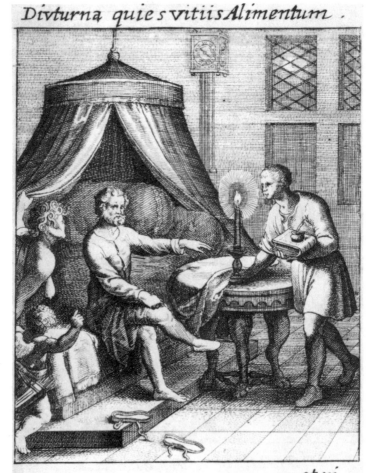

Figure 24
Hollar's emblem "Divturna quies vitiis Alimentum" [A long rest is food for vices].   A man rises early (at the fifth hour according to his clock) from a canopied bed.   To his left are Cupid and Envy who are ignored in favour of the servant who brings a lighted candle, pen and ink, and a book. (Hollar Collection, Thomas Fisher Rare Book Library, University of Toronto, P 453). Reproduced by courtesy of the University of Toronto.

Nihil silentio vtilius
Harpocratem hic vides silentij Deum,
digito labellum, quamquam media
jnter vina, et Iram, compescentem.

Figure 25
Hollar's emblem "Nihil silentio vtilius" [Silence is useless] in *Emblemata Nova*. The winged Harpocrates (the god of silence) sits, his finger on his lips, and holding a banner on which is a centaur and the inscription "S P Q R". Behind, to his left, a man addresses a crowd of women from some steps. (Hollar Collection, Thomas Fisher Rare Book Library, University of Toronto, P 454). Reproduced by courtesy of the University of Toronto.

Figure 26
Hollar's emblem "Principijs Obsta" [I resist beginnings] in *Emblemata Nova*. A dropsical man with a heavily-bandaged leg sits in a chair drinking, while his physician examines a flask (?containing the sick man's urine). (Hollar Collection, Thomas Fisher Rare Book Library, University of Toronto, P 455). Reproduced by courtesy of the University of Toronto.

Quis diues? Qui nil cupit ·

Rex est qui posuit metus, Et nunquam stabilis fauor
Et diri mala pectoris? Vulgi præcipitis mouet
Quom non ambitio impotens Qui tuto positus loco
⌐Infra se videt. omnia

Figure 27
Hollar's emblem "Quis diues? Qui nil supit" [Who is rich? He who
desires nothing] in *Emblemata Nova.* A man holding a club is
crowned with a halo-circled crown and laurel wreath by Minerva
(?Fortune). Persons to his left offer him more crowns. Beneath
his left foot lie three putti. One has a bow and arrow; one
clutches a bag (?of money); and one reaches for a crown and
scepter. The ground is covered with coins. (Hollar Collection,
Thomas Fisher Rare Book Library, University of Toronto, P 456).
Reproduced by courtesy of the University of Toronto.

Figure 28
Otto van Veen's emblem "In Medio Consistit Virtvs" [Virtue con-
sists in moderation] in *Quinti Horatii Flacci Emblemata*
(Antwerp, 1612), pp. 18-19. Van Veen's emblem on moderation
was the source for that by Hollar in *Emblemata Nova* (see
Figure 22).

NOTES

1. Henri Stegemeier, "Problems in Emblem Literature," *Journal of English and Germanic Philology*, 45 (1946), 36; Mario Praz, *Studies in Seventeenth-Century Imagery*, 2nd ed. (1939, Rome: Edizioni di Storia e Letteratura, 1964), pp. 156-157; Rosemary Freeman, *English Emblem Books* (London: Chatto & Windus, 1948), pp. 54-55.

2. Information about this matter with regard to English practices is minimal. However, it is known that in the Antwerp printing house of Christopher Plantin the tasks of providing drawings and woodblocks or copperplates were usually separate. Thus for the 1565 edition of Hadrianus Junius' *Emblemata*, fifty-one of the designs were drawn by the Parisian draughtsman Geoffroy Ballain, and six by the Antwerp painter Pieter Huys, but the woodblocks were made by the Breda bookseller Gerard Janssen Van Kampen and Arnold Nicolai; for the 1564 edition of Joannes Sambucus' *Emblemata*, the painter Lucas d'Heere of Ghent provided 168 drawings (eighty of which had later to be redrawn by Pieter Huys) and the woodblocks were made by Van Kampen, Arnold Nicolai, and Cornelis Muller; and for the 1571 edition of Arias Montanus' *Humanae Salutis Monumenta*, designs for the seventy copperplates were by Pieter van der Borcht and Crispyn van den Broeck but the plates were made by the brothers Jan and Hieronymus Wiericx, Abraham de Bruyn, and Pieter Huys (see Leon Voet, *The Golden Compasses*, 2 vols. [Amsterdam: Vangendt, 1969, 1972], II, 195-203; and the same author's *The Plantin Press (1555-1589). A Bibliography of the Works Printed and Published by Christopher Plantin at Antwerp and Leiden*, 6 vols. [Amsterdam: Van Hoeve, 1980-83], I, 182-83; III, 1272-1276; V, 2026-2030).

3. *The Art of Drawing*, sig. A2b. Cf. Nicholas Hilliard's comments in his manuscript treatise of the "Arts of Limning" (ca. 1598-1603), quoted by John Pope-Hennessy in "Nicholas Hilliard and Mannerist Art Theory," *Journal of the Warburg and Courtauld Institutes*, 6 (1943), 92.

4. Among the foreign engravers who worked in England during this period were Franz and Remigius Hogenberg, Theodor de Bry, Jodocus Hondius, Francis Delarum, Simon and Willem van de Passe, John and Martin Droeshout, Cornelis Boel, Jan Barra, and Robert van Voerst.

5. *Minerva Britanna* (1612), sig. A3a; and *The Compleat Gentleman* (1622), p. 199.

6. *The History of the Worthies of England* (1662), p. 77.

7. See Francis R. Johnson, "Notes on English Retail Book-prices, 1550-1640," *The Library*, 5th ser., 5 (1950), 90, 103, 108, 112.

8. Voet, *The Golden Compasses*, II, 381.

9. Gordon S. Haight, "The Publication of Quarles' *Emblems*," *The Library*, 4th ser., 15 (1934-35), 101. For further information on the prices of seventeenth-century English copper plates and illustrated books and prints, see Alexander Globe's study of *Peter Stent, London Printseller Circa 1642-1665* (Vancouver: University of British Columbia Press, 1985), pp. 26-33.

10. See Philip Gaskell, *A New Introduction to Bibliography* (Oxford: Clarendon, 1972), p. 159.

11. Voet, *The Golden Compasses*, II, 228.

12. Voet, *The Golden Compasses*, II, 384. For the actual fee per block paid to the woodblock maker for this book, see *The Golden Compasses*, II, 221n.

13. Whitney's presence in Leiden, like his dedication of his book to Leicester, probably had political motives as well. Leicester had just arrived in the Low Countries and his supporters on both sides of the North Sea appear to have been working towards his assuming something akin to sovereign status. Whitney was a member of the party of Janus Dousa, one of the ambassadors sent to England by the States General to seek the aid of Elizabeth against Spain. On Whitney's possible involvement in all this, see John Franklin Leisher, "Geoffrey Whitney's *Choice of Emblemes* and Its Relation to the Emblematic Vogue in Tudor England," Diss. Harvard University, 1952, pp. 362-76; Frank B. Fieler's introduction to the facsimile edition of *A Choice of Emblems*, ed. Henry Green (New York: Blom, 1967), pp. xii-xiii; and Mason Tung, "Whitney's *A Choice of Emblemes* Revisited: A Comparative Study of the Manuscript and the Printed Versions," *Studies in Bibliography*, 29 (1976), 37.

14. Tung, pp. 42, 78-85. Tung does not discuss how the woodblocks employed by Whitney got from Antwerp to Leiden. By the time Whitney arrived in Leiden, Plantin himself had already returned to Antwerp leaving his son-in-law Raphelengius in charge. It appears that the blocks were sent to Leiden after Plantin's return to Antwerp in 1585 since during his absence the Antwerp press published editions of Alciati (1584), Sambucus

(1584), Paradin (1583), Faerno (1585), and Junius (1585). The blocks for these works (as well, perhaps, as those of the 1577 and 1584 Alciati) must have then been sent to Leiden at the end of 1585 or early in 1586. Following the publication of Whitney's book in 1586, the Leiden press then published editions of Alciati (1591, 1593, 1599, 1608, 1610), Junius (1595, 1596), Paradin (1600, 1615), and Sambucus (1599). As well, an edition of Junius was published in two issues in 1585 (each under Christopher Plantin's name), one in Antwerp and one in Leiden. By 1589 the Leiden press possessed, according to documents dealing with the deceased Plantin's estate, 1,578 woodblocks and 461 copperplates. Following the liquidation of the Leiden press in 1619, however, most of these blocks (but not the plates) were bought by the Plantin-Moretus house in Antwerp which subsequently published editions of Alciati in 1622 and 1648. Today the Plantin-Moretus Museum possesses 13,794 original woodblocks and 2,881 copperplates. These include the blocks for editions of the emblem books by Alciati, Junius, Sambucus, Paradin, and others. Thus, most of the original blocks for Whitney's work are still in existence. For the above matters, see Voet, *The Golden Compasses*, I, 165-166, 174, 177, 426, and *passim*; and *The Plantin Press*, I, 27; III, 1271-85; IV, 1813, and 2026-30. I wish to acknowledge the assistance of Dr. F. de Nave, Curator at the Plantin-Moretus Museum, who provided me with information about the Museum's collection of emblem books and supplied call numbers for some of the surviving sets of emblem book woodblocks.

15. Bodleian Library, MS. Rawlinson poetry 146; British Library, MS. Harleian 6855, art. 13; British Library, MS. Royal 12A, LXVI; and Folger Shakespeare Library, MS. V. b. 45.

16. On this matter, see the discussion by James Clarke in "Henry Peacham's *Minerva Britanna* (1612): A Bibliographical Description and Analysis," Diss. University of Leeds, 1977.

17. The only parallel to Peacham that comes to mind, insofar as printed emblem books are concerned, is Otto van Veen, who was poet, painter, and engraver. However, though he may have designed his own pictures for his emblem books, he did not, as was once thought, engrave them, but left that task to members of his studio (see John Landwehr, *Emblem Books in the Low Countries 1554-1949: A Bibliography* [Utrecht: Haentjens Dekker & Gumbert, 1970], nos. 678 and 693). The pictures in one of Whitney's manuscript emblem books (Harvard College Library, MS. Type 14) were presumably drawn by him, but, as already

noted, he does not appear to have been involved in cutting his own blocks. In the late nineteenth century, Robert Louis Stevenson designed and cut the woodblocks for his emblem book. In the preface to a later edition in 1921, his stepson Lloyd Osbourne told the fascinating story of how the woodcuts were produced (see *Moral Emblems and Other Poems* [London: Chatto & Windus, 1921], pp. v-xviii).

18. *A Collection of Emblemes* (1635), sig. A1b. Wither's title-page names Augustine Mathews as his printer. The engraved frontispiece to *A Collection of Emblemes* was by William Marshall, a prolific engraver, who in the same year provided some of the plates for Francis Quarles's emblem book, an emblematic engraving for Heywood's *The Hierarchie of the Blessed Angels*, and the engraved emblematic title-page for the English translation by J. Maxwell of one of Du Plessis's works entitled *Emblema Animae or Morrall Discourses*. He also did the engravings for Quarles's *Hieroglyphikes of the Life of Man* (1638), the emblematic title-page for Drexel's *The Considerations of Drexelius upon Eternitie* (1636), the emblematic title-page and one emblematic illustration for Drexel's *School of Patience* (1640), a title-page and three plates for the English edition of Drexel's *The Forerunner of Eternitie* (1642), the engraved emblematic title-page for Thomas Blount's translation of Henri Estienne's *The Art of Making Devises* (1646), the plates (in conjunction with Michel van Lochem) for Christopher Harvey's *Schola Cordis* (1647), and the title-page and four plates for another emblem book, Mildmay Fane's *Otia Sacra*, printed in London by Richard Cotes in 1648. In 1662 Peter Stent, the London print-seller, was advertising (among "Books of Sorts") "Six Emblemes" engraved by William Marshall, a work later acquired and advertised by John Overton in 1673 (see, Globe, *Peter Stent*, pp. 127 and 181). Marshall's contribution as a maker of *picturae* for English emblem books is doubtless something that needs further investigation.

19. Gaskell, *A New Introduction to Bibliography*, pp. 157-158.

20. The identity of H. G. was ascribed by W. C. Hazlitt to Sir Henry Goodere or Godyere, and this suggestion has been subsequently accepted by Rosemary Freeman, Mario Praz, and others. However, it was questioned by Henry Green in his edition of *The Mirrour of Maiestie* (Manchester: Holbein Sociey, 1870), pp. 93 and 96, by I. A. Shapiro, "*The Mirrour of Maiestie*" (*T. L. S.*, 5 Feb. 1949, p. 89), and by Martin R. Smith in "The *Apologia* and Emblems of Ludovico Petrucci," *Bodleian Library Record*, 8

no. 1 (July 1967), 45. I am indebted to Smith's article for the information about the alleged piracy of Petrucci's emblems by H. G.

21. From Preface to "Candido Lettore," *Apologia* (1619, 2nd issue), sig. *4b (Cambridge University Copy, Syn. 7. 61. 85).

22. Ibid., "nell'istesso tempo che questa Apologia mezo manuscritta, & mezo stampata doueuo al Brittan Cesare presentare, contro la diuina & humana giustitia venni per l'altrui macchinationi incarerato" (Preface to "Candido Lettore").

23. *Apologia*, manuscript letter to the Earl of Pembroke, appended to the Bodleian Library copy (4° Rawlinson 550), quoted by Smith, p. 44.

24. To the examples of Quarles and Wither may be added the somewhat earlier case of Thomas Jenner's *The Soules Solace* (1626), a work that employed thirty engravings (one of them used twice) and that evidently proved popular, given its further editions in 1631 and 1639 (this last containing an additional engraving on tobacco). It is not known how Quarles's emblems were received on first publication, but they evidently were sufficiently successful to encourage him to write the *Hieroglyphikes* (1638), which was published with the *Emblems* in 1639, and in a considerable number of editions thereafter.

25. A. W. Pollard, "Some Notes on English Illustrated Books," *Transactions of the Bibliographical Society*, 6 (1901), 29, 31; and R. B. McKerrow, *Printers' and Publishers' Devices in England and Scotland 1485-1640* (London: Bibliographical Society at the Oxford University Press, 1913), pp. xli-xlii.

26. There is some evidence to suggest that Hollar may have been working for Merian somewhat earlier than has been supposed. See Antony Griffiths and Gabriela Kesnerová, *Wenceslaus Hollar: Prints and Drawings* (London: British Museum, 1983), p. 7, n. 7.

27. Graham Parry, *Wenceslaus Hollar in England* (Oxford: Ashmolean Museum, 1977), p. 3; and the same author's *Hollar's England: A Mid-seventeenth-century View* (Salisbury: Russell, 1980), pp. 13-14.

28. Hollar did, however, make drawings of at least fifty-nine paintings from Arundel's collection during this period since he later produced this number of etchings marked "ex collectione Arundeliana" along with forty-eight copies of the Leonardo grotesques from originals in the collection (see Richard Pennington, *A Descriptive Catalogue of the Etched Work of Wenceslaus Hollar* [Cambridge: Cambridge University Press, 1982] pp. xxvii-

xxviii).   The original claim that Hollar was engaged by Arundel
to make copies of the Arundel collections was made by George
Vertue (see Pennington, p. xxviii).

29. Their first joint work, "Seleucus and son," is dated 1637.

30. James Dallaway, for example, in his *Inquiries into the
Origins and Progress of the Science of Heraldry in England* (Glou-
cester, 1793) claimed that Arundel was Peacham's patron and
retained him in his family (p. 340).

31. Alan R. Young, *Henry Peacham* (Boston: Twayne, 1979),
pp. 26, 70).

32. *The Compleat Gentleman* (1634), p. 107.

33. "Seleucus and Son" (1637); frontispiece emblem to
Peacham's *The Valley of Varietie* (1638); "En Surculus Arbor"
(1641); "The World is Ruled and Governed by Opinion" [?1641];
"Royal Exchange" (1644); "Sir Thomas Cromwell" [undated]; and
undated states of "Greenwich"; and "Richard II.   Virgin and
Child."

34. Without definitive evidence this must remain an assumption.   Indeed, John Aubrey's statement that Hollar's son was
born at Tart Hall, an Arundel property, suggests that Hollar's
links with Arundel may not have been totally severed (see Griffiths and Kesnerová, p. 43).

35. For the period 1637-41 there are about sixty extant dated
Hollar etchings.   For the period 1642-44 there are 139 (Pennington, pp. xxvii, xxx; cf. Parry, *Hollar's England*, p. 19).   Hollar
returned to England in about 1651 or 1652 and remained there
until his death in 1677.   During this later and very productive
period, he does not appear to have returned to emblems as a
subject for his skills.

36. No ascription is given to Drexel in the 1618 edition.
There was a German translation of this edition with the same
illustrations published in Munich in 1619.   A later Munich edition,
printed by Nicolas Heinrich in 1629 has different engravings.

37. Other editions appeared in Cologne in 1622, 1624, and
1633, according to G. Richard Dimler, S. J., who is currently
preparing a bibliography of Jesuit emblem books.   See Dimler,
"Short Title Listing of Jesuit Emblem Books," *Emblematica*, 2
(1986), 139-187.   See also, Carlos Sommervogel, *Bibliothèque de
la Compagnie de Jésus* (Brussels & Paris, 1892), III, i, 184.4; and
Karl Pörnbacher, *Jeremias Drexel: Leben und Werk eines Barock-
predigers* (Munich: Seitz, 1965), pp. 170-71.

38. Students of Hollar's work have, however, long been aware of the earlier title-page. See Pennington, P 183-195. Copies of this earlier title-page exist in the Hollar collections at the Thomas Fisher Rare Book Library (University of Toronto), the Kinsky Palace (Prague), and the Royal Library (Windsor).

39. Subsequent references to the text of this first edition are consequently in fact based on the text of the later 1647 edition.

40. On the popularity of Drexel's works in England, see J. M. Blom, "A German Jesuit and his Anglican Readers: The Case of Jeremias Drexelius (1581-1638)" in *Studies in Seventeenth-Century English Literature, History and Bibliography.* Festschrift for T. A. Birrell, ed. G. A. M. Janssen and F. G. A. M. Aarts (Amsterdam: Rodopi, 1984), pp. 41-51.

41. Ibid. pp. 45-46.

42 Ibid. p. 47. Blom points out that Le Cousturier's activities are linked with those of the English Jesuit College Press.

43. Ibid. p. 47. Blom is aware only of the later 1647 edition.

44. Preface "To the Reader," sig. *2a.

45. Sigs. A 4a, and I 1a-I 8a.

46. The Cologne edition is 16° but Hollar is working in 12°. The Cousturier is 12° but larger than Hollar's.

47. The Cologne engraving may depict a whip of ropes rather than a bundle of rods, but the text refers to rods.

48. 1647 London edition "Printed for William Willson," sig. I 2a. A later edition and fresh translation into English by R. W., Fellow of Trinity College, Cambridge, was published in London ("Printed for R. Best") with the title *The Hive of Devotion* (1647). This independent Protestant work used engravings by Thomas Cross. Apart from the title-page, which appears to be based on the Cologne edition, Cross's engravings are copies of those by Hollar (including Emblem 3), and for Emblem 10 he kept the figure of the old man but showed him dragging rods and whips instead of a cross. Later, this edition was re-issued with a new letter-press title-page as *A Spiritual Repository* (1676).

49. Curiously, the device of the crown and two palms occurs as an emblem in Sebastian de Covarubias de Orozco's *Emblemas Morales* (1610) with the motto "Negata Macrum Donata Reddit Opimum" (Centuria III, no. 41). The motto is based on Horace *Episotola*, Bk. II. 1. 181): "Palma negata macrum, donata reducit opimum."

50. For a bibliographical description, see Pennington, P 446-456; and Globe, nos. 429. i-xi.

51. On the matter of Hollar's distinctive script, see Pennington, p. xxi.

52. Another state of the Antwerp edition of 1607 exists in which only Latin verse and prose appears. This does not appear to have been noted by Van Veen's bibliographers (see, for example, Landwehr, *Emblem Books in the Low Countries 1554-1949*, no. 678), but two copies are to be found in the British Library (86. g. 1; and C. 76. d. 6).

53. For example, where the 1607 text has "quam fronte" and "Venenum auro" on p. 74, the 1612 text, which is followed by Hollar, has "fronte quam" and "Auro venenum," and on p. 80 of the 1607 text there is a line absent in both the 1612 text and Hollar's text.

54. See the emblems with the mottoes "Mortis Formido," "In medio consistit virtus," "Innocentia vbique tuta," and "Nihil silentio vtilius."

55. See the emblems with the mottoes "Mortis Formido" and "Quis Dives?   Qui nil cupit." The quotations in question come from Seneca.

56. See the emblems with the mottoes "Fructus Laboris Gloria" and "Nihil silentio vtilius."

57. Globe, p. 119.

58. Ibid. pp 174-186.   Globe discusses and reprints both advertisements. The fact that Stent did not offer the full number of Hollar's plates may be due to damage or extra wear sustained by those plates that had been used in other publications.

59. Ibid. pp. 172, 181.

60. Pennington, p. 66

61. The French translation was by Marin Le Roy de Gomberville and titled *La Doctrine des Moeurs, tirée de la Philosophie des stoiques* (Paris, 1646). During the revival of interest in emblem literature in the nineteenth-century in England, led by such bibliophile collectors as Sir William Stirling Maxwell, a privately printed edition of Van Veen's work was published in 1876, entitled *'Ut Pictura Poesis' Or An Attempt to Explain, In Verse, The Emblemata Horatiana of Otho Vaenius*. The unsigned Preface and English explanatory verses were apparently by James Ford and there is a bibliographical introduction by Stirling Maxwell. Six copies were printed on the recto only so that the pages could be interleaved with a copy of Van Veen (see Glasgow University Library. Stirling Maxwell Collection, Nos. 1873; 1874; 1875).

EDMUND ARWAKER'S TRANSLATION OF THE *PIA DESIDERIA*: THE RECEPTION OF A CONTINENTAL JESUIT EMBLEM BOOK IN SEVENTEENTH-CENTURY ENGLAND

G. RICHARD DIMLER, S.J.
Fordham University

The enormous impact of Hermann Hugo's *Pia Desideria* (Antwerp, 1623) both on the Continent and in England is an acknowledged fact. The *Pia Desideria* was one of the most popular books of the seventeenth century, with its numerous editions and reprints including translations such as Edmund Arwaker's *Pia Desideria: Or Divines Addresses, in Three Books* and Francis Quarles's *Emblemes*.[1] Although Georgette de Montenay's Protestant *Emblemes ou Devises Chrestiennes* (Lyons, 1571) is usually referred to as the first religious emblem book, it was the Jesuit Hugo's book, inspired by Otto van Veen's *Amoris Divini Emblemata* (Antwerp, 1615), which had the greatest impact on the Continent and in Protestant England. Though Hugo was undoubtedly attracted by the humanist preoccupation with enigmatic Egyptian hieroglyphics and the mythology of Greece and Rome, his emblem book reveals the considerable influence of Ignatius Loyola's *Spiritual Exercises* (Rome, 1548), as does much seventeenth-century Catholic devotional literature.[2]

Both Mark Carter Leach[3] and Karl Josef Höltgen[4] have shown that the *Pia Desideria* clearly belongs to a sub-genre of religious emblem literature: the meditational emblem book. The prime purpose of an emblem book such as Hugo's was persuasion; through the emblem book the reader will come to know and converse with the divinity by means of the classical tripartite meditational structure of the purgative, illuminative and unitive paths derived from Bonaventure. Moving away from the esoteric nature of the earlier emblem books of the sixteenth century with their concern for Egyptian hieroglyphics, Hugo along with other Jesuit writers seeks to bring out the moral and spiritual nature of the emblems.[5] For this reason Hugo relates his emblems to sacred scripture, in contrast to van Veen's religious emblem book, *Amoris Divini Emblemata*, which retains the structure of his earlier book of love emblems, *Amorum Emblemata* (Antwerp, 1608), based on the commonplace themes of love expressed through the classical symbolism of Psyche and Amor. Although the illustrations in Hugo and van Veen are similar, they stem from different traditions. Van Veen is within the Alciati tradition where there is an immediate connection between word and image, where the

epigrams are shorter and the approach non-devotional. Hugo
stands within the tradition of illustrated devotional literature
where the picture is not so much an end in itself as it is a
means to an end, the stirring of devotion in the reader.[6]

Accompanying each emblem picture in *Pia Desideria* is a poem
which can extend to two or three pages, as compared to van
Veen's three- to eight-line epigrams. Hugo adds a concluding
meditation in prose, three to four pages in length, with numerous
citations from the early Church Fathers (see Appendix). Many of
Hugo's concluding prose passages seem like compact homilies with
their many references and their centering around an initial biblical passage. As Praz notes, the great success of the *Pia Desideria* was due in part to Hugo's marked ability to choose texts
that were well suited to early seventeenth-century sentiment, such
as the Song of Songs and the Psalms.[7] Of Hugo's forty-five
mottoes, for example, twenty-two are from the Psalms, thirteen
from the Song of Songs and five from the Book of Job. On the
other hand, the prose passages of the *Pia Desideria* are more a
mixture of quotations from both scripture and the Church Fathers.
A typical emblem, Book II, Chapter 3, "Perfice gressus meos in
semitis tuis," [Keep my steps in your paths] has citations from
the Psalms, Ambrose, Origen, Gregory the Great, Augustine,
Chrysostom, Bernard and Jerome.[8] This sermon-like aspect in
Hugo undoubtedly appealed to seventeenth-century Protestants for
whom the sermon, with its emphasis upon man's radical sinfulness
and corruption of the heart as a preparation for conversion, had
such an attraction.[9]

Hugo's purpose is to induce the reader to meditate and to
converse with God in accordance with the colloquies which take
place between the Soul and Amor Divinus in each chapter. In
van Veen's book, however, there is merely a simple correlation
between word and picture. The prose meditation in Hugo tends
to be more of a biblical homily for which the emblem is the
starting point, while in van Veen the correlation between the
word and image is more "referential"; i. e., the reader is con-
stantly referred back from the accompanying text directly to the
picture. In Hugo the distance between word and image is more
pronounced. The word in Hugo is primarily used as an exemplum,
a parable, or a sermon, and the prose meditation at the end of
each emblem takes the form of a devotional summary. It is not
our purpose here to explore the devotional structure of the *Pia
Desideria*; nevertheless, these devotional aspects must be recog-

nized since they are pertinent in any study of Francis Quarles's or Edmund Arwaker's books. Arwaker's statement in his Preface, where he speaks of his desire to translate Hugo's book, is to the point: "And finding that not any pen had been employ'd about the Work, . . . rather than it should remain undone, and such an excellent piece of Devotion be lost to those who would prise it most, the Religious Ladies of our Age: I resolv'd to engage in the attempt; and the rather, because the Subject was suitable to my Calling, as a Clergyman."[10]

The personal qualities, the heavy reliance on sacred scripture and the devotional aspects of Hugo's spirituality no doubt appealed to both Quarles and Arwaker and to their English readers. The effect of Hugo's spirituality on the English Protestant mentality is demonstrated by the number of published editions of Quarles's *Emblemes and Hieroglyphics*, fifty in all, and the four editions of Arwaker's book, which appeared between the years 1686 and 1712. When one reflects on the rudimentary state of the emblem book and the art of engraving in England at that time, the statistics are not merely surprising, they are astonishing.[11]

As we trace the history of the introduction of the *Pia Desideria* into England, we encounter the figure of Edward Benlowes (1602-1676), a former Roman Catholic turned violent antipapist. His brother, William, was a student of the Jesuits at St. Omer and Douai, whereas Edward was educated at Cambridge. It was during his visit to Europe (1627-1630) that Edward first encountered the Christus-Cupido tradition of Hugo, which he eventually introduced to Quarles.[12] Interestingly, in 1630 Benlowes was in Antwerp, the city where the two sources of Quarles's *Emblemes*, the *Typus Mundi* and the *Pia Desideria*, were first published; it was also to become the city which would publish the largest number of Jesuit Emblem Books, seventy-three in all.[13] Would Quarles have accepted the urging of Benlowes to write accompanying verses to Hugo's plates if Benlowes had remained a Catholic? As Höltgen indicates, the problem did not arise because Benlowes had converted to Anglicanism before he met Quarles.

Quarles's reworking of the *Pia Desideria* into English became Books III-V of the *Emblemes*, while he based Books I and II on the *Typus Mundi*.[14] The *Emblemes* is composed of clumsy copies of Boetius Bolswert's original engravings and Quarles's free translation of Hugo's prose and poetry, a fact which did not escape the eye of Arwaker in his Preface: "Mr. Quarles only

borrow'd his Emblems, to praefix them to much inferior sense"
(B2r = [A2r]). Thus Quarles's use of Hugo's plates was discovered
at least as early as 1686. It is not our purpose to analyze
Quarles's rendition; suffice it to say that Arwaker's rather severe
criticism of Quarles is not without some justification. Since
Quarles's book is, however, not really a translation of the *Pia
Desideria*, it is unfair to attack him on these grounds. Nevertheless, some critics feel that the quality of Quarles's poems is
second-rate at best.[15] Whether Arwaker's own translation succeeds remains to be seen.[16]

　　　Edmund Arwaker (1655-1730), the Elder--not the Younger as
Rosemary Freeman states (p. 229)--is not listed in the *Dictionary
of National Biography*. He is given only brief mention in *The
Poets of Ireland*.[17] Here we learn that he was an alumnus of
Kilkenny College, chaplain of the Duke of Ormond and later
Archdeacon of Armagh. His only claim to fame, apart from the
translation of the *Pia Desideria*, is a collection of translations
from Aesop and an elegy to the Duchess of Ormond on the invention that made sea-water fresh.

　　　Arwaker also used copies of Bolswert's plates, but his text
comes much closer to a translation than Quarles's. Scholars have
somewhat harshly censured Arwaker's translation as pedantic,
monotonous and boring, and criticized his use of rhyming couplets
which alter the meanings in various parts of the *Pia Desideria*.
However, Rosemary Freeman's claim that "Arwaker's translation
of Hugo was an afterthought probably stimulated by the popularity
of Quarles. . ." (p. 206) is questionable.[18] Because Quarles placed
less emphasis on the original text, he could experiment more in
poetic forms. The distinct impression one gains from Arwaker's
statements in his Preface, which is supported by the text, is of
a conscious, deliberate translation for a specific religious purpose.

　　　Although Quarles's version of the *Pia Desideria* established
the baroque devotional form of the Amor Divinus and Anima
emblems in England, Arwaker's book must also be considered if
one wishes to analyze in detail the English reception of a Continental emblem book such as Hugo's. Since Arwaker considered
himself to be primarily a translator of Hugo, the changes he felt
necessary to adapt Hugo's book for English readers are in many
ways more revealing than Quarles's freer rendition, and they may
ultimately tell us why the *Pia Desideria* proved to be so popular
among English Protestants.

Arwaker purports to be an conscientious translator. He states in his Preface: ". . . all the other variations and additions may be known to the English Reader by their being printed in the Italick Character," but this is confusing since he italicizes not just variations but also words that he wishes to emphasize. In fact, he is not really a literal translator in twentieth-century terms. His translation might be best characterized as a paraphrase of the Latin, although in general it adheres to the sense of the original Latin more closely than Quarles's. Arwaker, for example, simplifies and shortens Hugo's long poetic passages. He cites in abbreviated form only one author from the prose commentaries in Hugo.[19] But what substantive changes, if any, did Arwaker, the Anglican priest, make in the Catholic emblem book? Are there doctrinal discrepancies? Do we find traces of distaste for Roman Catholic theology and Hugo's more academic and learned poetry? Did the *Pia Desideria* appeal to the Anglican audience because it stresses a subjective, almost pietistic spirituality rather than a more doctrinaire Catholicism? To answer such questions we must turn to the text itself and examine Arwaker's treatment of Hugo's original references to classical mythology and literature, his treatment of Hugo's theology, and the general tone of his translation.

In his Preface, Arwaker provides us with some pointers for each of these areas of investigation. In general, he criticizes Hugo for being "a little too much a Poet, and [who] had inserted several ficticious stories in his Poems, which did much lessen their gravity, and very ill become their Devotion; and which, indeed, would take from them that prevalency which they ought to have, as serious Addresses from the Soul to God, over the affections of all that read them" (B2r = [A2r]). Arwaker's outlook, which can be described as devotional and non-doctrinaire, is apparent in the first paragraph of his Preface, where he feels the subject is suitable to his calling as a Clergyman and because of its "divine" sense. To strengthen the devotional quality of the work Arwaker simplifies many of Hugo's abstruse references; in particular, he substitutes scriptural references for classical ones. In his Preface, for example, Arwaker draws attention to "the first Poem of the second Book, where the Author brings in Phaeton as an example of mens desiring Liberty in choosing, tho their choice proves oftentimes their ruin; I have used the Prodigal Son, as more suitable to the design, and I am sure to the gravity of the Poem" (B3v = [A3v]). Similarly, in Book III, Chapter 2 Arwaker substitutes Eve's seduction by the Serpent for the deception of Cydippe by Acontinius with an apple.

For the following analysis we have chosen ten chapters from Arwaker's translation.[20] In Book I, Chapter 2 entitled "Human Folly," (Arwaker, pp. 10ff. [Figure 1], Hugo, pp. 9ff.) Arwaker introduces Moses (A. 12. 3.) together with the Queen of Sheba, neither of whom is mentioned by Hugo. Arwaker also refers to the Tower of Babel (A. 13. 10), which replaces Hugo's (H. 10. 7) "caleoque educimus arces" [from the heavens we brought forth peaks]. Hugo makes reference to the Horatian quotation from the Epodes (H. I. 7. 23) where Horace makes fun of counterfeit money used on the Roman stage. This is completely omitted by Arwaker (A. 11. 18-19). There is a characteristic change of Hugo's final two verses (H. 11. 30-31), which in translation read: "Therefore, my guardian of patrons, bring me sanity or grant that I myself will be watchful over my own folly." Arwaker translates these lines and stresses emotion and subjectivity with:

O then, some kind PROTECTION, Lord assign
This ideot Soul! But 'twill be best in Thine. (A.14.14-15)

In Book I, Chapter 3, "Divine Physician" (Arwaker, pp. 17ff. [Figure 2], Hugo, pp. 19ff.) Arwaker omits Hugo's reference to the Greek doctors and sons of Asclepius, Machaon and Podalyrius (H. 19. 10-11), and to Epidaurus, the centre of the cult of Asclepius in the ancient world, and substitutes for them "Bethesda's Pool" and the "Balm of Gilead." Of the numerous prose commentaries from the Church Fathers following Hugo's poem, Arwaker has chosen only one: the more personal and devotional quotation from Augustine, "The whole World, from East to West, lies very sick; but to cure this very sick World, there descends an Omnipotent Physician, who humbled himself even to the Assumption of a mortal Body, as if he had gone into the Bed of the Diseased" (A. 21). Hugo's final couplet has once again been recast by Arwaker. Hugo's lines translates as follows:

If this cannot be done, infuse your healing essences,
My health will grow with water and wine,

and they become in Arwaker:

Then take me home, lest if I here remain,

My Foes return, and make thy succour vain. (A. 20. 15-16)

Here again we see Arwaker's tendency to replace Hugo's impersonal lines with his own more pietistic phrasing.

Book I, Chapter 4: "Slavery of Sin and Eternity of Hell" (Arwaker, pp. 23ff. [Figure 3] and Hugo, pp. 31ff.) finds Arwaker translating Hugo's "humilitatem" and "laborem" from Psalm 24 as "adversity" and "Misery" respectively, which intensifies the more subjective or plaintive aspect of the Psalm (A. 23). Arwaker also inserts the name of his monarch, Charles I, in place of King Menelaus,

> . . . our Fam'd Martyr, in his Murd'rers stead,
> Bow'd to a Rebel Ax His Sacred Head. (A. 23. 17-18)

In his Preface, Arwaker somewhat self-consciously comments on his introduction of Charles I into his translation of Hugo. "More might be urg'd in behalf of my Author on this account, but that he needs no apology and I have enough to excuse myself, for 'tis not improbable I shall be accus'd of an indecorum as to Chronology, in the fourth poem of the first Book, in bringing the glorious Saint and Martyr King Charles I, with our late Monarch, for examples of the misfortune that oftentimes attends the greatest and best of men, instead of Menelaus and Dionysius: . . ." (A3v). Classical allusion makes way for subjective regionalism.

Hugo's final line (H. 31) of Book I, Chapter 4 is expanded into four lines by Arwaker (A. 24. 13-16). His translation has a subjective flavour lacking in the original and comes closer to the theme of the illustration, which shows Anima drawing the wheel in endless motion. The terror of Ixion, who was attached to a revolving wheel for his attempt on the chastity of Hera, is replaced by the "guilty souls in Hell" and "their never-ending Pains" (A. 25. 17-18). Arwaker expands the last Hugo couplet into four lines by inserting references to "Hand" and "Pain," thereby giving the final lines a more devotional and personal ring:

> Look on, O see if causes I complain!
> O hold thy HAND, and mitigate my PAIN! (A. 25. 21-22)

In the following chapter (5), "Frailty of Existence" (Arwaker, pp. 27ff. [Figure 4], Hugo, pp. 41ff.) our main interest focuses on the long scriptural insertion by Arwaker into his translation

(A. 27. 5ff.).   Hugo's straightforward, classically austere lines
describing man's beginnings become a longer, biblical digression
on the Creator and his creation of man in Arwaker's translation.
Of particular note is the peculiar Protestant inversion of the
Ignatian or Salesian meditational mode.   In Ignatian contemplation
the exercitant is urged to put himself in the very biblical scene,
to apply himself to the subject of the meditation.   In Protestant
meditation the procedure is reversed.   The applicant applies the
subject of the meditation to the self, frequently combined with
the Calvinist penchant for emphasis upon self-loathing and sinfulness.[21] We find traces of this in Arwaker:

> But things of finest texture first decay,
> And Heavens great Master-piece is brittle Clay;
> Ruin'd by that which does its worth advance,
> And dash'd to pieces by the least mischance.
> This frail, this transitory thing am I,
> Who only live, to learn the way to die:
> So soon shall Fate to its first Matter turn,
> The curious Structure of this living Urn.   (A. 28. 17-25)

Book II, Chapter 1, "Man's Freedom of Choice" (Arwaker,
pp. 79ff. [Figure 5],   Hugo, pp. 141ff.) finds Arwaker omitting
Hugo's reference to Phaeton and Icarus (H.142.1ff.), classical
examples of hubris.   Arwaker replaces them with the Prodigal Son
(A. 80. 13ff.).   Once again Arwaker changes the meaning of the
last couplet in Hugo, which in translation reads: "O God either
let my heart not be warmed by any fire or let it warm with love
of your law alone." Arwaker renders it as:

> O my dear God! let not my Soul incline
> To any Love, or let that Love be thine! (A. 81. 19-20)

Arwaker's mistranslation of the introductory Psalm is noteworthy in Book II, Chapter 4, "A Holy Fear of God Impedes Sin"
(Arwaker, pp. 95ff. [Figure 6], Hugo, pp. 171ff.).   The Latin
"confige timore tuo carnes meas" [transfix with your fear my
flesh] becomes "My flesh trembleth for fear of thee. . .", a much
more personal rendering.   This recurring emphasis on the self and
its subjectivity is heightened through Arwaker's frequent use of
the first person singular where Hugo uses either an impersonal
Latin form or the third person singular.

Hugo's reference to the sorrowful stripes of Orbilius (H. 171. 9) and to Cadmus (H. 171. 13), who first introduced writing into Greece, are both dropped by Arwaker. The allusions to Caesar's guilt at Pharsalus and to Orestes, the Avenger of Agamemnon, are replaced by Cain and Abel (A. 97. 20ff.). Likewise dark Avernus, a gloomy lake which leads to the underworld in classical mythology, is replaced by "Hell." Arwaker loosely translates Hugo's final two couplets (H. 173. 11ff.), but eagerly repeats the term "fear" three times in the last couplet as an antidote to sin. Once again we note the Protestant tendency to concentrate on the self and its sinfulness rather than on the subject of the meditation (A. 82. 1ff.).

In Book II, Chapter 12 entitled: "Longing, Searching, Finding" (Arwaker, pp. 133ff., Hugo, pp. 251ff.) Arwaker omits the reference both to Pyramus and Thisbe (H. 252. 1ff.) and Pylades and Orestes and instead speaks in terms of a more personal love:

Then hopeless, back my pensive course I steer'd,
But still no tidings of my Lover heard; (A. 133. 8ff.)

In the last four lines of the Arwaker text we find once again a rather free translation of the original. Indeed, the substitution of "complain" for the Latin "quaereris" and the translation of "cito liber" with the words "unkind, ungrateful" (A. 136) represent a misrendering. But these alterations have the effect of reinforcing the subjective colouring so typical of Arwaker's rendition.

Similarly, Arwaker dispenses with Hugo's reference to the tyrant of Sicily and his love for the priestess at Delphi (H. 307. 5ff.) in Book III, Chapter 3: "True and False Love" (Arwaker, pp. 165ff. [Figure 7], and Hugo, pp. 307ff.). The two famous classical examples of the inconstancy of love, Paris and Oenone and Jason and Hysiphle, are omitted and replaced with the words:

Of happy lovers no Records can boast
Their bliss was counterfeit, or short at most. (A. 166. 11-12)

Hugo's final verses

Pascitur in riguis, ubi candent, lilia, campis,
Et sua Vergineos ducit in arva greges.
Scilicet aethereum decet his flos purus Amorem,
Et bene tam castas pascit hic ortus oves (H. 309. 25ff.)

may be translated as follows:

> Love cultivates lilies shining in the moistened meadows
> And leads his virginal flocks to pasture
> Thus this pure flower befits a heavenly love
> And this grove well feeds such chaste sheep.

These lines receive a very different and passionate rendering in Arwaker (A. 167. 19ff.), where he speaks of the "Paradices of delight," "enamell'd Meads," "Emblems of our pure desires" and "mutual fires."

Hugo's reference to Agnes in Book III, Chapter 4: "God's Enduring Love" (Arwaker, pp. 169ff. [Figure 8], Hugo, pp. 319ff.), the daughter of Romulus (H. 320. 3ff.), is in fact to St. Agnes of Rome, a virgin and martyr of the Roman Catholic Church. She is also mentioned in the Roman Catholic Canon of the Mass. Acccording to St. Ambrose, the Roman prefect Sempronius wished her to renounce her Christian faith and marry his son. Arwaker replaces this element of Roman Catholic martyrology with the words:

> No, no my soul, fix my thoughts on high;
> Thou hast no equal match beneath the sky.
> My HYMEN shall no other Torches Bear,
> Than what have each been lighted at a Star. (170. 13-16)

Arwaker has substituted "my soul" for Agnes, has kept the marriage motif between Agnes and her "Ausonian suitor," Sempronius' son in line A. 170. 15, and replaced Hugo's reference (320. 17-20) to the Phoenician ships being guided by the constellation Ursus Minor with line A. 170. 16, quoted above. This is a clear case of Arwaker's tendency to compress Hugo's longer classical and religious references and create more succinct and personal poetry. The last four lines also take on a more personal flavour, and the classical allusions and the topos of the magnetic compass are dropped. The iron needle of the compass becomes the "blest Vision" (A. 171. 12).

In Book III, Chapter 8: "Personal Guilt of First Parents" (Arwaker, pp. 193ff. [Figure 9], Hugo, pp. 359ff.) Arwaker understandably omits Hugo's autobiographical references (360). Hugo was born on May 7th, the Kalends of May, and he refers to his mother as Rebecca, thus alluding to the advanced age of his mother at the time of his birth. Arwaker at this point details the circumstances of his own birth:

'Twas JULY's Month, the loveliest of the Year,
(Tho' all my Life DECEMBER did appear:)
The TWENTY-SEVENTH; Oh! had it been my last,
I had not mourn'd nor that made too much haste.
That was the fatal day that gave me breath.

Once again we note the Protestant emphasis on self-abasement and sinfulness. Arwaker also inserts the reference to "Cain" (A. 195. 7) in place of lightning and thunder, and "Babel Monarchs breast" (A. 195. 21) for "Rex" (H. 361. 11). He drops the classical references to Titan (the sun) and Cynthia (the moon) (H. 360. 17).

For the most part Arwaker found Hugo's catholicism acceptable from a doctrinal standpoint. Arwaker's statement in the Preface to his book is worth repeating: "'Tis true the Title-page in the Latine declares him of the Society of Jesus, but his book shows nothing either of his Order, or particular opinion in Religion, but that he is an excellent Christian in the main: And indeed he seems to me to have designedly avoided all occasion of offence to his Readers of different judgment; for tho in the fourteenth Poem of the first book, he had a fair opportunity of mentioning Purgatory, he wholly declines it, and takes no notice at all of such a place. And in the twelfth Poem of the third Book he says nothing of Transubstantiation, tho he had occasion to mention the Sacrament of the Eucharist."[22] A close inspection of the text indicates that Arwaker accepted the following theological elements in Hugo: the eternity of Hell (A. 25. 18-19); the account of creation, which Arwaker reworks into scriptural phraseology and pedestrian terminology (A. 27. 5ff.); a final judgment of the soul after death (A.70.8); the immortality of the soul (A. 69. 20); eternal life (A. 70. 19); freedom of the will and freedom of choice (A. 80. 1ff.); original sin on the part of the first parents (A. 194. 1ff.); and individual guilt and responsibility (A. 193. 1ff.). There is an implicit acceptance of sacramental confession and the forgiveness of sins (A. 33. 10ff.).

By way of conclusion, we might summarize our analysis as follows: Arwaker invariably replaces Hugo's classical and mythological references with scriptural quotations and prototypes. In general, he accepts the theology of the *Pia Desideria*, although as he states in the Preface, he would have rejected the catholic doctrines of transubstantiation and purgatory. The tripartite theological structure in Hugo comprising the three ways likewise appears in Arwaker; however, the purgative, illuminative and unitive ways are overriden by typical Protestant forms of colloquial prayer with an emphasis on sin and self-loathing. He renders the Hugo texts in a more personal manner, in particular the final couplets. We might thus characterize his translation as being more affective, pietistic, and subjective. In general he manifests an aversion for the intellectual aspects, the classical allusions, the academic poetry and certain doctrinaire tendencies in the *Pia Desideria*.

Although Praz and Freeman criticize Arwaker for his pedantry and monotonous tone, this is to some extent unjustified. Arwaker's translation has a certain charm and subjective grace, and it obviously held an appeal for an Anglican audience in the late seventeenth century. His translation is basically a close paraphrase of Hugo's Latin, generally retaining the sense of the original. Arwaker consciously strove to be pious, devotional, and non-doctrinaire, and in this he succeeded. Finally, his devotional attitude toward Hugo's text manifests the typical seventeenth-century Protestant devotional structure: an emphasis on the word of scripture as nourishment for the soul. Rather than the soul losing itself in contemplating the subject of the meditation, the soul itself becomes the object of contemplation in its radical sinfulness, its depravity, and its need for repentance and redemption.

APPENDIX: ARWAKER'S PROSE COMMENTARIES

I. 1- *Bernardus in Cantica Sermo 75*
I. 2- *Chrysostum in Joannem Homilia 4*
I. 3- *Augustinus de Verbo Domini Sermo 59 capitulum 11*
I. 4- *Augustinus in Psalmos XXXVI*
I. 5- *Rupertus in Jeremiam liber 1 capitulum 4*
I. 6- *Gregorius in 7 capitulum Job liber 8 capitulum 23*
I. 7- *Ambrosius Apologia pro David*
I. 8- *Hieronynus in Jeremiam capitulum 9*
I. 9- *Ambosius liber 4 in capitulum 4 Lucae/ Idem, de bono mortis*
I. 10- *Bernardus Sermo 6 super Beati qui, &*
I. 11- *Ambrosius Apologia pro David capitulum 3*
I. 12- *Ambrosius in Jeremiam capitulum 9*
I. 13- *Hieronymus ad Paulam Epistola 12*
I. 14- *Augustinus Soliloquia capitulum 3*
I. 15- *Chrysostum in Psalmos 115*

II. 1- *Augustinus Soliloquia capitulum 12*
II. 2- *Augustinus Soliloquia capitulum 4*
II. 3- *Ambrosius de fuga saeculi capitulum 1*
II. 4- *Bernardus Sermo 26*
II. 5- *Augustinus Soliloquia capitulum 4*
II. 6- *Hugo de Sancta Victoriau in Arrha animae*
II. 7- *Hieronymus Epistola ad Hesiod 1*
II. 8- *Gilbertus in Cantica Homilia 18*
II. 9- *Bonaventura Soliloquia capitulum 1*
II. 10- *Gregorius in Ezechielem Homiliae 19*
II. 11- *Ambrosius de Virginitate liber 3*
II. 12- *Beda in Cantica capitulum 3*
II. 13- *Augustinus in Psalmos 36*
II. 14- *Honorius in capitulum 2 Cant apul Delr*
II. 15- *Augustinus Meditationes capitulum 35*

III. 1- *Rupertus in Cantica*
III. 2- *Gislenus in Cantica capitulum 2*
III. 3- *Bernardus in Cantica Sermones 71*
III. 4- *Bernardus Meditationes capitulum 9*
III. 5- *Augustinus Soliloquia capitulum 34*
III. 6- *Augustinus Soliloquia capitulum 20*

III. 7- *Augustinus Sermones 43*
III. 8- *Ambrosius in Psalmos CXVIII*
III. 9- *Chrysostum Homilia 55 ad populum Antiochenum*
III. 10- *Gregorius in capitulum 7 Job*
III. 11- *Cyril in Joannem liber 3*
III. 12- *Augustinus in Psalmos 42*
III. 13- *Ambrosius Homilia capitulum 7*
III. 14- *Bonaventura Soliloquia capitulum 4*
III. 15- *Ambrosius de bono Mortis capitulum 5*

Authors cited by frequency:

Augustinus (12), Ambrosius (8), Bernardus (5), Chrysostum (3) Hieronymus (2), Gregorius (2)

Figure 1
Edmund Arwaker, *Pia Desideria:
Or Divine Addresses*, Book I,
Chapter 2, "Human Folly."
Reproduced by courtesy of
Fordham University.

*O God, thou knowest my Sim=
plicity, and my faults are not
hid from thee. Psal: 69.5.*

P. 10.

*Haue mercy upon me O Lord,
for I am Weak: O Lord heal me,
for my bones are vexed. Psal: 6. 4*

P. 16.

Figure 2
Edmund Arwaker, *Pia Desideria:
Or Divine Addresses*, Book I,
Chapter 3, "Divine Physician."
Reproduced by courtesy of
Fordham University.

Figure 3
Edmund Arwaker, *Pia Desideria:
Or Divine Addresses*, Book I,
Chapter 4, "Slavery of Sin."
Reproduced by courtesy of
Fordham University.

Figure 4
Edmund Arwaker, *Pia Desideria:
Or Divine Addresses*, Book I,
Chapter 5, "Frailty of Existence."
Reproduced by courtesy of
Fordham University.

Figure 5
Edmund Arwaker, *Pia Desideria:*
Or Divine Addresses, Book II,
Chapter 1, "Man's Freedom of
Choice." Reproduced by cour-
tesy of Fordham University.

My soul breaketh out for the very
fervent desire that it hath allways
to thy Iudgments. Psal:119. 20.
178.

My flesh trembleth for fear of
thee, and I am afraid of thy Iudgments. Psal:119. 120.
P. 194.

Figure 6
Edmund Arwaker, *Pia Desideria:*
Or Divine Addresses, Book II,
Chapter 4, "A Holy Fear of
God." Reproduced by courtesy
of Fordham University.

My Beloved is mine, and I am his;
he feedeth among the Lillies
Cant. 2.16.

P. 164.

Figure 7
Edmund Arwaker, *Pia Desideria:
Or Divine Addresses*, Book III,
Chapter 3, "True and False
Love." Reproduced by courtesy
of Fordham University.

I am my Beloved's, and his desire
is towards me. Cant. 7.10.

P. 168.

Figure 8
Edmund Arwaker, *Pia Desideria:
Or Divine Addresses*, Book III,
Chapter 4, "God's Enduring
Love." Reproduced by courtesy
of Fordham University.

O wretched man that I am! who
shall deliver me from the body
of this death? Rom. 7. 24.

P. 192.

Figure 9
Edmund Arwaker, *Pia Desideria:
Or Divine Addresses*, Book III,
Chapter 8, "Personal Guilt."
Reproduced by courtesy of
Fordham University.

222 G. Richard Dimler

NOTES

1. Karl Josef Höltgen, *Francis Quarles 1592-1644. Meditativer Dichter, Emblematiker, Royalist. Eine biographische und kritische Studie* (Tübingen: Max Niemeyer, 1978), p. 205, states that there were over forty Latin editions and just as many translations of the *Pia Desideria* into other languages. For a synopsis of the structure of Ignatian meditation and that of the meditative or devotional emblem of Hugo and Quarles, see Höltgen's *Aspects of the Emblem* (Kassel: Edition Reichenberger, 1986), p. 49. Mario Praz, *Studies in Seventeenth-Century Imagery*, 2nd ed. (Rome: Edizioni di Storia e Letteratura, 1964), p. 143, lists some eleven editions between the first edition in Antwerp, 1624 and 1647, that is, within a span of of twenty-three years.

2. Louis L. Martz, *The Poetry of Meditation. A Study in English Religious Literature of the Seventeenth Century* (New Haven and London: Yale University Press, 1962), pp. 25ff. G. Richard Dimler, "The Egg as Emblem: Genesis and Structure of a Jesuit Emblem Book," *Studies in Iconography*, 2 (1976), 86-87. Mark Carter Leach, "The Literary and Emblematic Activity of Hermann Hugo, S.J. (1588-1629)." Diss. University of Delaware, 1979. (Ann Arbor, Michigan, University Microfilms, 1979), pp. 111f.

3. See note 2.

4. See note 1.

5. A typical Jesuit emblem writer, Maximilian Sandaeus (van der Sandt, 1578-1650), devoted the entire fourth book of his *Theologia Symbolica* (Mainz, 1626) to the discovery of emblems in sacred scripture and in the created world. See Leach, "Hugo," p. 113.

6. Leach, "Hugo," p. 122.

7. Praz, *Studies*, p. 145.

8. *Pia Desideria libri III*, Mit einer Einführung von Ernst Benz, "Emblematisches Cabinet." Herausgegeben von Dmitrij Tschizewskij und Ernst Benz. Vol. I (Hildesheim and New York: Georg Olms, 1971), p. 161. This is a reprint of the Antwerp, 1632 edition. All references to the *Pia Desideria* are to this volume.

9. Barbara Kiefer Lewalski, *Protestant Poetics and the Seventeenth-Century Religious Lyric* (Princeton: Princeton University Press, 1979), p. 158.

10. *Pia Desideria Or, Divine Addresses, In Three Books, Illustrated with XLVII. Copper-Plates. Written in Latine by Herm. Hugo. Englished by Edm. Arwaker, M.A. The Second Edition, with*

Alterations and Additions (London: Henry Bonwicke, 1690.), B2r
= [A2r].

11. Praz, *Studies*, p. 156, Höltgen, *Quarles*, p. 196.

12. Höltgen, *Quarles*, p. 184.

13. This is based on my computerized listing of all known Jesuit emblem books. This data base includes places of publication for over 500 Jesuit emblem books. The next cities which published large numbers of Jesuit emblem books are Cologne with fifty-two titles and Munich with forty-three. See Dimler, "Short Title Listing of Jesuit Emblem Books," *Emblematica* 2 (1987), 139-187.

14. *Typus Mundi in quo ejus Calamitates et Pericula nec non Divini, humanique Amoris Antipathia, Emblematice proponuntur a RR. C. S. I. A.* (Antwerp, 1626), is a work of the College of Rhetoric of the Jesuits at Antwerp. See Praz, *Studies*, pp. 158-159 and Gordon S. Haight, "The Sources of Quarles's Emblems," *The Library*, 16 (1936), 188-209. Lewalski, *Protestant Poetics*, regards Quarles as creating a new "Protestant narrative sequence on the spiritual life which deliberately undermines the orderly progressions of the Jesuit devotional books," p. 192. This begs the question since in the final analysis Quarles actually follows Hugo's sequence in Books III to V of the *Emblemes* as Höltgen points out in *Aspects of the Emblem*, pp. 53-54.

15. See Praz, *Studies*, p. 163. Rosemary Freeman, *English Emblem Books*, 2nd rpt. (New York: Octagon Books, 1970), p. 115.

16. In the Preface Arwaker refers to his book as a "translation" (B2r = [A2r]).

17. *The Poets of Ireland, A Biographical and Bibliographical Dictionary of Irish Writers of English Verse*, by D. J. O'Donaghue, (Dublin: Hodges Figgis and Co., 1912), p. 13.

18. Freeman, *English Emblem Books*, p. 206. Arwaker does not directly claim "that he was bettering the work" of Quarles as Freeman states, p. 132.

19. The appendix lists each of Arwaker's prose commentaries.

20. Leach's dissertation has been of considerable help in the following analysis, especially pp. 135ff. In the textual references that follow, the first number refers to the page in Arwaker or Hugo, the second number refers to the line in the text. Thus H 10. 7 = Hugo, page 10, line 7, and A 12. 3 = Arwaker, page 12, line 3.

21. Lewalski, *Protestant Poetics*, p. 149.

22. Höltgen, *Quarles*, p. 207 cites two respected nonconformist ministers in London from about 1808 commenting on Quarles's "translation": "The poem appears to be, in the main, very consistent with the evangelical doctrines, and not a little adapted both to please and profit those who wish to have their hearts called off from the present world, and fixed upon a better."

COLLARED STAGS AND BRIDLED LIONS: QUEEN ELIZABETH'S HOUSEHOLD ACCOUNTS

MICHAEL BATH
University of Strathclyde

The Bodleian Library contains a fragmentary manuscript consisting of five title-pages from the household accounts of Queen Elizabeth I. The actual accounts have not been preserved, and the remaining title-pages were collected by Francis Douce presumably for the sake of their decorated initials, which take the form of emblematic line drawings in pen and ink.[1] Such household accounts, drawn up in this case twice a year by the successive Controllers of the royal household who are named on the title-pages, contained lists of wines and household provisions with prices paid, and are usually plain, practical documents lacking any decoration. In this case the status of the royal person to whom they would have been presented has dictated the unusually elaborate decoration of the surviving pages.

These five folios are of no great artistic value in themselves, and my reason for drawing attention to them is largely in order to trace the origins of some of the motifs which they contain. A mapping of the sources of particular emblematic motifs illustrates something of the relationship between emblem books proper and other types of documents which shared their iconography. It is worth noting the early date of the these five pages from the royal accounts, 1577 and 1580-81, some five or more years before the appearance of the first English emblem book. The fact that two of these decorated initials use motifs copied directly from Continental emblem books is one more piece of evidence for the influence of particular emblem books in England before Whitney. Of the taste for emblems at court there is plenty of evidence, much of it assembled by Rosemary Freeman.[2]

The decoration of each of these folios includes scroll-work, cornucopias and foliage, and two of them have decorated borders of flowers and insects. Enclosed within each initial is the emblematic drawing. The first of these shows a man in a simple tunic with a scrip at his waist carrying a lamb on his shoulders (Figure 1). He is the Good Shepherd, drawn in the style of Georgette de Montenay's *Devises chrestiennes* which had appeared in 1571, though he does not have a source in that book. The second folio depicts a winged stag with a collar of the same pattern as the crown above its head, and the motto HOC CAESAR ME DONAVIT

[Caesar gave me this] on a scroll from its mouth (Figure 2). This is a reverse copy, slightly enlarged, of an emblem from Paradin's *Devises heroiques* of 1551, the winged stag device first appearing in the expanded second edition of 1557.[3]   The winged stag was the badge of the kings of France from the time of Charles VI, as Paradin's commentaries, which are a feature of all editions after the first, point out, quoting an anecdote from the chroniclers telling how Charles VI recaptured Caesar's deer in the forests of Senlis.   The following leaf shows a well-dressed man with a hat giving succour in the shape of a purse to a less fortunate fellow, with the motto BIS DAT QUI TEMPESTIVE DONAT [He gives twice who gives in good time] (Figure 3).   This is a reverse copy, again slightly enlarged, from Simeoni.   Simeoni's collection of imprese was often printed together with that of Paradin, and the composite Paradin/Simeoni volume was translated into English in 1591.   Whitney borrows this emblem of timely charity in 1586.[4]   The fourth emblem shows a lion rampant on a globe with erect sword, and shield with the cross of St George (Figure 4).   It is heraldic as much as emblematic.   The final folio shows a bare-breasted woman seated on a bridled lion, holding a pillar over her left shoulder (Figure 5).   This was a well-known allegory of Fortitude, and though the exact figure does not appear to have a source in emblem books, the image of the woman and bridled lion has a complex and interesting iconographic and semantic structure which I believe is worth mapping for its own sake.   This includes not just the specific allegory of Fortitude, but images of the Great Mother and of Justice which go back a long way in the mythological handbooks and are brought into the emblem tradition by Alciato.

My aim in what follows is to show something of the process of historical accretion and transformation which such symbols as the winged stag and the bridled lion have undergone, not just in emblem books proper, but in other contexts and documents which shared the same iconographic traditions.   Both images have their origins in pre-emblematic contexts which had developed their iconographic structure long before Alciato initiated the genre, and a study of these may realise something of the complex interrelations between different iconographic sources.   Both images, furthermore, raise problems of interpretation and exemplify some of the ways in which meaning gets fixed, or otherwise, in emblematic imagery.   The contexts in which each image developed supplied the *langue*, to suggest a Saussurian model, of which the individual emblem is but the *parole*. This is another way of saying that not all the received meanings of an image are present in the emblem, even when, as in the case of both these images, most of its history was known to Renaissance writers. The tradition of scholarly annotation, of which Alciato's commentators perhaps offer the best example, often enough involves the recovery of different parts of their iconographic *langue* from those which the original emblem exploited.

Two years before its appearance in Paradin's second edition of 1557, the winged stag had been described by Giovio in his *Dialogo dell'Imprese Militari et Amorose* (1555) as the device, not of the French kings, but of the Connétable de Bourbon. Editions after the first, which is not illustrated, show the badge with the motto CURSUM INTENDIMUS ALIS [We pursue our course with wings] (Figure 6). It is a particularly good example of Giovio's theory that the impresa symbolises a predisposition or intention, for Giovio jokes that none should have been surprised at the Connétable's notorious defection from the French king's side to that of the emperor after the Battle of Pavia, since his badge had always indicated his intention of flight. It is this conceit which accounts for Giovio's satirical motto, which is his own invention. Ercole Tasso must have had this particular device in mind when he wrote a comment on the propriety of unnatural attributes, which Mario Praz quotes: "Truth, however, can be enhanced by some hyperbolical adjunct: such as the wings added to stags, a device which is, however, derived from nature . . . the adjunct emphasizes their natural swiftness."[5] Tasso's comment relates to the important debate in emblem theory on the truth of emblems, an issue which was most notably to be taken up in the next century by Henri Estienne in his *L'Art de faire les devises*, which distinguishes between the medal as a record of things past or of things a man has done, and the device as an advertisement of things to come.

In the first half of the sixteenth century the winged stag was recognized as the Connétable's device. Maurice Scève has a dizain on the treacherous flight of the winged stag, and Jean Lemaire is credited with the Ballade which rejoices in the downfall of Charles, Connétable de Bourbon, and makes satirical capital out of the details of wings and collar.[6] The collar bore the motto *espérance* and the refrain rejoices that his hope has proved vain despite his alliance with the eagle. Like Icarus, who sailed too near the sun, he lost his wings. With the poetry of Pierre

Gringore we come closer to the late-medieval genre of political prophecy which uses animals as covert symbols for political realities and aspirations. The Prologues to his *Fantaisies de la mère sotte* includes Louis XII as the *porcepic*, François I as the salamander and Charles de Bourbon as the *cerf volant* or winged stag (Figure 7).[7] Its frontispiece illustrates all three. It is in such documents as these that we may see the immediate antecedents of the winged stag as the Bourbon device. The Connétable's own claims to the device are less easy to document, though it is known that in 1515 he entertained the king and queen with a spectacle on the river Saone, in which a large winged stag drew a barge in which the royal couple sat.[8] That various members of the Bourbon family appropriated the badge of their royal predecessors is suggested by the funerary chapel which Cardinal Charles de Bourbon built himself in Lyons cathedral in 1458, the balustrade of which is dominated by a carving of the winged stag encircled by a banderole with the motto ESPÉRANCE, motto of the order of chivalry founded by Louis de Bourbon in 1369, to which Jean Lemaire's satirical poem also alludes (Figure 8).

Though the winged stag device became thus associated with various Bourbon nobles in a way that affected sixteenth-century impresa iconography, its traditional and more strongly established iconography was as the royal badge, tracing its origins back to that hunting episode which the chroniclers recorded and which Paradin quotes from the reign of Charles VI.[9] Throughout the fifteenth century we meet it as the royal badge in a variety of sources including political poems, allegorical tapestries, royal entries, painting and sculpture. Its use appears to have been quite closely linked with the development of that curious and richly symbolic occasion known as the *lit de justice*.[10] On some of the earliest occasions to which this term was applied a conspicuous part was played by a large symbolic winged stag manipulated by concealed machinery. A version of this automaton is mentioned in various royal entries throughout the fifteenth century.

The poetic *scriptura*, which explicated the symbolism of the entries in which this model played a part several times, pun on the words *cerf* and *serve*, which became a rhetorical commonplace. The verses which greeted Louis XII on his 1498 entry into Paris exploited it, as did the inscription to the tableau of stag and unicorn which greeted the king at Rouen in 1508:

Quant la licorne et le grant cerf
Larmarye tiennent ensemble,
Il n'est ennemy qui ne tremble
Et qui'ilz ne rend a eux serf.[11]

The pun is common enough in the Middle Ages, frequently with
scant iconographic justification. At the beginning of his *Testament*, for instance, Villon protests that he is not the slave of
Thibault d'Aussigny: "Je ne suis son serf ne sa biche". Pierre
Gringore's pamphlet against Pope Julius II, *La chasse du cerf des
cerfs* puns in its title on the pontifical title of *servus servorum*.[12]
The pontifical stag stays in harbour whilst the hounds of Europe
hunt his triple crown: he is compared to Actæon, the proud man
devoured by his followers. In emblem literature this pun is picked
up by De La Perrière in the first French emblem book in 1539,
which has an emblem showing a herd of stags led by a lion con-
fronting a pride of lions led by a stag.[13] The moral that a brave
leader is worth a host of cowards is enforced by the pun: "Le
seul Lyon rendra les aultres serfz". Georgette de Montenay tried
her hand at the same pun, though with a different emblem, in
1571: a misguided prince has a stag's head, to show that he is the
slave of his slaves: "de ses serfs serviteur".[14] More usually in
Renaissance emblems the stag-headed man represents the figure
of Actæon.

The motto to Paradin's impresa of the winged stag, CAESAR
HOC ME DONAVIT [Caesar gave this to me], identifies it as
Caesar's deer. The legend of Caesar's deer is, if anything, more
curious and extensive than the history of the winged stag, with
which it is only intermittently identified. The chroniclers whom
Paradin's commentary cites certainly account for the origin of the
badge in terms of the legend. Whilst hunting near Senlis in the
year of his accession, Charles encountered a stag which bore a
collar with the Latin inscription. Thereafter the king adopted
the winged stag as his badge. Subsequent records of the motif
seldom identify it as Caesar's deer, however. The legend that an
emperor put a collar on a stag which lived to a miraculous age
and was recaptured by medieval kings and emperors is to be found
in various versions and forms throughout the Middle Ages, and
was sanctioned by similar legends in classical writers such as
Pausanias, Aristotle, Pliny and Solinus. Although it accreted
other symbolism it was, as I have argued elsewhere, fundamentally
a legend of imperial *renovatio*.[15] Some of the more celebrated

examples, certainly, overlaid this symbolism with quite different meanings. Petrarch, for instance, made it the basis of a love-conceit in a famous sonnet ("Una candida cerva") in which Laura is the white hind wearing a collar prohibiting capture and dedicated to Caesar. His editors unerringly identify this as a reference to the legendary deer which a Roman emperor had captured and given an inscribed collar, with the words, "Noli me tangere Caesaris enim sum" [Touch me not, for I belong to Caesar]. One of them tells the story of Charles VI's stag from the French chronicles, the same story that Paradin supplies.[16]   In 1566 Ruscelli used Petrarch's white hind with its Italian inscription ˜Nessun me tocchi˜ [Touch me not] as an impresa, which he dedicated to Lucrezia Gonzaga (Figure 9).[17]   Renaissance writers were likely to record versions of this legend when discussing various received ideas on the longevity of stags. These include the idea, which had come down from the ancient natural histories and bestiaries, that the stag prolonged its life by eating snakes and equally ancient topos of the Oldest Animals.[18]   All of these get picked up in emblem books in one form or another. Horapollo's influence must have helped to interest emblematists in such traditions, since in Horapollo the stag occupies a fairly prominent position as a hieroglyphic of longevity. In illustrations of Petrarch's *Trionfi* stags are frequently shown pulling the chariot of Time.[19]

In the documents surveyed so far--and they are by no means an exhaustive selection of the records of this motif which are known to have survived[20]--the collared stag can be seen to have enjoyed a status as, variously, an emblem or impresa; a royal device; a literary topos; a legend; and a myth of imperial *renovatio*. It can be shown, finally, to have enjoyed a more-or-less separate status in courtly hunting ceremonial and as a piece of folklore. The assumption that the winged stag had its origins in legend is prompted and surely justified by the hint of *mirabilia* about the chroniclers' accounts of Charles VI's encounter with the marvellous collared stag in the forest of Senlis. And yet nothing could be more matter-of-fact than the record in the royal accounts for a payment made two years later, in the year 1382, to one Colin le Serrurier for a branding-iron in the shape of a fleur-de-lis, to be used to mark (*signer*) a stag which the king had captured in the forest of Compiègne and later released with his mark.[21]   There seems to be no doubt that the practice of capturing a stag, and putting a collar, signature, or inscription on it, and then releasing it, was not uncommon. It seems to have been a practice reserved for royalty, or at least for those aspiring to imperial descent. At the beginning of the seventeenth century King Christian IV of Denmark claimed to have recaptured the stag on which a collar had been put with the inscription of one of his legendary ancestors who was thought to have reigned at the time of Christ's birth.[22] Some years later, Queen Sophie Magdalene is known to have sheltered a stag in the royal stables which she released with a collar inscribed with verses of her own composition. The collar, and what there is good reason to believe are the taxidermised remains of this stag, are preserved in Danish museums.[23] In 1611, whilst visiting the English court of James I, the Landgrave of Hesse was taken on a hunt in which, to honour the visitor, a stag was captured and a collar was fixed, before it was released.[24] As late as the year 1808 the emperor Napoleon is reported to have captured a large stag with nets in the forest of Vincennes, on which a collar was soldered with a dedicatory inscription to Empress Josephine before it was released. In 1839 Louis Napoleon, it is claimed, recaptured the same stag.[25] I have argued elsewhere that such a pattern was understood as establishing imperial descent, dynastic continuity, or a *translatio imperii*.[26]

The status of this motif as folklore is established by the nineteenth-century inn-sign at the village of King's Stag in the county of Dorset which still shows the following rhyme:

When Julius Caesar landed here
I was then a little deer.
When Julius Caesar reigned king
Round my neck he put this ring.
Whoever doth me overtake
Spare my life for Ceasar's sake.[27]

Similar verses were recorded in the seventeenth century in Yorkshire, and in the fifteenth-century book on armorial devices by Nicholas Upton, which tells of a stag caught in Windsor forest wearing a collar on which Caesar had obligingly written in Norman-French.[28] Remote though such examples might seem from the legend of the winged stag which we started with, Upton cites the same classical legends of collared stags on which the Senlis anecdote was modeled, and which sanctioned Paradin's emblem. The diversity of these sources and applications should not lead us

into the error of supposing that what we are studying is not a
single image.

Much the same is true of the image of the bridled lion, for
it can be shown that there are connections between all its diverse
applications. As with the winged stag emblem, the form which
this image takes in the Household Accounts identifies it with a
particular allegorical commonplace. It has an exact analogue in
the so-called Mantegna Tarot, where it is explicitly identified as
Forteza [Fortitude] (Figure 10).[29] But the image of the woman
with the lion has a variety of other meanings in Renaissance
mythologies and emblem books. In Book Five of *The Faerie
Queene* Mercilla sits on a throne with a lion, bound with an iron
chain and collar, beneath her feet. Jane Aptekar first drew
attention to the similarity between this and an emblem in Ripa of
Force subdued by Justice, and the idea that Mercilla's lion repeats
a familiar emblem of Justice has rapidly become the standard gloss
to *Faerie Queene*, V.ix.33.[30] When one looks at Ripa, however,
the evidence for this emblem of Justice, at least in anything like
the fixed form which is characteristic of the image of Fortitude
for instance, rapidly vanishes. The emblem which Aptekar illustrates is from the Padua, 1618, edition of Ripa, and it appears
there for the first time (Figure 11). The only one of the earlier
editions which Spenser could have seen is the unillustrated 1593
first edition. Though this describes several bridled lions, none
of them has anything to do with Justice. For Ripa, Justice is
simply a crowned maiden, first illustrated in the second edition
of 1611. This edition also shows Reason as a young woman
holding a sword in one hand and the bridle of a lion in the
other: the bridled lion is explained as signifying the subjected
senses (Figure 12). The earliest editions of Ripa also show
Ethics holding a bridled lion, meaning that Ethics bridles the
animal part of human nature, and in another emblem the virtue
of self-mastery is depicted as a man riding a lion. There are
various other lions in Ripa, who likes the formula of an allegorical
figure standing in front of the appropriate animal.

Ripa's 1618 emblem of Justice suppressing Force is based, as
the commentary makes clear, on a description in Valeriano (1556)
of a "recently discovered" antique medal. Under the motto
IUSTITIAE CULTUS [Respect for justice] one face of this medal
showed Justice as a crowned, seated woman reaching toward the
hilt of a sword. The reverse showed an almost naked woman,
with her hand on the mane of a seated lion and the motto LEO-

NIS HUMILITAS [The humility of the lion]. When later editions of Valeriano came to illustrate this they showed the woman actually riding the lion (Figure 13). Valeriano's first Book, which treats of the hieroglyphic significance of the lion, also shows a man riding a bridled lion with the motto ANIMI DOMITOR [The tamer of the will], which is the source for Ripa's emblem of self-mastery. It also includes hieroglyphs of the Sun and Earth, which are shown separately as a woman riding a lion and a man doing the same, with rays descending from the one and ascending to the other (Figures 14, 15). The commentary tells us that these are the Syrian gods Adad and Adargatis. The meaning of the lion is not explained.

We get a clearer idea of the meaning of this hieroglyph if we turn from Valeriano's learned, but rather unilluminating account, to that of Vincenzo Cartari. The unillustrated first edition of Cartari's *Imagine dei Dei* (1556) describes the same gods Adad and Adargatis, and explains that the Syrians showed the sun with descending rays meaning that everything born on earth is created by virtue of the sun's light. The lion's presence is accounted for as a reference to Terra. Traditionally identified with Cybele, Ops, Berecynthia and the Great Mother, Terra was easily recognisable by virtue of her towered headdress, but she was also conventionally shown riding in a chariot drawn by lions, and Cartari refers the reader to his later description of the Magna Mater in her lion-drawn chariot. Cartari's eventual illustrator shows the Syrian goddess corresponding to Terra as a semi-nude woman sitting on a lion, with rays shining down on her from the sun god who stands beside her (Figure 16). Cartari's illustrator got this detail right, unlike Valeriano's, who confuses the sexes of the two, for Terra should be the woman, and Sol the man. The lion's presence is now explicitly justified as a syncretic reference to the received iconography of the Roman goddess, Magna Mater, in her lion-drawn chariot (Figure 17).

It would appear, then, that far from being an unequivocal symbol of Justice, the woman on the lion had a shifting and complex iconography in the sixteenth century. Rather than a single or unchanging meaning, it is polysemous. Ripa's icon of Justice goes back to Valeriano, where the lion has a variety of meanings, including the association with Terra which was sanctioned by ancient descriptions of the Magna Mater riding in her chariot.[31] We might think it important to distinguish between motifs which showed the lion as beneath a throne, being ridden, or harnessed to a chariot, but it seems that the Renaissance mythographers were less scrupulous. Often enough their commentaries are prepared to invoke whatever analogue seemed appropriate. In Alciato, for instance, the two lions yoked to a chariot are not a symbol of the Great Mother in any of her guises, but are indeed an icon of Justice, with the motto ETIAM FEROCISSIMOS DOMARI [Even the fiercest are tamed] based, as the epigram explains, on a metaphor used by Cicero to describe Mark Antony (Figure 18). But Alciato also adapted the image to a love emblem, based on a conceit in the Greek Anthology, in which blind Cupid, rather than Justice or Cybele, rides the chariot, demonstrating that love can tame even the most powerful (Figure 19). This emblem clearly did provide Spenser with a model for his description of Cupid at II.xxi.22:

> Next after her the winged God himselfe
> Came riding on a Lion ravenous,
> Taught to obay the menage of that Elfe,
> That man and beast with powre imperious
> Subdeweth to his kingdome tyrannous . . .

Wrath also rides a lion at I.iv.33 in the procession of the Seven Deadly Sins.

In 1566 Ruscelli illustrated an impresa showing a disembodied hand holding the bridle of a lion, with the motto DIES ET INGENIUM [Time and wit] (Figure 20). The motif really looks quite different from any of those we have examined, yet the commentary acknowledges it as a version of the chariot-pulling lions of Alciato, and quotes the same classical texts in its support. The lion represents the pride of the mistress which time and ingenuity will eventually bridle.

Spenser's emblem of Justice would seem, therefore to be based on images which were more fluid and shifting than Aptekar's account seems to acknowledge. The images of the subjected lion have diverse meanings and forms which do not harden into a fixed iconographic commonplace even when their affiliations with each other are acknowledged. Though there seems to have been an association with ideas of Justice from Alciato onwards, this is by no means the only nor perhaps the central application of the motif. The example illustrates rather well the dangers of snatching a random analogue from emblem books or mythologies to serve as a gloss on a literary text. It might seem that what

we need for the purposes of literary scholarship and art history
in such cases as these is less a motif-index, indispensible though
that is, than a transformational grammar.

As far as the Household Accounts of Queen Elizabeth I are
concerned, the effort to fix meanings might in any case seem
redundant, for it would be difficult to say on the evidence of the
five surviving folia whether the emblematic initials had anything
more than a decorative function. The manuscript does, however,
confirm what plenty of other evidence suggests, namely that
Continental emblem books were well known in England sometime
before the appearance of the first English emblem book. Whatever
the use to which they were being put on these title-pages, all
these motifs are speaking pictures which carried a heavy weight
of received meaning. If we are going to use emblem books and
related documents as evidence for our glosses on Renaissance
allegories, it is important to be aware of dates, and of the
different states of successive editions of the most popular source
books. Aptekar often writes as though all emblem material was
synchronous, and much of her evidence is drawn from later
editions of Ripa which Spenser could not have seen. The truth
is that the meaning and structure of particular motifs was con-
tinually developing as each new manual or each edition of Alciato,
Valeriano or Ripa adopted, expanded or transformed the material
of its predecessors. Alongside this diachronic development,
however, it seems clear that complex motifs such as the two I
have been examining here have at any one time a synchronic
structure, defined by contingent motifs and topoi. Such contingent motifs define not simply the meaning, but the very identity
of particular images.

Figure 1
Household Accounts of Elizabeth I, 1577. MS Douce bl. fol. 1.
Reproduced by courtesy of The Bodleian Library, Oxford.

Figure 2
Household Accouts of Elizabeth I, 1578. MS Douce bl. fol. 2.
Reproduced by courtesy of The Bodleian Library, Oxford.

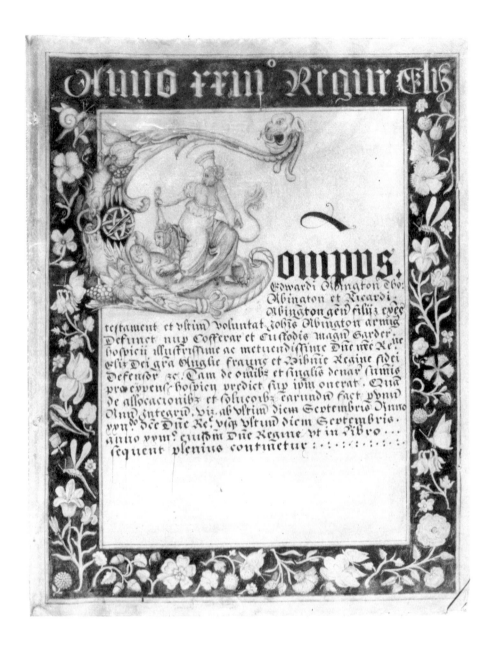

Figure 3
Household Accounts of Elizabeth I, 1579. MS Douce bl. fol. 3.
Reproduced by courtesy of The Bodleian Library, Oxford.

Figure 4
Household Accounts of Elizabeth I, 1580. MS Douce bl. fol. 4.
Reproduced by courtesy of The Bodleian Library, Oxford.

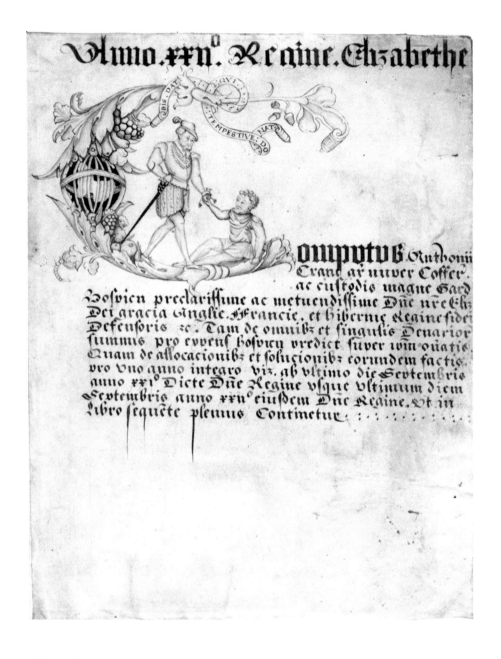

Figure 5
Household Accounts of Elizabeth I, 1581. MS Douce bl. fol. 5.
Reproduced by courtesy of The Bodleian Library, Oxford.

Figure 6
Paolo Govio *Dialogo
del'Imprese Militari et Amorose*
(Lyons, 1559), fol. 11. Reproduced by courtesy of The University of
Glasgow.

Figure 7
Frontispiece to
Piere Gringoire,
*Fantaisie de la
Mère Sotte* (Paris,
1516). Reproduced
by courtesy of
The University of
Glasgow.

Figure 8
Balustrade of Bourbon Chapel, Lyons Cathedral   Reproduced courtesy of Musée des Monuments Français.

323

LVCRETIA

GONZAGA.

VESTA IMPRESA MOSTRA SENZA
alcun dubbio d'effer tratta da quel bel Sonetto del
Petrarca,
  Vna candida Cerua fopra l'erba
    Verde , m'apparue,con due corna d'oro;
    Fra due riuiere à l'ombra d'un'Alloro,
    Leuando il Sole à la ftagion'acerba .
Ma perche il Petrarca con quel Sonetto volle narrar la pura iftoria dell'innamoramento fuo fotto
quella bella allegoria,& ui ebbe da narrar le due riuiere,Sorga,& Druen-
za, & per le corna d'oro intefe le trecce di Laura,quefta Signora nella fua
Imprefa n'ha tolto folamente quello, che fa al propofito dell'intétion fua,
cioè la candidezza della Cerua,l'ombra dell'Alloro,& ancora il monile al
collo,che pur nella fua defcriue il Petrarca,
  Neffun mi tocchi, al bel colle d'intorno
    Scritt'auea di Diamanti , e di Topati,
    Libera farmi al mio Cefare parue.

SS 2

Figure 9
Girolamo Ruscelli, *Le Imprese Illustri* (Venice, 1566).
Reproduced courtesy of The University of Glasgow.

Figure 10
The Mantegna Tarot "Forteza."
Reproduced by courtesy of The British Museum.

Figure 11
Justice, Caesae Ripa, *Iconologia* (Padua, 1618), p. 207.
Reproduced by courtesy of The University of Glasgow.

Figure 12
Ragione, Caesare Ripa, *Iconologia* (Padua, 1618), p. 451.
Reproduced by courtesy of The University of Glasgow.

Figure 13
Piero Valeriano, *Hieroglyphica* (Basle, 1556), fol. 15^r.
Reproduced by courtesy of The University of Glasgow.

Figure 14
Piero Valeriano, *Hieroglyphica* (Basle, 1556), fol. 15ᵛ.
Reproduced by courtesy of The University of Glasgow.

Figure 15
Piero Valeriano, *Hieroglyphica* (Basle, 1556), fol. 15ᵛ.
Reproduced by courtesy of The University of Glasgow.

Figure 16
Vincenzo Cartari, *Le Imagini dei Dei degli Antichi* (Venice, 1571), fol. 78ᵛ. Reproduced by courtesy of The University of Glasgow.

Figure 17
Vincenzo Cartari, *Le Imagini dei Dei degli Antichi* (Venice, 1571), p. 207. Reproduced by courtesy of The University of Glasgow.

Figure 18
Andrea Alciato, *Emblematum Liber* (Lyons: Roville, 1548), p. 32.
Reproduced by courtesy of The University of Glasgow.

Figure 19
Andrea Alciato, *Emblematum Liber* (Lyons: Roville, 1548), p. 84.
Reproduced by courtesy of The University of Glasgow.

483

GIOSEPPE
ANTONIO
CANACEO.

VESTA IMPRESA DEL LEONE COL
freno alla bocca, & sù'l collo,& col Motto,

DIES, ET INGENIVM,

Si vede chiaramente esser formata da quella cele-
bratissima sentenza di Catullo Poeta,nella quarta
Elegia del primo libro,
Longa dies homini docuit parere Leonem,
Longa dies molli saxa peredit aqua,
Oue è posta la parola *DIES* nel suo communissimo modo della lingua
Latina, cioè, che significa,non vn giorno precisamente, ma Tempo,ò sta-
gione,come lunga stagione,per lungo tempo disse il Petrarca,
Lunga stagion di tenebre vestito.

PPP 2

Figure 20
Girolamo Ruscelli, *Le Imprese Illustri* (Venice, 1566), p. 483.
Reproduced by courtesy of The University of Glasgow.

NOTES

1. MS Douce b1. According to the librarian it is almost but not quite certain that the MS belongs in the collection bequeathed to the Bodleian Library by Francis Douce (1757-1834), though it is not described in the 1840 printed catalogue of the Douce collection, perhaps because it was considered an unimportant fragment. On Douce, see A. N. L. Munby, *Connoisseurs and Medieval Miniatures 1750-1850* (Oxford: Clarendon Press, 1972), pp. 35-36.

2. *English Emblem Books* (London: Chatto & Windus, 1948), p. 49.

3. For details of the emblem books mentioned in this essay the reader is referred to the standard bibliographies by Mario Praz and John Landwehr.

4. Whitney (1586), p. 190.

5. *Studies in Seventeenth-Century Imagery* (Rome: Edizioni di Storia e Letteratura, 1964), p. 69.

6. *Délie*, no. 21; Jean Lemaire de Belges, *Oeuvres*, ed. J. Stecher (Louvain: J. Lefever, 1882-91), IV, 358.

7. Pierre Gringore, *Les Fantasies de Mère Sote*, ed. R. L. Frautschi (Chapel Hill: University of North Carolina Press, 1962).

8. Published by G. Guigue, *L'entrée de François Ier à Lyon en 1515* (Lyons: Chez le trésorier-archeviste de la soc., 1899), based on MS Wolfenbüttel 86.4.

9. This anecdote is first recorded by the chronicler Juvenal des Ursins, the standard edition of whose chronicle is in Joseph François Michaud, *Nouvelle collection de mémoires relatif à l'histoire de France* (Paris: Didier, 1854-1857), II, 242. It found its way thence into the sixteenth-century chronicles compiled by Robert Gaguin. The history of the winged stag as royal badge has been studied by Bath, "The white hart, the *cerf volant* and the Wilton Diptych" in *Beast Epic, Fable and Fabliau*, ed. J. Goossens and T. Sodmann (Cologne: Bohlau, 1981), pp. 25-42; Collette Beaune, "Costume et pouvoir en France à la fin du Moyen Age: les devises royales vers 1400," *Revue des sciences humaines*, 4 (1981), 125-146; and Jean-Bernard de Vaivre, "Les cerfs ailés et la tapisserie de Rouen," *Gazette des beaux-arts*, 100 (1982), 93-108.

10. The evolution of the *lit de justice* and the use of the winged stag model are studied by Sarah Hanley, *The "lit de justice" of the Kings of France; constitutional ideology in legend, ritual, and discourse* (Princeton: Princeton University Press, 1983).

11. Descriptions of these entries are in J. A. Buchon, *Collection des chroniques* (Paris: Verdière, 1824-1828), x, pp. 205-6; B. Guenée and F. Lehoux, *Les entrées royales françaises de 1328 à 1515* (Paris: Éditions du Centre national de la recherche scientifique 1968), p. 132, pp. 160-1; P. le Verdier, *L'entrée du roi Louis XII et de la Reine Anne à Rouen, 1508* (Rouen: Léon Gy, 1900).

12. *Oeuvres complètes*, (Paris, 1858), i, pp. 157-167.

13. Emblem 39.

14. P. 20.

15. See Bath, "The legend of Caesar's deer," *Medievalia et Humanistica*, n.s. 9 (1979), pp. 53-66, and my forthcoming article "Imperial *renovatio* symbolism in the *Très riches heures*," in *Simiolus*.

16. Petrarch ed. Daniello da Lucca (1541), fol. 120^v.

17. *Le Imprese Illustri* (Venice, 1566), p. 323.

18. See Bath, "Donne's 'Anatomy of the world' and the Legend of the Oldest Animals," *Review of English Studies*, 32 (1981), 302-8.

19. See for instance Raimond van Marle, *Iconographie de l'art profane* (The Hague: M. Nijhoff, 1931), II, fig. 143, which illustrates one of the Vienna *Trionfi* tapestries; or E. H. Gombrich, *Symbolic Images*. Studies in the Art of the Renaissance (London: Phaidon Press, 1972), fig. 143, from a fifteenth-century engraving. There are numerous further examples.

20. Most, though not all, of the surviving examples are mentioned in the articles cited in note 9 above.

21. The record is preserved in L. C. Douët-d'Arcq, ed. *Comptes de l'hotel des rois de France aux xive et xve siècles* (Paris, 1865).

22. See Bath, "The legend of Caesar's deer," note 15 above, p. 63.

23. The remains of this stag, the skin showing clear marks of a collar, is preserved at Hørsholm, Denmark, Jagd- og skovbrugsmuseet; Queen Sophie Magdalene's engraved collar is in the neigbouring Egns Museum.

24. The record of this visit is preserved in Kassel, Landesbibliothek, Quarto MS Hass. 68, fols. 87^r-^{v}. I am indebted to Professor Karl Josef Höltgen, who has examined the MS, for drawing my attention to it, and to Professor Alan Young for a transcript of the relevant passage.

25. The Napoleonic anecdote was noted by Kenneth Blaxter in *The British Veterinary Journal*, 135 (1979), 595.

26. See Bath, note 15 above.

27. Bath, "King's Stag and Caesar's Deer," *Proceedings of the Dorset Natural History and Archaeological Society*, 95 (1974), 80-83.

28. *Memorials of John Ray*, ed. Edwin Lankester (London: Ray Society, 1846), pp. 139-40; Nicholas Upton, *De Studio Militari*, ed. Edward Bysse (London, 1654), p. 159.

29. See Arthur M. Hind, *Early Italian Engraving* (London: Published for M. Knoedler & Company, New York, by Bernard Quaritch, Ltd., 1938), IV, pl. 355. Further examples are listed in Guy de Tervarent, *Attributs et symboles dans l'art profane,1450-1600* (Genève: Droz, 1958), I, col. 243. De Tervarent's numerous examples of the lion as attribute of Justice in the adjacent column supply a better context for the iconography of Mercilla's throne in the sense required by Jane Aptekar than anything in Ripa.

30. *Icons of Justice: Iconography and Thematic Imagery in Book V of The Faerie Queene* (New York: Columbia University Press, 1969), pp. 53-66.

31. The Great Mother is one and the same with Cybele, Ops and Berecynthia. Her iconography was established by Saint Augustine's description in *Civitas Dei*, VII, 24, where her defining characteristic is the tower on her head, signifying the cities of the earth. She is usually shown in the Middle Ages with a bell or cymbals. Augustine says that Cybele is shown with an unbound and tame lion beside her to show that there is no land too wild to be cultivated. Already in the later Middle Ages, however, she appears seated on a chariot drawn by lions, as in Virgil manuscript illuminations reproduced in Millard Meiss, *French Painting in the Time of Jean de Berry: The Limbourgs and their Contemporaries* (London: Thames and Hudson, 1974), fig. 248. The justice symbolism of Terra's bridled lions is already established in Vasari's account of the mythological program of the Palazzo Vecchio, Florence, in 1558, and in Cartari's description of Ops, which are compared by Jean Seznec, *Survival of the Pagan Gods; the mythological tradition and its place in Renaissance humanism and art*, transl. by Barbara F. Sessions (New York: Pantheon Books, 1953), p. 289. Both Vasari and Cartari explain the yoked lions as showing that the kings of the earth are subject to the law. Spenser's own description of Cybele in *Faerie Queene*, IV.xi.28, mentions the castellated headdress and the chariot but not the lions. She stands for London as Troynovant because of *Aeneid*, VI, 784-7, in which the towered crown of Berecynthia is

associated with the prophecy of Rome's foundation. Virgil, too, mentions the chariot but not the lions.

I am grateful to the Carnegie Trust for the Universities of Scotland for help towards the cost of obtaining photographs to illustrate this article.

INDEX OF NAMES (AUTHORS)

INDEX OF ARTISTS

INDEX OF NAMES (MODERN SCHOLARS)